Rigolo 1

Tea ook

Amanda Collins

Assessment sections: Julie Green

OXFORD
UNIVERSITY PRESS

OXFORD
UNIVERSITY PRESS

Great Clarendon Street, Oxford, OX2 6DP,
United Kingdom

Oxford University Press is a department of the University of Oxford.
It furthers the University's objective of excellence in research, scholarship,
and education by publishing worldwide. Oxford is a registered trade mark
of Oxford University Press in the UK and in certain other countries

First Edition published by Nelson Thornes Ltd in 2008
This edition published by Oxford University Press in 2014

British Library Cataloguing in Publication Data
Data available

ISBN: 978-0-19-835608-0

12

Paper used in the production of this book is a natural, recyclable product
made from wood grown in sustainable forests. The manufacturing process
conforms to the environmental regulations of the country of origin.

Printed by Ashford Colour Press Ltd.

Acknowledgements

Illustrations by: Mark Draisey

Page make-up by Pantek Arts Ltd

The authors and publisher would like to thank the following people and companies,
without whose support this book would not have been possible:

Julie Green – series editor and assessment author
Jim McElwee – manuscript consultant
Joyce Morrison – consultant for Scottish curriculum
Sara McKenna – teaching notes editor
Recordings produced by Footstep Productions Ltd.
Music composed and produced by Steven Faux

Oxford OWL

For school
Discover eBooks, inspirational
resources, advice and support

For parents
Helping your child's learning
with free eBooks, essential
tips and fun activities

www.oxfordowl.co.uk

Rigolo 1

Contents

Foreword

Rigolo is an exciting new course for Key Stage 2. It is not a traditional language course as it combines a variety of new and traditional media. Its structure serves the dual purpose of making French accessible and exciting to pupils, and of providing the classroom teacher with a flexible route through the range of resources.

Rigolo is also a new venture into Blended Learning; that is, a combination of traditional and new media, allowing the planning of taught lessons and flexible learning with the suite of multimedia materials. It is also particularly suitable for use with an interactive whiteboard, so that the whole class can work on the activities, particularly useful where time is precious. The course is closely matched to the Key Stage 2 Framework, both in its selection of teaching and learning activities, and in its promotion of language-learning strategies and development of knowledge about how the language works.

Background to the Virtual Teacher

A unique feature of *Rigolo* is the Virtual Teacher. She is there not as a surrogate teacher, but as a support assistant to the classroom teacher. The Virtual Teacher was developed as part of a three-year project, funded by the European Commission, called *Primary Letter Box*, which looked at ways of integrating reading into the primary foreign language programme. The project considered, among other things, the importance of showing children the link between sound and spelling, so that they could acquire fluent reading skills.

Recent research has shown that one of the factors influencing the sense of failure in the early years of secondary school is pupils' inability to decipher the correct pronunciation of French. This impinges on their ability to understand texts, since they are too concerned with its actual appearance. Experiments with primary school children showed that they were capable of responding to the Virtual Teacher and acquire good levels of pronunciation and intonation. Where the classroom teacher did not have high quality pronunciation, the children took the Virtual Teacher as their role model, but this did not detract from their professional relationship with their classroom teacher. Indeed, teachers often felt relieved that they could confidently point to their virtual colleague! It was found that children learnt and retained vocabulary more effectively with this method than those who were taught the same language in a more traditional way.

Presenting new language in *Rigolo*

Rigolo presents new language against an interactive backcloth, rather like an animated flashcard.

Children click on any part of the screen and the Virtual Teacher says the word. In a departure from common practice over the last 20 years, the text also appears as it is spoken, although it may be turned off if desired. It was found in *Primary Letter Box* that children who interacted with the Virtual Teacher in order to learn new language retained it much more easily than those who were taught in a more linear way with flashcards and an OHP.

Moreover, children remembered the spelling of words even though these had not been pointed out to them. As one Year 4 pupil explained, "I watched the lady's mouth and I noticed the word underneath her face, and then when I thought of the picture, I could remember the spelling and how to say it." This is a naïve, but very succinct definition of the holistic nature of multimedia learning. Trials of *Rigolo* found the same phenomenon, with children noticing the spellings of words and also making observations such as *souris* being the only animal that was *une*.

We need to pursue the logic of this new approach and ensure that children are seeing the relationship between the sound and spelling of words, as the Key Stage 2 Framework demands: 'Recognise how sounds are represented in written form' (Year 3). *Rigolo* has the added function of presenting selected phonemes and graphemes in each unit.

Introducing literacy skills

Primary Letter Box also experimented with exploring words at text level. Research showed that children could cope with texts particularly well when they were presented on an interactive whiteboard. They were able to apply very sophisticated logic to texts and deduce the meanings of prepositions (*dans, sur*) and conjunctions (*et, mais*) from the context and illustrations. This meant that they also began to make inferences about sentence structure, an important step in developing writing skills.

Again, *Rigolo* includes a range of interactive exercises that help children to move into reading and writing. Regular animated stories use graphics and audio alongside the text to develop the engaging storyline, which is continued in the separate Big Books. Exploring the written form of the language at word, sentence and text level contributes to the acquisition of Knowledge about the Language (KAL) and Language Learning Strategies (LLS), both of which underpin the teaching activities set out in the Key Stage 2 Framework. Classroom teachers will be pleased to find that many of the activities reflect their experiences with the National Literacy Strategy, and *Rigolo* complements work in literacy, as indeed it does in other areas of the curriculum.

Learning away from the whiteboard

Let's not forget that ICT isn't everything! The *Rigolo* Resource Pack provides several excellent ways to extend the fun beyond the whiteboard. Children relate to the *Rigolo* characters, and the puppets bring these characters to life. Moreover, the Big Books offer the possibility, not only for enjoyment, but also for seeing and hearing the language in a different way. Children should be encouraged to try to read parts of the Big Books aloud. The simplicity of the storylines means that children can become immersed instantly in the action, and the clear illustrations support understanding of the language on each page. The songs are also a very powerful way of developing children's affective learning: they quickly learn and remember not just the whole song but also its elements. Singing is a very effective way of learning longer pieces of text by heart, and it helps to encourage recycling of language in new contexts.

Rigolo has the twofold aim of providing a route to excellence and of promoting enjoyment. We hope that those teachers who find the idea of teaching French somewhat daunting will find that the *Rigolo* Virtual Teacher and plethora of resources will help them to do the job with confidence.

Jim McElwee

Series Consultant to Rigolo
Modern Language Consultant for Redcar & Cleveland
Redcar & Cleveland Primary MFL Regional Support
Group Co-ordinator

How to use *Rigolo*

What is *Rigolo*?

Overview

Rigolo is a ground-breaking new Key Stage 2 French course. It provides a wealth of exciting activities for pupils, and as much or as little support for teachers as they need. It fully meets the requirements of the Key Stage 2 Framework for Languages.

The course is chiefly aimed at pupils in Years 3–6, with *Rigolo 1* covering Years 3 and 4, and *Rigolo 2* Years 5 and 6. However, if schools are starting French earlier or later (for example, in Year 1 or Year 5) they can still use *Rigolo 1* as it is designed to cover the first two years of learning French across a range of ages.

Course components

The *Rigolo* course is based on a CD-ROM, for delivery primarily on an interactive whiteboard. The *Rigolo 1* CD-ROM contains approximately 150 whiteboard activities, and 175 class activities which may be used away from the screen.

The CD-ROM also includes several other teaching and planning tools:

- Flashcards: approximately 130 colour flashcard images with matching text captions to use either on the whiteboard or to print out and use around the class.

- Worksheets: eight differentiated worksheets for each unit, providing further practice in reading, writing and speaking skills.

- Teacher's notes: notes for each of the lessons and units of *Rigolo 1* are stored on the CD-ROM for quick reference.

- Scheme of Work and mapping grids: a full medium-term planning scheme for *Rigolo*, plus correlation documents showing how *Rigolo 1* meets the Key Stage 2 Framework and 5–14 guidelines requirements.

- Certificates and portfolios: certificates for pupils and teachers to track their progress through *Rigolo*. There are specific *Rigolo* certificates, and also ones using the European Language Portfolio and Language Ladder 'can-do' statements.

Rigolo 1 also includes a Resource Pack, sold separately, containing six Big Books, three hand-puppets and an audio CD featuring readings of the Big Book stories and songs from the course.

Course structure and aims

The course is planned carefully so that non-specialist language teachers can easily follow a structured progression through Key Stage 2, covering the Year 3 and 4 objectives from the KS2 Framework for Modern Languages in *Rigolo 1*. For those teachers used to the QCA Scheme of Work for Primary Languages, *Rigolo* also covers the language from the units in the scheme. Activities, lessons and units are mapped against the 5–14 guidelines for Scotland and the levels from the Languages Ladder. Cross-curricular opportunities are also flagged throughout, so that teachers can find activities to use in other curriculum time outside the French lesson.

Rigolo 1 is divided into 12 units: six units per year, or two per term. Each unit is then divided into four or five lessons. The course combines whiteboard activities with class activities using the flashcards, Big Books and puppets for whole-class teaching, so there is a varied approach across different learning styles.

Rigolo aims to enable pupils to meet the suggested DfES target of reaching National Curriculum Level 4 by the end of Key Stage 2. *Rigolo 1*, however, works mainly at Levels 1–2 (Breakthrough: Grades 1–2 of the Languages Ladder).

Rigolo storyline

Rigolo 1 has a central storyline of an English family moving to France, where they make new friends and learn about life in a different country. This story runs through the CD-ROM as well as the Resource Pack, which features puppets of the three main characters and Big Books continuing the adventures of the family. Most activities and stories focus on the two English children, Jake and Polly, and their pet dragon Bof. As the story progresses they make friends with Didier, Nathalie and Olivier, and constantly cross paths with Didier's aunt Madame Moulin, the cantankerous housekeeper of Château Rigolo.

Teacher support

Teacher support in *Rigolo* is very thorough and provided at three levels. For non-specialists and those teachers with less knowledge of French, *Rigolo* features the unique Virtual Teacher: video clips accompanying each activity on the CD-ROM. These present new language visually and aurally, showing correct pronunciation and gestures to reinforce understanding, and also provide instructions to pupils and a response to their answers. More specialist teachers can switch off the Virtual Teacher if they do not need this much support.

There are also short on-screen instructions in English to explain how each activity works, and to act as a quick reminder in the lesson. Finally, to back up each activity in *Rigolo*, there are detailed teaching notes explaining how to deliver these in the classroom.

Delivering lessons with Rigolo

As mentioned above, each unit of the course contains four or five lessons, each designed to last approximately 45 minutes. The teaching notes clearly indicate how long to allow for each activity, so these can easily be broken up into shorter lessons depending on how much time you have to teach French.

Each unit is based on an animated story, which introduces the new language of the unit in the context of the *Rigolo* storyline.

Each lesson is framed by starter and plenary activities to refresh pupils' memory of language learnt previously or to reflect on what has just been learnt. Most lessons proceed to introduce a set of new language – usually only five to eight words or short phrases at a time – in a Presentation. The new language is then practised in a mixture of whiteboard and class activities, the latter using puppets, flashcards and other props where appropriate.

Each unit also features an *Extra* section, containing resources and activities to further practise the language and content. This includes eight differentiated worksheets for every unit, as well as a Project Work activity. Every other unit also contains a set of

Sound/spelling activities focusing on French sounds encountered in the preceding two units, and a set of Assessment activities to gently test pupils' progress through Key Stage 2 (see below for more details on both Sound/spelling and Assessment).

Cross-curricular opportunities are clearly highlighted throughout *Rigolo*. The teaching notes on each lesson summarise the other areas of the KS2 curriculum that are covered.

How to use *Rigolo* features and activities

This section explains in more detail how to use the various different types of activities and recurring features found in *Rigolo 1*.

a) Standard features

Virtual Teacher

The Virtual Teacher (VT) offers an unparalleled level of support for primary teachers who lack confidence or practice in French.

In Presentations, the VT will also pronounce each item of language when it is selected on the screen, usually giving an associated gesture at the same time. You can click on *Replay* to play this clip again, or *Zoom* if you want to focus more closely on the teacher's mouth movements to aid pronunciation.

When pupils complete activities, the VT will also react to their answers in French, depending on whether they are right or wrong. Again, you can click on *Replay* to repeat these clips.

The VT panel appears in the top-right corner of the screen on every whiteboard activity. She will give brief

instructions in French of what to do in the activity, so that pupils get used to hearing classroom instructions in the target language. At any other time while using the activity, you can click on *Task* to hear the instructions one more time.

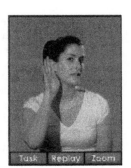

While the VT is a valuable support, more experienced teachers might not want to have her enabled. To switch off this feature, click on the *Virtual Teacher off* button in the bottom right corner of the activity screen.

Text bar

In the Animated story and Presentation activities, you have the option of viewing the story or new language in written form on the text bar at the bottom of the screen. To disable this, click on the white *Turn text off* tab above the text bar. To turn it back on, click on *Turn text on*.

Instructions

In any activity, you can click on the *Instructions* button at any time to find out how to complete the activity. This will display short instructions in English. You can find out more detail on how to use the activity in the classroom in the teaching notes. Click on the cross to close this window.

Allez, Encore and *Continuez* buttons

To start most activities, click on the *Allez* green light icon. Press *Allez* again to move from one question to the next. This will flash every few seconds until it is clicked.

In listening activities, you can click on the *Encore* button to hear the audio again. In some activities, you can also click on *Encore* to see the animation a second time when pupils have got an answer right.

In some Presentations, when you select an object the display will "zoom in" to a particular part of the screen to show more detail. As above, you can use *Encore* to hear the new language again. A *Continuez* button will appear to enable a return to the initial display.

Random order

Each time you use any activity, questions will appear in a different, random order.

b) Whiteboard activities

Animated stories

There is one Animated story in each unit of ***Rigolo 1***, which introduces the new language of the unit in the context of a short narrative featuring the characters from the ***Rigolo*** storyline.

Each story has two distinct halves with discrete new language, and you can watch these shorter clips as part of two of the lessons of the unit, so that pupils see the language in action that they are about to study. These clips are launched using the Animated story buttons in the lesson folder, usually in Lesson 1 and Lesson 3.

When you start the story, you will firstly see the instructions in French and the Virtual Teacher, if activated, reading these out. Click on the cross button in the corner of this panel to close this. The *Play* button will flash at the bottom of the screen to start the story.

Use the *Forward* and *Rewind* buttons to move through the story more quickly to a particular spot. Selecting *Pause* will pause the story at the current point until you click *Play* to restart. If you click on *Stop* the story goes back to the beginning.

Presentations

Most lessons in ***Rigolo*** are centred on a Presentation which introduces the core new language that is then practised in the accompanying activities. The Presentations are some of the most versatile teaching tools in ***Rigolo***: they allow pupils to hear and see the new language pronounced by the Virtual Teacher, and also to see it illustrated in a fun, animated context where they (and the teacher) choose which language they want to discover.

You will firstly see the instructions given in French on screen and by the Virtual Teacher, if enabled. Close this panel by clicking on the cross.

There will always be around five to eight items of language in each Presentation, represented by clickable icons or images in the display. These work like interactive, animated flashcards. The images will flash automatically soon after you start the activity, and when you hover over them the cursor will change to a pointing finger. When you select an item it will be animated, and you will then hear the word or phrase spoken either by the Virtual Teacher, or by the audio if the VT is not enabled. Wherever appropriate, the VT will give a gesture to accompany each word to reinforce understanding. Pupils should be encouraged to repeat this gesture to help them remember the new language.

Click on the same image again to repeat the sequence above, or *Replay* on the VT panel just to hear her repeat the word(s).

There are several other options on the Presentation to further explore the new language, as below.

Spell

To hear and see the new words spelt out, click on the *Spell* button once you have selected an item in the main display. The relevant letters will be highlighted as they are spoken, to reinforce knowledge of the alphabet.

The alphabet is introduced formally in Unit 5, but if you have taught this earlier, or after you have finished this unit, you can practise spelling skills using this feature in all the Presentations from Unit 1.

Sound

You can focus on sound/spelling links and improve pupils' pronunciation using this feature. Click on the *Sound* button and relevant sounds will be highlighted in red.

Click on one of the sounds to hear and see the Virtual Teacher pronounce this in isolation, then ask pupils to repeat the sound, imitating her mouth movements. Pupils will recognise many of the common sounds as they recur through the Presentations, and are practised further in the separate Sound/spelling activities.

Word

This feature helps focus on grammar terms and word classes. After selecting an item, click on the *Word* button to see and hear the Virtual Teacher describe what word class it falls into (noun, verb, adjective etc.), together with an accompanying gesture corresponding to those recommended for Key Stage 2 Literacy.

Please note that the above options are not enabled for those language items where they are not appropriate. You cannot use the spelling feature for whole phrases, for example, and some words do not have relevant sounds to highlight.

Oracy activities

Oracy activities separately practise either speaking or listening skills.

The speaking activities in **Rigolo** are designed to practise pupils' understanding and pronunciation of new language. In each activity pupils are given visual prompts for a particular word or phrase.

To start these activities or move between questions, click on the *Allez* button.

You can check pupils' answers by clicking on the audio check icon in the speech bubble (as above) that will appear. If pupils have given the correct answer, click on the tick, or click on the cross if not. If possible, it is better to give your own immediate feedback to pupils' answers and wait before clicking on the audio icon to reveal the answer, so that the activity can last longer.

Listening activities in **Rigolo** practise pupils' understanding of new language and their skills in listening for specific information. Pupils will hear various audio prompts, and have to select the relevant image on-screen to demonstrate their comprehension.

Click on the *Allez* button to start the activity and move between questions, and on *Encore* to hear any audio line repeated.

In some cases pupils will have three 'lives', represented by hearts (see picture overleaf). They will 'lose a life' for any incorrect answer, and the game ends once all three hearts have disappeared.

Literacy activities

The whiteboard Literacy activities mainly focus on reading skills, with (hand)writing skills practised largely on the Worksheets. The exceptions to this are the regular animated sentence activities, which practise word order in short phrases and are a useful way to model the writing process.

As elsewhere, click on the *Allez* button to start most of the activities or to move between questions. Pupils will see a visual prompt of either text or pictures, and have to select or drag and drop the corresponding text or image. As with Oracy activities, occasionally Literacy activities will also feature 'lives', to make activities more fun.

In the animated sentence activities (see above), pupils can experiment with building sentences or short phrases. To do this they drag the various words into the machine and click on the *Fini* button to see their meaning animated, if they are in the correct order. If not, then the machine will 'malfunction' and produce smoke. Once they have created a first sentence, pupils can drag and drop different words into position to produce new meanings.

Songs

There is one song in every unit of **Rigolo**, which revisits some or all of the language from the unit with music and movement, to reinforce learning and understanding.

The songs feature a unique set of 'karaoke' controls, so that pupils can sing along to the music on its own or listen to the words without the backing music instead.

The animations that accompany the **Rigolo** songs also feature movement and animations to illustrate the meaning of the songs. Pupils should be encouraged to mimic the dancing and movements in time with the song, wherever appropriate, thereby reinforcing their understanding of the language via kinaesthetic learning.

Each song can be used in either *Practice* or *Sing* mode. In *Practice* mode, you can play and practise one or two lines of the song in isolation, advancing to the next line(s) once pupils are ready. Click on *Whole lyrics* to see a whole verse at a time without the animation in the background. In *Sing* mode you can hear and see the song and animation all the way through.

The controls at the bottom of the screen operate in a similar way to those in the Animated story: *Play* starts the song; *Pause* halts it (*Play* starts it again); *Rewind* and *Forward* move quickly back or ahead; and *Stop* returns to the beginning. In Practice mode, *Previous* and *Next* move forward or back line by line.

To allow pupils to sing along to the music without hearing the words, click on the *Lyrics on/off* button. Click on it again to turn the words back on again. Similarly, to focus on the words in isolation, you can turn the backing music on and off using the *Music on/off* button.

Sound/spelling activities

After every even unit there is a Sound/spelling activity, to practise pronunciation and recognition of one of the key sounds that has been met in the preceding two units.

These activities are each made up of two sections: the first (*Practice*) to practise the sound(s) in question, and the second (*Activities*) to practise recognising it aurally and in writing.

Firstly select which section of the activity you want to use. In the *Practice* section, listen and watch the Virtual Teacher (if enabled) pronounce the particular sounds. You will hear the sounds firstly in isolation, and then used in several familiar words from the preceding units.

The activities are all slightly different, but are based on listening out for the relevant sounds in the audio and matching them to the text on-screen.

c) Worksheets

There are eight differentiated worksheets in each unit, providing further practice of the new language. These can be used alongside the separate lessons or at the end of the unit as a summative exercise. They cover a range of skills, but principally writing. Reading and writing activities on the worksheets also often progress on to pairwork speaking activities.

The worksheets in each unit are divided into four pairs, each at two different levels of difficulty. Worksheet A is for less able pupils, while Worksheet B is for the more able ones.

These may be used to allow some quiet time away from the whiteboard, set as homework tasks, or used in a cover lesson. In mixed year groups you can also give one half of the class some worksheets to complete while you use different whiteboard activities with the other half.

How to use the *Rigolo* teacher tools

On the Rigolo 1 menu screen are links to the main 'teacher tool' sections of the course:

- Teacher support
- Flashards

Below is a quick overview of what each section provides:

Teacher support

This section provides various levels of support for teachers using **Rigolo**, so that you don't have to always turn to the Teacher's Book. It also provides more video-based support for teachers to learn how to use the course and also to remind themselves of the new language, and its pronunciation, that they will encounter in **Rigolo**.

The Video case studies demonstrate how to use some of the main parts of the course, including the Animated stories, Presentations, Oracy and Literacy activities and Songs. The short video clips show the course being used in genuine classroom situations so that teachers can understand how the different activities can work with pupils, and also to see examples of good teaching practice with Primary MFL.

From the *Teacher support* area you can also display or print off any unit from the Teacher's notes, or a unit's worth of Worksheets. There are also files of the Mapping grids from the back of this book, and copies of certificates and language portfolios to mark pupils' progress through *Rigolo*.

Flashcards

There are numerous class activities in *Rigolo* which use the supplied Flashcards as visual prompts for pupils to practise the new language in the course. You can display accompanying Flashcards for a particular activity by clicking on the link in the class activity screen that appears when you launch the activity from the Lesson menu.

To print off the Flashcards, it is easier to use the Flashcards tab in the Teacher Support section. Once you have launched this section, you can choose which unit of Flashcards you would like to print out.

Each Flashcard consists of a picture and separate card with the accompanying word or phrase.

Using *Rigolo* to measure pupil's progress

As mentioned above, *Rigolo* as a whole covers National Curriculum levels and Language Ladder grades 1–4. There are various ways in which you can measure how pupils progress through Key Stage 2.

Assessment activities

There is a group of assessment activities after every even unit in *Rigolo*, launched from the *Extra* section of the Lesson menu. This consists of four worksheets, one focusing on each of the four main skills: listening, speaking, reading and writing. Each worksheet contains three or four individual activities.

The activities move through a graded progression: for example, in the first half of *Rigolo 1*, the activities start by working towards National Curriculum level/Languages Ladder Grade 1, then move up towards Level/Grade 1–2. For more information, see the teaching notes on these activities.

Assessment in Key Stage 2 is best kept fairly informal, without focusing pupils' attention on the levels at which they are working. Please note that these assessment tasks are not intended to certify that pupils have reached a certain level, but rather that they are working towards this point. However, for transition to Key Stage 3, it could well be useful to have a record of which levels pupils are working towards using *Rigolo*.

Assessment for learning opportunities

There are numerous ways to address Assessment for Learning (AfL), or Formative assessment, using *Rigolo*. AfL provides feedback to pupils on what has been achieved and also on which areas need further work, and can be used to inform your lesson planning. Below are several ways you can regularly incorporate this into teaching with *Rigolo*:

- Share the objectives of each unit and lesson with pupils before you start teaching, so that they are aware of the nature and purpose of the work they will be doing. At the end of the lesson, you can review with pupils whether they feel they have achieved these objectives and what they feel unsure about.

- Use the Presentations to allow pupils to compare their pronunciation with the model audio and video.

- Similarly, pupils can compare their pronunciation in the Songs and Animated stories.

- Use the Worksheets to measure pupils' progress, discussing the answers to each activity in class so that pupils are aware of where they have made mistakes and how they could improve. This acts as useful preparation for the Assessment worksheets at the end of every other unit.

Certificates and portfolio information

Pupils can keep track of their own progress using the supplied *Rigolo* certificates, accessible in the Teacher support area of the CD-ROM. These come at the end of every two units, roughly every term. Pupils can check off the various can-do statements listing the skills and language that they should be able to produce at this point. There is also a column for their partner, so that they are encouraged to discuss their progress and level of ability.

Rigolo also provides checklists to use with the national Languages Ladder or the European Languages Portfolio (ELP). The former provides a list of the can-do statements for the first two grades of the ladder, which pupils can keep to mark their progress at the end of each year of the course. The latter provides a copy of the relevant ELP can-do statements for the two stages of *Rigolo*. This can be used more frequently for pupils to track their progress, although please note that it does not tie into specific units of *Rigolo*.

Transition to Key Stage 3

Planning transition between primary and secondary French lessons requires careful co-ordination between schools in a local area. *Rigolo* aims to ease this process by providing the means to record each pupil's progress using the certificates, portfolios and assessment materials listed above.

Using *Rigolo* with the Scottish curriculum

Rigolo is an exciting interactive course which appeals to all types of learners. The Curriculum for Excellence Review Group recommends that young people should be "successful learners, confident individuals, responsible citizens and effective contributors" and *Rigolo* encourages young learners to achieve success and be confident in their learning of the French language. The variety of activities and the visual impact of the CD-ROM is relevant and stimulating and makes learning enjoyable. This has a positive effect on children's self-esteem and promotes positive attitudes to language learning at present and in the future.

The course progression provides worksheets, games and follow-up activities for reinforcement and extension work. The fact that it can be used for all stages of ability adds to its value. Assessment is built into the programme and allows children to know what the Learning Intentions are (unit objectives) and thus know when and precisely what they have achieved. They can then go on to set their own goals, which is an aim of the Assessment is for Learning Programme – itself a major focus in Scottish schools.

The Scottish 5–14 guidelines recommend that the teaching and learning programme for Modern Languages should provide "broad and balanced learning, coherent links and connections, continuous pathways for learning and a progressive development for learning". *Rigolo 1* is a course that meets these aims in a fun, comprehensive way. It links to the Listening, Speaking, Reading and Writing attainment outcomes and provides a framework for the development of the knowledge, understanding and skills identified within the strands A–C.

The included Appendix 3: *Rigolo 1* 5–14 guidelines mapping grid matches the 5–14 strands to the different units in *Rigolo 1* at the relevant levels, allowing teachers to identify activities easily for their planning and, at a glance, enables them to focus on certain strands across some or all of the units.

Joyce Morrison
Class teacher
Ancrum Road Primary School
Dundee

Flashcards

Unit 1
Nouns
1 un piano
2 une guitare
3 une trompette
4 un tambour
5 une flûte à bec
6 un garçon
7 une fille
8 un dragon
Greetings
9 Salut!
10 Bonjour, Monsieur. / Bonjour, Madame.
11 Au revoir, Mademoiselle. / Au revoir, Monsieur.

Unit 2
Classroom objects
1 un sac
2 un cahier
3 un crayon
4 une règle
5 une trousse
6 un livre
7 une gomme
8 un stylo
Colours
9 marron
10 rose
11 rouge
12 jaune
13 orange
14 bleu

Unit 3
Parts of the body
1 les yeux
2 le nez
3 la bouche
4 les oreilles
5 les cheveux
6 la jambe
7 le bras
8 la tête
Eyes and hair
9 les cheveux longs
10 les cheveux courts
11 les yeux verts
12 les yeux bleus
13 les yeux marron

Unit 4
Animals & pets
1 un chien
2 un chat
3 un lapin
4 un oiseau
5 un dragon
6 une souris
7 une tortue
Character descriptions
8 sévère
9 grand / petite
10 petit / grande
11 drôle
12 timide
13 bavard / bavarde
14 sympa

Unit 5
Household items
1 le DVD
2 le CD
3 le jeu vidéo
4 le lecteur de CD
5 l'ordinateur
6 la machine
7 la table
8 la chaise
Family
9 mes parents
10 mon père
11 ma mère
12 mon frère
13 ma sœur

Unit 6
Food and drink
1 une pomme
2 une banane
3 un jus d'orange
4 un sandwich
5 une pizza
6 un gâteau
Months of the year
7 janvier / février / mars / avril / mai / juin / juillet / août / septembre / octobre / novembre / décembre

Unit 7
Nationalities
1 Il est français. / Elle est française.
2 Il est britannique. / Elle est britannique.
3 Il est canadien. / Elle est canadienne.
Characteristics
4 Il est intelligent.
5 Elle est intelligente.
6 Il est sévère.
7 Elle est sévère.
8 Il est sportif.
9 Elle est sportive.
10 Il est timide.
11 Elle est timide.
Flags
12 canadien / canadienne
13 britannique
14 français / française

Unit 8
Leisure activities
1 Je joue au tennis.
2 Je joue au football.
3 Je regarde la télé.
4 J'écoute mes CD.
5 Je regarde un DVD.
6 J'écoute la radio.
Telling the time
7 Il est une heure.
8 Il est deux heures.

9 Il est trois heures.
10 Il est quatre heures.
11 Il est cinq heures.
12 Il est six heures.
13 Il est sept heures.
14 Il est huit heures.
15 Il est neuf heures.
16 Il est dix heures.
17 Il est onze heures.
18 Il est douze heures.

Unit 9
Festivals
1 le Nouvel An
2 la Fête des Rois
3 la Saint-Valentin
4 Pâques
5 la Fête Nationale
6 Noël

Unit 10
Weather
1 Il fait chaud.
2 Il fait froid.
3 Il neige.
4 Il pleut.
5 Il fait beau.
Directions
6 Tournez à gauche.
7 Tournez à droite.
8 Allez tout droit.
9 Arrêtez.

Unit 11
More food and drink
1 du pain
2 du fromage
3 de la limonade
4 de la crème
5 des fraises
6 des tomates
Party activities
7 On mange.
8 On boit.
9 On danse.
10 On chante.
11 On s'amuse.

Unit 12
Countries
1 la France
2 le Sénégal
3 le Maroc
4 le Canada
5 la Suisse
6 la Martinique
Clothes
7 un pantalon
8 une veste
9 une chemise
10 un t-shirt
11 un chapeau
12 une jupe

Unit 1: Bonjour!

National criteria

KS2 Framework objectives

O3.1　Listen and respond to simple rhymes, stories and songs
O3.2　Recognise and respond to sound patterns and words
O3.3　Perform simple communicative tasks using single words, phrases and short sentences
O3.4　Listen attentively and understand instructions, everyday classroom language and praise words
L3.1　Recognise some familiar words in written form
L3.2　Make links between some phonemes, rhymes and spellings, and read aloud familiar words
L3.3　Experiment with the writing of simple words

QCA Scheme of Work

Unit 1　Je parle français

Language ladder levels

Listening:	Breakthrough, Grade 1
Reading:	Breakthrough, Grade 1
Speaking:	Breakthrough, Grade 1
Writing:	Breakthrough, Grade 1

5–14 guideline strands　　　　　　　　　　　　　　　　　　　　　　Levels A–C

Listening		**Reading**	
Listening for information and instructions	A, C	Reading for information and instructions	A, C
Listening and reacting to others	A, B, C	Reading aloud	A, C

Speaking		**Writing**	
Speaking to convey information	A, C	Writing to exchange information and ideas	A, C
Speaking and interacting with others	B, C	Writing to establish and maintain personal contact	A, C
Speaking about experiences, feelings and opinions	A, B	Writing imaginatively/to entertain	n/a

Unit objectives

- greet and say goodbye to someone
- ask someone's name and give your own
- ask how someone is and respond to the same question
- count numbers 1–10
- identify musical instruments

Key language

- greetings: *bonjour, salut, au revoir; Madame, Monsieur, Mademoiselle*
- say and ask names: *Comment t'appelles-tu?; Je m'appelle...*
- say and ask how you are: *Ça va? Ça va bien, Ça ne va pas, Comme çi comme ça*
- numbers 1–10: *un, deux, trois, quatre, cinq, six, sept, huit, neuf, dix*
- musical instruments: *une trompette, une guitare, une flûte à bec, un piano, un tambour, un dragon, une fille, un garçon, un dragon*

Grammar and skills

- first notions of gender
- ask and answer questions
- recognise cognates

Unit outcomes

Most children will be able to:

- use spoken French to greet others and introduce themselves
- understand and use numbers 1–10
- begin to recognise, read and pronounce sounds of combinations of letters, words and set phrases

Some children will also be able to:

- write and say phrases from memory, with clear pronunciation and meaning
- identify nouns using the correct gender
- combine numbers and nouns together in a short phrase

1

Unit 1   Lesson 1

Context
Saying hello and goodbye

National criteria
KS2 Framework: **O3.1, O3.2, O3.3, O3.4, L3.1, L3.2, L3.3, IU3.1, IU3.2, IU3.3**
Attainment levels: **AT1.1, AT2.1, AT3.1**
Language ladder levels:
  Listening: **Grade 1**; Reading: **Grade 1**
  Speaking: **Grade 1**

Cross-curricular links
PSHE: different ways of greeting people in different cultures; how we feel in unknown situations
Geography: looking at francophone countries around the world

Key vocabulary
Greetings: *Bonjour* (Hello), *Salut* (Hi), *Au revoir* (Goodbye)

Language structures and outcomes
Bonjour (Monsieur/Madame…, etc.), Salut, Au revoir (Monsieur/Madame…, etc.)

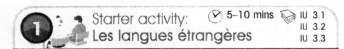

1 Starter activity: ⏱ 5–10 mins   📖 IU 3.1
Les langues étrangères   IU 3.2
                                 IU 3.3

Materials
World map and/or globe, map of Europe/France

Description
Discussion of foreign languages.

Delivery
● Begin by checking pupils' awareness of foreign languages. Ask pupils which languages they speak at home, which languages other people in their family speak, whether they have heard different languages on holiday, on TV, and so on.

● Ask if pupils think it is important to speak different languages, and why/why not. Ask if they can guess how many languages are spoken in the world (answer: approximately 6800) and which ones are most widely spoken (generally held to be Mandarin Chinese, Spanish and English).

● If French hasn't already been specifically mentioned, ask if anyone has been to a place where French is spoken, and if they already know any words. Referring to the map/globe, ask which countries use French, and invite pupils to come up and locate the countries on the map. (French is the main language spoken in 35 countries; English in around 50.)

Extension
● Pupils prepare a project on a French-speaking country they know.

● Encourage pupils to introduce themselves using *Je m'appelle…* (the Virtual Teacher models this language on the CD-ROM in the Language Presentation of Lesson 2).

● Use the internet to obtain up-to-date facts and figures on languages.

2 Animated story: ⏱ 15 mins   📖 AT1.1 O3.1
Le Château Rigolo (1)   AT3.1 O3.4
                                      L3.1

Materials
CD-ROM

Description
Watch and listen to this interactive animated story presenting the language for Lessons 1–3. You can pause and rewind the story at any point.

Delivery
● This animated story can be used for both starter and plenary activities – the whole animation can be played at the end of the unit so that pupils can gauge their improved understanding.

● At this point, pupils watch the first half of the story only; the second half is in Lesson 4.

Scene 1 (arrival of van and family)

● Play the scene, then pause the screen and ask pupils to describe what is happening.

● Ask where the family are from (clue: flag on van), and what they think the family is going to do in France (are they on holiday? are they going to live here?). Who will the family meet first?

Scene 2 (at the front door)

● Repeat as for Scene 1. Ask the class if they can tell you how the characters are saying 'hello' to each other. Play the scene again for pupils to check their answers.

● Ask more confident groups to listen for the names of characters; otherwise tell your class who is who, i.e. Jake, Madame Moulin, Mrs Mills, Didier, Bof.

Scene 3 (Jake and Didier)

● Repeat as above, this time adding the question 'How do we say "goodbye" in French?'

3 Presentation: ⏱ 15 mins   📖 AT1.1 O3.2
Bonjour et au revoir   AT2.1 O3.4
                               AT3.1 L3.1
                                      L3.2

Materials
CD-ROM

Description
Click on the doors to hear and see the correct pronunciation when characters exchange greetings. Use the additional features to practise sound/spelling links **and spelling.**

Delivery
● Start by asking pupils if they know, or can remember from the animation, how to say 'hello' or 'goodbye' in French. Ask the class to listen carefully during this activity to see if they were right.

● Ask several pupils, in turn, to choose and click on a door on the whiteboard. After hearing each greeting, repeat all together. Click on the *Encore* button to listen again. Repeat chorally, copying the Virtual Teacher's gestures as you say the words.

● Ask pupils to practise the greeting they have just heard with the pupil next to them.

● Once you have finished practising the scene behind each door, click on the *Continuez* button to return to the main view of the house.

● Continue until each door has been opened at least once. Repeat the activity as often as you feel is necessary.

Extension
● Choose another set of pupils to click on each of the doors in turn. Point to each door and ask the class what greeting they will hear, then click to see if they were right.

● Contrast the exchanges between Didier and Jake, or between Polly and Bof, with the others. Ask pupils why they think the characters might say 'hello' and 'goodbye' in a different way to different people (due to formality).

Spelling
● For groups who have already covered the alphabet: click on a greeting and ask pupils to say and spell the word. Check answer by clicking on the *Spell* icon.

● To simply introduce the concept of spelling in French, click on a word, then on the *Spell* icon, and get pupils to follow the letters as they are spoken/highlighted. Repeat, this time asking the whole class to join in. Continue in the same way with all the words.

Sounds
To further reinforce accurate pronunciation, and to introduce some basic reading skills:

● Point to each greeting on the text bar and ask the class to say the word.

● Focus on the text on screen, click on the *Sound* icon, and click on the different highlighted sounds to hear and see the Virtual Teacher saying them.

● Repeat all together.

4 Oracy activity: **Bonjour, Monsieur**   ⏱ 10 mins 📖 AT1.1 O3.3 AT2.1 O3.4

Materials
CD-ROM

Description
Click on *Allez* to hear each question. Listen to what the first character says in the dialogue and click on the correct speech bubble (A or B) for the answer.

Delivery
● Click (or invite a pupil to click) on the *Allez* button to start the activity.

● Ask pupils to listen to the possible answers in the speech bubbles (A and B). They will hear two different greetings, only one of which is correct.

● Ask the class, or an individual pupil, to say the correct answer, then click on button A or B. There will be an appropriate automatic response. If wrong, then pupils can click on the other option.

● Click on the *Allez* button again to go on to the next greeting (there are a total of six).

● To play the game again click on the *Jouez encore?* ✓ button.

Extension
● Split the activity into two parts, each with three sets of greetings, then do the activity as a team game and see who gets most correct answers.

Support
● Model the three different greetings (*Salut, Bonjour, Monsieur*, etc.), and *Au revoir*) with pupils before they start the activity.

 Knowledge About Language

Social conventions
● French uses similar and also different social linguistic conventions compared to English, and it is worth pointing these out to pupils as they learn.

● In this lesson, point out how the children say *Salut!* to each other, but *Bonjour, Madame* or *Bonjour, Monsieur* to adults.

● Ask pupils to compare this with English, where they might say 'Hi!' to their friends or family, but 'Hello' to people they know less well.

 **5** Plenary activity: **Salut! Au revoir!**   ⏱ 5 mins 📖 AT2.1 O3.3 IU3.3

Materials
Unit 1 Flashcards 9–11 (Greetings), character puppets, and/or a selection of the following: school caps/baseball-style caps, ladies' hats, gentlemen's hats

Description
Role-play activity to practise the greetings introduced so far.

Delivery
● Use the greetings flashcards to elicit the various greetings that have been covered in this lesson.

● Show the puppets to the class. Ask pupils to think how the characters could greet each other, and to practise in pairs or threes for one or two minutes.

● Invite small groups of pupils to the front to use the puppets to perform their role-play for the rest of the class.

Extension
● Call out two pupils to the front of the class. You can either hand them each a hat, or let them choose one each. They must then greet each other in the appropriate way (e.g. two pupils in school or baseball caps would be expected to say *Salut!* to each other; someone wearing a lady's hat would be addressed *Bonjour, Madame*, and so on).

Support
● You can use the Virtual Teacher at any time to refresh pupils' memory of the target expressions in Activity 3.

Unit 1 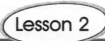 Lesson 2

Context
Asking and saying your name

National criteria
KS2 Framework: **O3.2, O3.3, O3.4, L3.1, L3.2, L3.3**
Attainment levels: **AT1.1, AT2.1, AT3.1, AT4.1**
Language ladder levels:
  Listening: **Grade 1**; Reading: **Grade 1**;
  Speaking: **Grade 1**; Writing: **Grade 1**

Cross-curricular links
PSHE: different ways of greeting people in different cultures; how we feel in unknown situations

Key vocabulary
Greetings: *Comment t'appelles-tu?* (What's your name?), *Je m'appelle...* (My name is...)

Language structures and outcomes
Comment t'appelles-tu?, *Je m'appelle...*

---

 1 Starter activity: ⏱ 5–10 mins 📖 AT2.1 O3.3 O3.4
Les noms

Materials
Character puppets

Description
Role-play revision activity using puppets.

Delivery
● Hold up a puppet and say 'hello' to the class, getting them to say 'hello' back. Make the puppet answer (with gestures where possible!).

● Act out the phrase *Je m'appelle* (e.g.) *Bof. Comment t'appelles-tu?* between the puppet and yourself, making sure you answer using the full *Je m'appelle...* phrase. Then ask pupils the same question in turn with the puppet.

● Repeat with the other puppets.

● Invite a pupil to choose a puppet and to stand at the front of the class. The whole class says 'hello' and asks the puppet its name; the pupil 'makes' the puppet give an answer.

● Repeat a few times with different pupils and different puppets.

2 Presentation: ⏱ 10 mins 📖 AT1.1 O3.2 AT2.1 O3.4 AT3.1 L3.1 L3.2
Comment t'appelles-tu?

Materials
CD-ROM, puppets (for extension activity)

Description
Click on the pictures to hear and see the correct pronunciation when characters introduce themselves to each other. Use the additional features to practise sound/spelling links.

Delivery
● Invite pupils to click on the pictures one by one, then encourage the class to repeat the questions and answers. Ensure they imitate the intonation as accurately as possible.

● After clicking on each picture, click on *Continuez* to return to the main picture of the gallery.

● Click on *Encore* to hear each question/answer a second time.

● Use the Virtual Teacher at any time to compare intonation.

Extension
● Using two puppets, make them ask and answer their names using the model from the presentation. Invite pairs of pupils to the front of the class. Hand them a puppet each, and ask them to ask and answer what their names are.

● Ask a pupil *Comment t'appelles-tu?* Once they have replied, they must ask the pupil next to them, and so on around the group.

● In larger groups, you can ask two pupils: one at the front of the class, one from the back. The 'chain' of questions continues until it meets somewhere in the middle!

Sounds
To further reinforce accurate pronunciation, and to introduce some basic reading skills:

● Point to each question and answer on the text bar and ask the class to repeat them.

● Focus on the text on screen, click on the *Sound* icon, and click on the different highlighted sounds to hear the Virtual Teacher saying them.

● Repeat all together.

 3 Oracy activity: ⏱ 10 mins 📖 AT2.1 O3.3
Les présentations

Materials
Hats and other props to help indicate 'age' of role-play characters; whistle or hooter to indicate when to change groups (or the end of the activity)

Description
Pairwork/role-play activity practising introductions.

Delivery
● Put the pupils into pairs/small groups and ask them to do mini role-plays using the language that they have learned so far i.e. for saying 'hello' and giving their name. Encourage them to include a mix of characters and ages by using props; this will ensure they cover all the target language.

● After five minutes, blow the whistle or clap your hands, to indicate that pupils should move into new groups and repeat the same activity with new characters.

● You can use the Virtual Teacher on the CD-ROM at any time to refresh your memory of the target expressions.

4 Plenary activity: ⏱ 10 mins 📑 AT3.1 L3.1
Je m'appelle Bof   AT4.1 L3.2
                                   L3.3

Materials
Blank paper and pens, magazine pictures of fictional characters (optional)

Description
Literacy activity practising reading and writing your name.

Delivery
● Write the model dialogue *Comment t'appelles-tu?/Je m'appelle...* on the board for pupils to copy.

● Get pupils to choose a character from *Rigolo*, or another fictional character, and write out the dialogue giving that as their name. They can then draw a picture of their chosen character below the dialogue, or stick a magazine picture there instead.

● Separate the pictures from the dialogues and mix them up. One by one, pupils have to find the matching pairs of picture and dialogue, then read the question and answer aloud.

Unit 1 (Lesson 3

Lesson summary

Context
Asking and saying how you are

National criteria
KS2 Framework: **O3.1, O3.2, O3.3, O3.4, L3.1, L3.2, L3.3, IU3.3**
Attainment levels: **AT1.1–2, AT2.1–2, AT3.1–2, AT4.1**
Language ladder levels:
  Listening: **Grade 1–2**; Reading: **Grade 1–2**;
  Speaking: **Grade 1–2**; Writing: **Grade 1–2**

Cross-curricular links
PSHE: different ways of greeting people in different cultures; how we feel in unknown situations

Key vocabulary
Asking and saying how you are: *Ça va?* (How are you?), *Oui, ça va bien.* (Yes, I'm well.), *Comme ci comme ça.* (I'm so-so.), *Non, ça ne va pas.* (No, I'm not doing well.).

Language structures and outcomes
Ça va?; *Oui, ça va bien*; *Comme ci comme ça*; *Non, ça ne va pas*

1 Starter activity: ⏲ 5–10 mins 📖 AT2.1 O3.3
                                          O3.4
Bonjour, comment   IU3.3
t'appelles-tu?

Materials
Character puppets, and/or a selection of the following: school caps/baseball-style caps, ladies' hats, gentlemen's hats

Description
Revision of role-play game using puppets and/or basic props.

Delivery
● Invite pairs/small groups of pupils to the front to wear the puppets and to perform a greetings role-play for the rest of the class, saying 'hello' to each other and asking their names.

Extension
● Call out two pupils to the front of the class.

● You can either hand each of them a hat, or let them choose one each. They must then greet each other in the appropriate way (e.g. two pupils in school/baseball caps would be expected to say *Salut!* to each other; someone wearing a lady's hat would be addressed *Bonjour, Madame*, and so on). They can invent their own names.

Support
● Model each dialogue using puppets and/or hats before getting pupils to perform them.

2 Presentation: ⏲ 10 mins 📖 AT1.1 O3.2
                                    AT2.1 O3.4
Ça va?   AT3.1 L3.1
                                           L3.2

Materials
CD-ROM

Description
Click on the doors to hear and see the correct pronunciation when characters ask and say how they are. Use the additional features to practise sound/spelling links.

Delivery
● Tell the class that they are going to learn how to ask and say how they are in French. Ask if anyone already knows how to say this – you can either comment on their answers now, or simply ask the class to listen carefully to the presentation to check if their suggestions were correct.

● Choose different pupils to click on each door in turn. Listen to what is said, with or without using the Virtual Teacher, and repeat all together. Then listen again to the Virtual Teacher to practise pronunciation, or do this yourself if you prefer. Make

sure that everyone also copies the Virtual Teacher's gestures – this will help pupils remember much more easily.

● Click on *Continuez* to return to the main view of the Château.

Sounds
● This is a good opportunity to practise sound/spelling links. See the Introduction for notes on how to use this feature of the Language Presentation.

 Language Learning Strategies

Using the Virtual Teacher to aid learning
The *Rigolo* Virtual Teacher illustrates various important ways in which pupils can benefit from watching language being spoken in front of them:

● Pupils should imitate the native speaker pronunciation by listening to and repeating what the Virtual Teacher says.

● Encourage pupils to look at the Virtual Teacher's face as she speaks and to focus on how she moves her mouth when she pronounces different sounds. Use the *Zoom* feature to enlarge her mouth, or you can model this yourself instead.

● For many words or phrases, the Virtual Teacher gives an accompanying gesture to reinforce the meaning. This is a kinaesthetic aid to learning for pupils, and you should encourage them to repeat this gesture when they repeat the words. You can also get them to respond with the gesture when you say the word.

---

3 Oracy activity: ⏲ 15 mins 📖 AT1.1 O3.2
                                          O3.4
Ça va bien

Materials
CD-ROM

Description
Listen to each character say how they are, then click on the appropriate button to indicate if the response is happy, neutral or sad.

Delivery
● Click on *Allez* to start the activity. You will hear each character being asked the question *Ça va?* and their response

will also be heard, but without seeing their facial expression. The pupil must decide if the response is happy, sad, or neutral, and then click on the appropriate 'face' icon on screen. If unsure, the pupil can click on the *Encore* button to hear the response a second time.

● There will be an appropriate reaction from the Virtual Teacher, if activated, depending on whether the answer is right or wrong. If wrong, pupils can have another attempt.

Extension
● You can turn this activity into a team game by forming two groups and inviting pupils (in turn) from each group to click on a character. Keep scores of the correct answers.

Support
● Play each scene twice using the *Encore* button before asking pupils to respond.

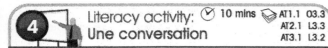

4 Literacy activity: 🕙 10 mins 📖 AT1.1 03.3 / AT2.1 L3.3 / AT3.1 L3.2
Une conversation

Materials
CD-ROM

Description
Drag the word tiles into the machine to answer the questions. Press the *Fini* button when you have completed each answer, and watch the machine illustrate them using animation.

Delivery
● The question *Comment t'appelles-tu?* is on the first screen. The pupil must select any of a number of correct combinations of answer tiles and drag them into the machine.

● Ask the whole class if they agree with the selected answer.

● The pupil now presses *Fini*. If the combination was correct, a mini-animation of the character they chose will appear. In the case of incorrect-order combinations, the machine blows out black smoke.

● Proceed to the second question, *Ça va?* A response must be dropped into the machine and the pupil presses *Fini* to see the character appropriately animated.

● Invite another pupil to come to the board and create another response to either the first or second question, using a different character or a different answer to *Ça va?* Repeat as above until all characters and scenarios have been covered.

Extension
● Invite pupils to recreate the dialogues at the front of the class using the puppets.

5 Literacy activity: 🕙 10 mins 📖 AT2.1 03.3 / AT3.1 L3.1 / L3.2
Au château

Materials
CD-ROM

Description
Watch each animation and drag the correct speech bubble to the character.

Delivery
● Click on *Allez* to start the activity. Watch each mini-animation, and ask pupils to work out which is the correct speech bubble, then say it aloud. You can either give them feedback yourself, or let pupils come to the whiteboard and try dragging the sentence into the empty speech bubble.

● There will be an appropriate reaction from the Virtual Teacher, if activated.

● Click on *Allez* to continue to the next mini-animation. Repeat as above until all characters have been covered at least once.

Extension
● Pupils can copy out their favourite scenario from the activity, writing the appropriate phrases into speech bubbles.

Support
● Go through each of the options with pupils, reading them aloud and giving the gestures already learnt. Ask pupils e.g. *Salut – oui ou non?* until they have agreed what the correct answer is.

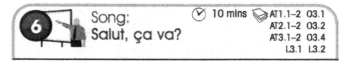

6 Song: 🕙 10 mins 📖 AT1.1–2 03.1 / AT2.1–2 03.2 / AT3.1–2 03.4 / L3.1 L3.2
Salut, ça va?

Materials
CD-ROM or Audio CD, track 07

Description
Watch and listen to the interactive karaoke song. Choose either *Practice* or *Sing* mode: the former to go through the song line by line, the latter to sing it all the way through. Switch the music and words on or off as you prefer.

Delivery
● Ask pupils to listen out for the greetings and questions, which appear in the song.

● Play the song straight through once, in *Sing* mode. Afterwards, ask pupils to tell you as many of the greetings and questions as they can remember.

● Go back and play the song in *Practice* mode, focusing on one line at a time. Repeat chorally and to check comprehension.

● When pupils are comfortable with the lyrics, divide the class in two groups – one group will sing each part in the different verses.

● Swap over roles for each verse.

See the Introduction for more notes on the Song features.

7 Plenary activity: 🕙 5–15 mins 📖 AT2.1 03.3 / AT4.1 L3.3
Les presentations

Materials
Names or cut-out pictures of famous characters known to pupils (e.g. Harry Potter, Hermione, Bart Simpson, Horrid Henry, Matilda, The Gruffalo); a cloth bag or hat to hold the name/picture cards; blank paper for drawing cartoon dialogues (extension activity).

Description
Role-play revision activity for Lessons 1–3 using famous characters from books and films.

Delivery
● Place the name/picture cards in the bag or hat.

● Invite pupils to come up, two at a time, to choose a card each. Continue until all pupils have a card.

● Pupils then sit down together in their pairs and create a dialogue between their two characters.

● Pupils can either write down the dialogue, as in a mini-play, or create a short cartoon by drawing the characters and speech bubbles, or sticking cut-out pictures on the paper.

Support
● To simplify this activity, you could prepare a basic cartoon outline and photocopy one for each pair: draw two boxes, with two 'stick' characters in each box. Pupils then just need to stick or draw on the faces and add speech bubbles or text.

Unit 1  Lesson 4

Context
Nouns (musical instruments)

National criteria
KS2 Framework: **O3.1, O3.2, O3.3, O3.4, L3.1, L3.2, L3.3**
Attainment levels: **AT1.1, AT2.1, AT3.1, AT4.1**
Language ladder levels:
  Listening: **Grade 1**; Reading: **Grade 1**;
  Speaking: **Grade 1**; Writing: **Grade 1**

Cross-curricular links
Music

Key vocabulary
Instruments: *un tambour* (drum), *une guitare* (guitar), *un piano* (piano), *une trompette* (trumpet), *une flûte à bec* (recorder)
Miscellaneous: *une fille* (girl), *un garçon* (boy)

Language structures and outcomes
n/a

---

1 Animated story: ⏱ 10 mins 📖 AT1.1 O3.3 / AT3.1 O3.4 / L3.1
Le Château Rigolo (2)

Materials
CD-ROM

Description
Watch and listen to this interactive animated story presenting the language for Lessons 4–5. You can pause and rewind the story at any point.

Delivery
● This animated story can be used for both starter and plenary activities – the whole animation can be played at the end of the unit so that pupils can gauge their improved understanding.

● At this point pupils only watch the second half of the story; the first half is in Lesson 1.

Scene 4 (in the Great Hall of the castle)

● Pause the screen before viewing each scene and ask pupils to guess what objects are hidden under the cloths.

● Play the scene all the way through, without stopping. Ask pupils if they correctly guessed the instruments and the storyline. Summarise together what happened in this scene.

● Replay the counting of each lot of instruments. Alternatively, you can do this at the start of Lesson 5.

● You can replay the scene again now, or wait until later in the section to enable pupils to see how much more they understand.

2 Starter activity: ⏱ 5 mins 📖 AT2.1 O3.3 / AT3.1 L3.1
Un piano

Materials
Unit 1 Flashcards 1–5 (musical instruments)

Description
Revision of musical instruments presented in animated story.

Delivery
● Ask pupils to recall which instruments featured in the animation.

● As they say each one, hold up the relevant picture flashcard (and stick on board/wall if possible).

● Encourage pupils to say the word in French, but don't worry if they can't remember all of them as this is covered in the next activity.

Extension
● Introduce the word Flashcards to go with the pictures, and play a matching game between picture and word.

3 Presentation: ⏱ 15 mins 📖 AT1.1 O3.2 / AT2.1 O3.4 / AT3.1 L3.1 / L3.2
Les instruments de musique

Materials
CD-ROM

Description
Click on the language objects to hear and see the correct pronunciation. Use the additional features to practise sound/spelling links, word classes and spelling.

Delivery
● Choose pupils to come up, in turn, and click on a character or an instrument.

● The whole group repeats the word and copies the Virtual Teacher's gestures, if activated.

● When each instrument has been covered a couple of times, make two teams, and ask each team (in turn) to say the word when you point at an instrument. Click on the picture to check whether the answer is correct, and give a point for each correct answer.

● Ask pupils to click on the remaining three images (Jake, Polly, and Bof) and repeat the words for 'boy', 'girl', and 'dragon'.

Spelling
● You can practise spelling using the language in this presentation. See the Introduction for notes on how to use this feature of the Language Presentation.

Sounds
● This is a good opportunity to practise sound/spelling links. See the Introduction for notes on how to use this feature of the Language Presentation.

Word class
● This is a good opportunity to practise word classes. See the Introduction for notes on how to use this feature of the Language Presentation.

Knowledge About Language

Genders

● This lesson features the first notion of different gender nouns in French. For more confident pupils, you can take the opportunity to investigate this in class.

● In the Presentation above, with the text bar activated, ask pupils if they can work out what the word for 'a' is in French (*un* or *une*).

● Then ask pupils if they can work out what the words on the left-hand side of the screen have in common, and likewise for the words on the right (the words on the left are masculine and use *un*, while the words on the right are feminine and use *une*).

● Explain that nouns in French are divided into two groups using either *un* or *une*. They will see words in different groups like this throughout *Rigolo*.

Word classes

● The *Word* feature in the *Rigolo* Presentations enable you to focus on grammar terms in French. In this case all the words presented are nouns.

● The first time you meet a word class, you might want to tackle this in English first, before introducing the equivalent French phrase (*C'est un nom* – it's a noun).

● Each word class has an associated gesture, as used in literacy activities. This is a good way to reinforce meaning.

4 Oracy activity: ⏱ 10 mins 📖 AT1.1 03.2
C'est quel instrument de AT3.1 03.4
musique?

Materials
CD-ROM

Description
Listen to the audio and click on the correct picture for each word.

Delivery
● Click on *Allez* to start the activity. You will hear a word. Ask a pupil to come up to the whiteboard and click on the corresponding picture.

● There will be an automatic response to the pupil's answer.

● Click on the *Encore* button to play the audio for each question again, or on the *Allez* button to proceed to the next question.

Extension
● Make two teams. The teams take it in turn to click on *Allez*, then on a picture and score a point for each correct answer.

Support
● Model the first few questions: after hearing the audio for each question, point to each object on the screen asking pupils *C'est un...? Oui ou non?*, until pupils agree the correct answer.

Language Learning Strategies

Cognates

● It is reassuring for pupils to point out that there is a lot of language shared between French and English. There are numerous cognates that come up in *Rigolo*.

● Ask pupils to concentrate on the words they have learnt so far in this lesson and to think of which words are similar to the English (*une trompette, une guitare, un piano, un dragon, une flûte à bec, un tambour*).

5 Literacy activity: ⏱ 10 mins 📖 AT2.1 03.3
Une trompette AT3.1 L3.1

Materials
Unit 1 Flashcards 1–8 (Nouns)

Description
Flashcard activity, matching words to pictures and/or articles to nouns.

Delivery
● Separate word and picture cards into two piles.

● Go through the picture cards one by one, and ask the class to tell you the correct word.

● Divide the group into teams and give each team a set of cards.

● Time how long it takes each team to match the cards correctly.

Extension 1 (articles)
● Cut up each word card so the article is separate from the noun.

● Repeat the above activity; this time pupils must also match the correct article in each case.

Extension 2 (Kim's game)
● Stick a set of flashcards on the board (either picture or word cards).

● Ask one or two pupils to leave the room for one minute.

● Ask a third pupil to come to the board and remove a card.

● Pupils 1 and 2 come back in and must identify the card which has been removed.

● Repeat as many times as desired!

Extension 3 (memory pairs)
● Give a set of picture and word cards to each group/table.

● Turn the cards over so the text/pictures are hidden

● Pupils in each group take it in turn to turn over two cards – if they match, they keep the pair. Otherwise, the cards are put back in the same place, and the next pupil has a go.

● Continue until all pairs have been found.

6 Plenary activity: ⏱ 5–10m 📖 AT2.1 03.3
C'est un tambour AT3.1 L3.3

Materials
Unit 1 Flashcards 1–8 (Nouns)

Description
Flashcard activity for practising gender and noun recognition.

Delivery
● Hold up a flashcard and ask *C'est un dragon ou un garçon?*; *C'est une trompette ou un piano?* etc.

● You may wish to make this into a team game, and give points for each correct answer.

Extension
● Hold up a flashcard and ask *Qu'est-ce que c'est?* Give the card to the pupil or team who answers correctly.

● Write *un* and *une* on either side of the board. Hold up a picture/word card (minus the article!) and ask a pupil to put it in the correct group.

Unit 1 (Lesson 5)

Context
Numbers 1–10

National criteria
KS2 Framework: **O3.1, O3.2, O3.3, O3.4, L3.1, L3.2**
Attainment levels: **AT1.1, AT2.1, AT3.1**
Language ladder levels:
  Listening: **Grade 1**; Reading: **Grade 1**;
  Speaking: **Grade 1**

Cross-curricular links
Numeracy, Music

Key vocabulary
Numbers 1–10: *un, deux, trois, quatre, cinq, six, sept, huit,*
neuf, dix

Language structures and outcomes
n/a

---

1 Starter activity: ⏱ 5–10 mins 📚 AT2.1 O3.3 / AT3.1 O3.1
Encore des instruments

Materials
Unit 1 Flashcards 1–8 (Nouns)

Description
Flashcard activity, to revise nouns from previous lesson.

Delivery
● Repeat one of the activities from Lesson 4, Activity 5.

2 Presentation: ⏱ 10–15 mins 📚 AT1.1 O3.2 / AT2.1 O3.4 / AT3.1 L3.1 / L3.2
Un, deux, trois

Materials
CD-ROM

Description
Click on the numbers to hear and see the correct
pronunciation. Use the additional features to practise
sound/spelling links.

Delivery
● Choose pupils to come up, in turn, and click on one number
at a time, starting from 1. The whole class repeats the number
and holds up the appropriate number of fingers each time.
Repeat until all the numbers have been covered.

● Invite another set of pupils to point to the numerals on
screen, as above. This time, ask the class to say the number
<u>before</u> they click, then listen to the audio/Virtual Teacher to
check if they were correct.

Spelling
● For groups who have already done the alphabet: point to a
number (word) and ask pupils to say/spell the word. Check
answers by clicking on the word then on the *Spell* icon.

● To simply introduce the concept of spelling in French, click
on a word, then on the *Spell* icon, and get pupils to follow the
letters as they are spoken/highlighted. Repeat, this time
asking the whole class to join in. Continue in the same way
with all the words.

Sounds
To further reinforce accurate pronunciation, and to introduce
some basic reading skills:

● Point to each number on the text bar and ask the class to
say the word.

● Focus on the text on screen, click on the *Sound* icon, and
click on the different highlighted sounds to hear the Virtual
Teacher saying them.

● Repeat all together.

NB. If the *Sound* icon is not illuminated, that means it is not
applicable for that particular word.

🦉 **Knowledge About Language**

Identifying sounds and phonemes
● The *Sound* feature in Presentations enables you to
examine pronunciation of new language in more detail,
to draw parallels between words in *Rigolo* and to
improve pupils' appreciation of sound/spelling links.

● For example, in this lesson pupils can meet the sounds
un, eu, oi, qu, r and *i* in the numbers, and recognise
how these sounds can be represented in written form.

---

3 Oracy activity: ⏱ 5 mins 📚 AT2.1 O3.1 / O3.3
Le rap des nombres

Materials
n/a

Description
Oracy activity practising numbers in a rap-style song.

Delivery
● Go through numbers 1–10, all together, clapping as you say
them

● Repeat as above, this time splitting the numbers as follows:
un, deux, trois,
quatre, cinq, six,
sept et huit,
neuf et DIX!

● Put the class into groups of 6–8, and ask each group to
make a rap out of the sequence you have just practised. Give
them no more than five minutes to prepare.

● Each group, in turn, performs their rap at the front of the
class.

● You could have a vote for the best rap!

Extension
● Each group could record their own *Rap des nombres*.

4 Oracy activity: ⏱ 10 mins 📚 AT1.1 03.2
Les nombres AT3.1 03.4

Materials
CD-ROM

Description
Listen to the audio, and drag the correct number to the object to match the phrase.

Delivery
● Click on *Allez* to start the activity. Ask pupils to come up to the board, in turn, to answer each question.

● You will hear a phrase combining numbers and objects (e.g. *trois pianos*). Pupils must drag the correct number to the correct image (in this case, number 3 to the piano picture).

● There will be an automatic response indicating whether the answer is right or wrong.

● Click on the *Encore* button to hear the audio again for each question, or the *Allez* button to move on to the next question.

● Repeat the activity as many times as necessary.

Extension
● Make two teams. The teams take it in turn to answer questions, and score a point for each correct answer.

Support
● Model the first few questions. Take the number in each phrase first, and ask pupils to locate it (e.g. *Cinq, c'est où?*). Then take the noun and get them to find this too (e.g. *C'est un piano – oui ou non?*). Finally get them to drag the correct number to each object.

 5 Literacy activity: ⏱ 10 mins 📚 AT3.1 03.2
Deux trompettes L3.1 L3.2

Materials
CD-ROM

Description
Play bingo in teams, either using completed cards, or filling your own cards in on screen, or using a printed grid. Then mark off the word on your card if you see the object appear on-screen. The first player or team with all their words marked off wins.

Delivery
There are three ways of playing the bingo game:

● *Ready to go*: the computer automatically completes two grids for each team. Team members mark off phrases on their grid as pictures appear on-screen.

● *Make your own*: as above, but teams complete their grids with their choice of phrases on-screen.

● *Print your own*: as *Ready to go*, but print off blank lotto grids from the CD-ROM, which pupils fill with their choice of instruments from those listed on-screen.

● When you are ready to start the game, call up a member of each team to click on the card.

● Click on *Allez* to make each item appear. When pupils hear a phrase from their grid, they must either click on the relevant square, or mark the square off on their printed grid.

● When the first on-screen grid is complete, there will be a celebratory animation.

● If playing with printed grids, then the first player to complete their grid calls out *Gagné!*

Support
● You can play with or without sound, by clicking on the *Audio on/Audio off* button on the taskbar at the bottom of the screen. With sound on, pupils will hear each phrase spoken as it appears.

 **6** Plenary activity: ⏱ 5 mins 📚 AT1.1 03.2
Les nombres 1–10 AT2.1 03.3
03.4

Materials
Bof (dragon) puppet, if available

Description
Game for revising numbers 1–10

Delivery
● Ask the class to choose a number between 1 and 10. This number will now be replaced with the word *Bof!* in the game.

● Go round the class, each pupil saying a number in the correct sequence. When a pupil has to say *Bof!*, they must collect the puppet from the teacher (or another pupil), and sit down. When number 10 is reached, go back to 1, and keep going until only one pupil is left standing.

● Change the *Bof!* number a few times, to keep pupils on their guard!

Extension
● Split pupils into two or three groups to make the activity quicker.

● Give pupils the option of saying just one number, or two – they can then use the numbers tactically to put someone out of the game!

Unit 1

Worksheet 1A
⏱ 10–15 mins 📖 AT2.1 O3.3
AT3.1 L3.1
AT4.1 L3.3

Description
Worksheet to give further practice on greetings and introductions.

Notes
1 You can go through Activity 1 as a whole-class activity, or let pupils work individually.
2 Put pupils in pairs and ask them to role-play the dialogue. You could choose some pairs to perform the dialogue, if time allows.

Answers
1 Completed bubbles:
 a Salut! Comment t'appelles-tu?
 b Je m'appelle Didier. Ça va?
 c Comme ci comme ça.
 d Au revoir, Polly.

Worksheet 1B
⏱ 10–15 mins 📖 AT2.1 O3.3
AT3.1 L3.1
AT4.1 L3.3

Description
Worksheet to give further practice on greetings and introductions.

Notes
1 You can go through Activity 1 as a whole-class activity, asking pupils for suggestions, or let pupils work individually.
2 Put pupils in pairs and ask them to role-play the dialogue. You could choose some pairs to perform the dialogue, if time allows. As an extension activity, pupils could change the names and responses and write their own dialogues.

Answers
1 Completed bubbles:
 a Salut!
 b Salut! Comment t'appelles-tu?
 c Je m'appelle Didier. Ça va?
 d Comme ci comme ça.
 e Au revoir, Didier.
 f Au revoir, Polly.

Worksheet 2A
⏱ 10–15 mins 📖 AT2.1 O3.3
AT3.1 L3.1
AT4.1 L3.3

Description
Worksheets to give further practice on greetings and introductions.

Notes
1 Encourage pupils to do Activity 1 individually, before reading through the dialogue together.
2 Pupils then read through the dialogue again in pairs.
3 This (finding the words in the grid) could be given as homework.

Answers
1 Completed dialogue:
 – Bonjour.
 – Salut!
 – Je m'appelle Bof. Comment t'appelles-tu?
 – Je m'appelle Jake.
 – Ça va, Jake?
 – Oui, ça va bien.

3
A	N	B	E	F	J	O	D
M	O	N	S	I	E	U	R
A	N	Q	C	Y	R	I	P
D	L	É	U	V	N	S	H
A	S	Ç	A	V	A	A	O
M	Z	G	A	M	V	L	I
E	B	O	N	J	O	U	R
C	O	M	M	E	N	T	J

Worksheet 2B
⏱ 10–15 mins 📖 AT2.1 O3.3
AT3.1 L3.1
AT4.1 L3.3

Description
Worksheets to give further practice on greetings and introductions.

Notes
1 Encourage pupils to do Activity 1 individually, before reading through the dialogue together.
2 Pupils then read through the dialogue again in pairs.
3 This (finding the words in the grid) could be given as homework.

Answers
1 Completed dialogue:
 – Bonjour.
 – Salut!
 – Je m'appelle Bof. Comment t'appelles-tu?
 – Je m'appelle Jake.
 – Ça va, Jake?
 – Oui, ça va bien.

2
N	O	N	A	O	R	J	A	N	E	U	F
G	U	I	T	A	R	E	M	G	E	O	D
A	I	E	S	E	P	O	A	I	R	O	V
R	I	E	Ç	B	I	L	D	E	U	X	A
Ç	B	L	A	E	S	S	A	E	E	N	U
O	O	N	V	E	T	A	M	B	O	U	R
N	N	M	A	I	C	N	E	A	I	J	E
E	J	D	O	N	C	T	A	N	T	S	V
M	O	N	S	I	E	U	R	V	E	A	O
C	U	U	Q	U	E	P	O	U	R	L	I
V	R	O	I	R	C	E	T	I	N	U	R
F	A	M	I	C	O	M	M	E	N	T	E

Worksheet 3A
⏱ 10–15 mins 📖 AT2.1 O3.3
AT3.1 L3.1
AT4.1 L3.3

Description
Worksheet to give further practice on numbers.

Notes
1 & 2 Let pupils work on these two questions individually and move round the class to help where needed.
3 Put pupils in pairs. Ask each pupil A to cover up cloud B, and each pupil B to cover up cloud A before they begin.

Answers
2 a cinq   d six
  b neuf   e trois
  c sept   f quatre

Worksheet 3B
⏱ 10–15 mins 📚 AT2.1 O3.3
                         AT3.1 L3.1
                         AT4.1 L3.3

Description
Worksheet to give further practice on numbers.

Notes
1 You could ask pupils to spell out the numbers after completing this activity, if they have covered the alphabet.

2 Correct this activity together, encouraging pupils to read out the sums and answers in French.

3 Put pupils in pairs. Ask each pupil A to cover up cloud B, and each pupil B to cover up cloud A before they begin!

Answers
1 Nathalie – 1 – un   Bof – 6 – six
   Mme Moulin – 2 – deux Mrs Mills – 7 – sept
   Mr Mills – 3 – trois   Polly – 8 – huit
   Didier – 4 – quatre   Mme Chanson 9 – neuf
   Olivier – 5 – cinq   Jake – 10 – dix

2 a trois + deux = cinq   d neuf – trois = six
  b cinq + quatre = neuf e sept – cinq = deux
  c un + six = sept   f dix – quatre = six

Worksheet 4A
⏱ 10–15 mins 📚 AT3.1 L3.1
                         AT4.1 L3.3

Description
Worksheet to give further practice on numbers and musical instruments.

Notes
1 Ask pupils to copy out the mystery word and hand it in to you!

2 If time allows, read through the answers together, to give extra reading and pronunciation practice.

Answers
1

Le mot mystère: TROMPETTE

2 a trois tambours   d huit trompettes
  b sept garçons   e quatre filles
  c cinq pianos   f neuf flûtes à bec

Worksheet 4B
⏱ 10–15 mins 📚 AT3.1 L3.1
                         AT4.1 L3.3

Description
A crossword covering language from the whole of Unit 1.

Notes
1 You may wish to cut off the answers at the bottom of the worksheet to see how pupils get on with the crossword without any prompts. They could do this activity in pairs.

Answers
1

Project work: French châteaux
⏱ 30–60 mins 📚 IU3.3

Description
Pupils discover information about a real French château, then prepare and deliver a presentation about it.

Materials
Books and pictures about French châteaux, holiday brochures, internet access

Delivery
● Using the animated story from Unit 1, discuss with the class what type of building Château Rigolo is – similar to a castle or stately home in the UK. Explain that there are a lot of châteaux like this one in France, and that you are going to find out more information about these.

● Divide the class into groups. Provide a list of suggested châteaux for the groups to investigate or, if confident, they can find one for themselves. A possible shortlist could be the Château Chenonceau and the Château Chambord in the Loire valley, and the Château de Versailles and the Château de Fontainebleau near Paris.

● Provide access to information via brochures or books and/or the internet, and ask each group to find some information on their chosen place.

● Pupils should then do some research and write up a short report on what they have discovered. Encourage them to add captions in French to any pictures where possible.

● Invite each group to come to the front of the class to deliver their presentation and display any visual aids. These could then be displayed around the classroom.

Support
● You can provide some suggested questions for the type of information they should look for, such as: Where is it? How old is it? How big is it? Who lived there?

Unit 2: En classe

National criteria

KS2 Framework objectives

O3.1 Listen and respond to simple rhymes, stories and songs
O3.2 Recognise and respond to sound patterns and words
O3.3 Perform simple communicative tasks using single words, phrases and short sentences
O3.4 Listen attentively and understand instructions, everyday classroom language and praise words
L3.1 Recognise some familiar words in written form
L3.2 Make links between some phonemes, rhymes and spellings, and read aloud familiar words
L3.3 Experiment with the writing of simple words

QCA Scheme of Work

Unit 1 Je parle français
Unit 2 Je me présente

Language ladder levels

Listening:	Breakthrough, Grade 1–2
Reading:	Breakthrough, Grade 1–2
Speaking:	Breakthrough, Grade 1–2
Writing:	Breakthrough, Grade 1–2

5–14 guideline strands　　　　　　　　　　　　　　　　　　　Levels A–C

Listening
Listening for information and instructions　　　A, C
Listening and reacting to others　　　　　　　A, B, C

Reading
Reading for information and instructions　　　A, C
Reading aloud　　　　　　　　　　　　　　　A, C

Speaking
Speaking to convey information　　　　　　　A, C
Speaking and interacting with others　　　　B, C
Speaking about experiences, feelings and opinions　A, B

Writing
Writing to exchange information and ideas　　A, C
Writing to establish and maintain personal contact　A, C
Writing imaginatively/to entertain　　　　　n/a

Unit objectives

- identify classroom objects
- identify colours, and describe an object's colour
- say your age
- recognise and repeat classroom instructions

Key language

- classroom objects: *une trousse* (pencil case), *un stylo* (pen), *une règle* (ruler), *un crayon* (pencil), *un cahier* (exercise book), *un livre* (text book), *un sac* (bag), *une gomme* (rubber)
- colours: *rouge* (red), *rose* (pink), *bleu* (blue), *jaune* (yellow), *marron* (brown), *orange* (orange)
- give your age: *J'ai... ans.*
- classroom instructions: *écoutez, regardez, lisez, asseyez-vous, levez-vous, écrivez, chantez*

Grammar and skills

- gender of different nouns
- ask and answer questions

- simple word order
- use context to determine meaning
- compare different languages
- take part in a simple dialogue

Unit outcomes

Most children will be able to:

- use spoken French to identify objects in the classroom
- understand and identify the different colours in French
- use spoken French to give their age
- respond to a range of instructions in French
- begin to recognise, read and pronounce sounds of combinations of letters, words and set phrases

Some children will also be able to:

- write and say phrases from memory, with clear pronunciation and meaning
- recognise different genders in French
- use colour adjectives together with nouns
- produce several simple phrases using *j'ai...*

14

Lesson summary

Context
Classroom objects

National criteria
KS2 Framework: **O3.1, O3.2, O3.3, O3.4, L3.1, L3.2, L3.3**
Attainment levels: **AT1.1, AT2.1, AT3.1, AT4.1**
Language ladder levels:
  Listening: **Grade 1**; Reading: **Grade 1**;
  Speaking: **Grade 1**; Writing: **Grade 1**

Cross-curricular links
Citizenship: comparing schools around the world
Literacy: labelling things
Numeracy

Key vocabulary
Classroom objects: *une trousse* (pencil case), *un stylo* (pen), *une règle* (ruler), *un crayon* (pencil), *un cahier* (exercise book), *un livre* (text book), *un sac* (bag), *une gomme* (rubber)

Language structures and outcomes
J'ai un/une...

---

1   Animated story: ⏱ 10–15m   📖 AT1.1–2 O3.1
À l'école (1)   AT3.1–2 O3.4
                                                         L3.1

Materials
CD-ROM

Description
Watch and listen to this interactive animated story presenting the language for Lessons 1–2. You can pause and rewind the story at any point.

Delivery
● This animated story can be used for both starter and plenary activities – the whole animation can be played at the end of the unit so that pupils can gauge their improved understanding.

● At this point pupils watch the first half of the story only; the second half is in Lesson 3.

Scene 1 (playground)

Pause the screen on the opening scene and ask the following questions:

● Where is Jake?

● Can they see any differences between a French school and school in their country (uniform? backpacks?)

● What would there be in their backpacks?

● Play the scene through, without stopping. Ask pupils whether their predictions were correct. Ask them to summarise briefly what happened.

2   Starter activity: ⏱ 5 mins   📖 AT2.1 O3.1
Les objets de classe   O3.2

Materials
Unit 2 Flashcards 1–5 and 8 (Classroom objects)

Description
Starter activity for learning classroom objects presented in animated story.

Delivery
● Ask pupils what was in Jake's backpack.

● As they say each one, hold up the relevant flashcard (and stick on the board/wall if possible).

● Encourage pupils to say any of the words in French, but don't worry if they can't remember them as this is covered in the next activity.

3   Presentation: ⏱ 5 mins   📖 AT1.1 O3.2
J'ai un sac   AT2.1 O3.4
                                                  AT3.1 L3.1
                                                         L3.2

Materials
CD-ROM

Description
Click on the language objects to hear and see the correct pronunciation. Use the additional features to practise sound/spelling links, word classes and spelling.

Delivery
● Select pupils to come to the board and click on an object. The whole class then listens and repeats the word.

● When the bat drops the object into Jake or Nathalie's bag they will say *J'ai* [*un crayon.*] ('I've got [a pencil.]'). Again, the whole class listens and repeats.

● Click on the *Replay* button on the Virtual Teacher to hear her pronounce the noun again on its own.

● Continue until all objects have been selected.

Extension
Once you have worked through the nouns on their own several times, move on to just using the phrase *J'ai un ...* instead. Use the question *Qu'est-ce que tu as?* and point to an object on the screen. Pupils must answer the phrase, e.g. *J'ai une trousse.* Click (or get a pupil to click) the object on the Whiteboard or check the answer.

Support
● Focus on the individual nouns only at first, and introduce the full phrase *J'ai un...* at a later stage.

Spelling
● You can practise spelling using the language in this presentation. See the Introduction for notes on how to use this feature of the Language Presentation.

Sounds
● This is a good opportunity to practise sound/spelling links. See the Introduction for notes on how to use this feature of the Language Presentation.

Word class
● This is a good opportunity to practise word classes. See the Introduction for notes on how to use this feature of the Language Presentation.

Knowledge About Language

Gender
● As in Unit 1, Lesson 4, in this lesson the notion of gender can be examined with pupils. The masculine nouns using *un* are positioned on the left of the screen, and the feminine ones using *une* are on the right.

Oracy activity: Qu'est-ce que tu as?
⏱ 10 mins   AT2.1   O3.2   O3.3   O3.4

Materials
CD-ROM

Description
Look at the objects Jake takes out of his bag. Guess what he is going to say, then click on the audio check button in his speech bubble to find out. Click on the tick or the cross to mark the class.

Delivery
● Click on *Allez* to start the activity. Polly asks *Qu'est-ce que tu as?* ('What have you got?') You will see Jake pick up one of his school items.

● Ask the class to answer the question (as in Jake's model sentences in Activity 3) using *J'ai [un stylo]*.

● Click on the audio check button in Jake's speech bubble if you want to hear the correct answer. If the class answers correctly, click on the tick button. If their answer was wrong, click on the cross.

● Click on *Allez* to proceed to the next question. To hear Jake's answer again, click on the audio check button in his speech bubble.

Extension
● Make two teams. Each team takes it in turn to answer a question and scores a point for each correct answer.

Support
● Model the first few answers with the class. Point to the object and ask what it is (*Qu'est-ce que c'est?*). Once pupils have answered correctly, ask them how they'd say that word using 'I have'.

Oracy activity: J'ai un stylo
⏱ 15 mins   AT1.1   O3.2   AT2.1   O3.3   O3.4

Materials
Objects from the classroom or Unit 2 Flashcards 1–9 (Classroom objects), scarf or blindfold (for extension activity).

Description
Oracy activity practising classroom objects, using realia or flashcards.

Delivery
● Hold up an object (or a flashcard) and say one of the target words (either simply as *[un stylo]* or *J'ai [un stylo]*).

● The class must respond *Oui* or *Non* according to whether your statement is true or false.

● Work through all the items in the same way.
● If time allows, invite a few pupils to make similar statements that the other pupils must respond to.

Extension
Put a selection of the smaller objects in a cloth bag. Blindfold a pupil and ask them to pull an object out of the bag, identify it, then say the word in French. This can be made into a team game if preferred.

Literacy activity: Dans mon sac
⏱ 5–10 mins   AT3.1   L3.1   AT4.1   L3.3

Materials
Unit 2 Flashcards 1–9 (Classroom objects), sticky labels

Description
Literacy activity labelling own classroom objects.

Delivery
● Display the flashcards on the board (word and picture cards in pairs).

● Hand out a few sticky labels to each table. Ask pupils to write out labels for as many objects as possible in the time allowed, and to stick them onto the relevant items on their table/in the room.

Language Learning Strategies

Writing new words
● Class activities such as Activity 6 are an ideal way for pupils to practise writing new French words as they learn them.

● There are many more opportunities to practise writing French in the *Rigolo* worksheets.

Plenary activity: Dans la salle de classe
⏱ 5–10m   AT2.1   O3.2   O3.3

Materials
Unit 2 Flashcards 1–9 (Classroom objects), clock/timer

Description
Pictionary-style game to revise the classroom objects vocabulary from this lesson.

Delivery
● Form two teams. Invite a pupil from Team A to come to the front. Show them a flashcard. They must then draw the object on the board for their team to guess in under 30 seconds. The team gets 2 points if they guess correctly and say the French word. Team B may win 1 point for a correct guess if Team A is unsuccessful.

● Repeat for Team B.

● Continue, selecting different pupils to be the 'artist' each time, until all the words have been covered. Hand out a few sticky labels to each table. Ask pupils to write out labels for as many objects as possible in the time allowed, and to stick them onto the relevant items on their table/in the room.

Support
● If necessary, use the flashcards to revise target words quickly before starting the game.

Unit 2  Lesson 2

Context
Colours

National criteria
KS2 Framework: O3.2, O3.3, O3.4, L3.1, L3.2
Attainment levels: AT1.1, AT2.1, AT3.1–2, AT4.1–2
Language ladder levels:
  Listening: **Grade 1**; Reading: **Grade 1–2**;
  Speaking: **Grade 1**; Writing: **Grade 1–2**

Cross-curricular links
Literacy (language patterns)

Key vocabulary
Colours: *rouge* (red), *rose* (pink), *bleu* (blue), *jaune* (yellow), *marron* (brown), *orange* (orange). Revision of classroom objects from Lesson 1.

Language structures and outcomes
un stylo rouge (etc.)

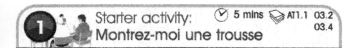
1 Starter activity: ⏱ 5 mins 📓 AT1.1 03.2 03.4
Montrez-moi une trousse

Materials
Unit 2 Flashcards 1–9 (Classroom objects), or realia for target words

Description
Starter activity for revising classroom objects presented in the previous lesson.

Delivery
● Ask pupils to put a selection of classroom objects out on their desk.
● Say *Montrez-moi [une trousse.]* ('Show me [a pencil case.]'). Pupils respond by holding up the correct object.

Extension
● If you're not afraid of a bit of a scuffle, select a group of pupils to stand around a table on which you have placed a selection of objects. (Make sure there is one fewer of each object than the number of pupils selected.)
● Call out (or ask another pupil in the class to call out) the name of an object. Everyone at the table tries to grab the object; the pupil who doesn't manage to do so is 'out' and is replaced by another pupil.

2 Presentation: ⏱ 10–15 mins 📓 AT1.1 03.2 / AT2.1 03.4 / AT3.1 L3.1 / L3.2
Un sac rouge

Materials
CD-ROM

Description
Click on the colours and coloured objects to hear and see the correct pronunciation. Use the additional features to practise sound/spelling links, word classes and spelling.

Delivery
● Select pupils to come to the board and click on a paint pot. The whole class then listens and repeats the colour. Continue for all the colours. (You may wish to go through each colour twice at this stage, but there will be more opportunity for practice later in the lesson.)
● Select a different set of pupils to click on the coloured objects in the classroom. Again, the whole class listens and repeats each object + colour. Continue until all objects have been selected.

Extension
● Ask a pupil to stand at the front, with their back to the board.

● Another pupil clicks on a coloured object. Pupil 1 listens to the phrase being said, then turns round and identifies the correct object.

Spelling
● For groups who have already covered the alphabet: click on a word and ask pupils to say/spell the word. Check answer by clicking on the *Spell* icon.
● To simply introduce the concept of spelling in French, click on a word, then on the *Spell* icon, and get pupils to follow the letters as they are spoken/highlighted. Repeat, this time asking the whole class to join in. Continue in the same way with all the words.
NB. If the *Spelling* icon is not illuminated, that means it is not applicable for that particular phrase.

Sounds
To further reinforce accurate pronunciation, and to introduce some basic reading skills:
● Point to each item on the text bar and ask the class to say the word.
● Focus on the text on screen, click on the *Sound* icon, and click on the different highlighted sounds to hear the Virtual Teacher saying them.
● Repeat all together.
NB. If the *Sound* icon is not illuminated, that means it is not applicable for that particular phrase.

Word class
● Having selected one of the objects, ask the group if they can remember what class of word it is in French (an adjective).
● Click on the *Word* icon to hear the Virtual Teacher say the word class.
● Repeat all together, copying the Virtual Teacher's gestures as you say the word class.

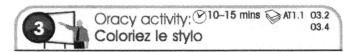
3 Oracy activity: ⏱ 10–15 mins 📓 AT1.1 03.2 03.4
Coloriez le stylo

Materials
CD-ROM

Description
Listen to the audio instructions. Click on the colour and object on the blackboard to colour it in correctly.

Delivery

● Click on *Allez* to start the activity. The audio will instruct you to colour in one of the target classroom objects.

● The pupil clicks on the correct colour and then on the correct object. There will be an automatic response. If they have not answered correctly, you can let them try again by clicking on the *Encore* button, or invite another pupil to the board to have a go.

● Continue until all the questions have been answered.

Extension

● Make two teams. Each team takes it in turn to answer a question and scores a point for each correct answer.

● Get pupils to record themselves saying each exchange, then compare their pronunciation with the original.

Support

● Before starting, run through the objects on the blackboard, asking pupils *Qu'est-ce que c'est?* for each one, to help them anticipate the vocabulary.

4 Oracy activity: ⏱ 15 mins 📚 AT1.1 03.3
C'est de quelle couleur?

Materials

Unit 2 Flashcards 1–8 (Classroom objects).

Description

Oracy activity practising classroom objects plus colours, using Unit 2 Flashcards (1–8).

Delivery

● Show all the flashcards before hiding one in a bag.

● Hold up the bag and ask *Qu'est-ce que c'est?* ('What is it?')

● The class must then make statements such as *C'est un stylo.* ('It's a pen.'), or *C'est bleu.* ('It's blue.'), to which you can only reply *Oui* or *Non*. The pupil who guesses the correct object/colour gets to keep the card for the duration of the game.

● Before handing over the card, say *Oui, dans mon sac j'ai [un livre rouge.]* ('Yes, in my bag I have [a red book]'). This is the model for the next sentence-building activity.

Extension

● If pupils are up to it, encourage precise guesses such as *un livre rouge.*

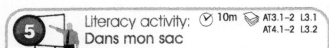

5 Literacy activity: ⏱ 10m 📚 AT3.1–2 L3.1
Dans mon sac   AT4.1–2 L3.2

Materials

CD-ROM

Description

Drag the words together to form a phrase. Press the *Fini* button when you have completed each answer, and see Bof illustrate the phrase with his machine.

Delivery

● Explain to the class how the machine works, and ask pupils to come up to the whiteboard to create a sentence. They need to select three tiles to form a phrase, dragging and dropping the tiles into the panels at the top of the machine, in the correct order, then click on the *Fini* button.

● If the combination is correct, Bof will activate the machine and an appropriately coloured object will appear on the conveyor belt. In the case of an incorrect answer, the machine blows black smoke and there is a negative response.

● Invite another pupil to come to the board and select another three tiles. Repeat as above until as many combinations as possible have been covered.

Support

● Model a sentence to start with, e.g. *J'ai un stylo bleu.*

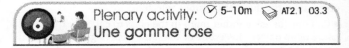
Language Learning Strategies

Comparing languages

● Word order is a simple way for pupils to compare how different languages work.

● Write on the board two or three phrases from the lesson using colours, e.g. *un crayon rouge*, *un stylo bleu*. Ask pupils what these mean in English and write these next to the French.

● Ask pupils if they can see what the difference is between the position of the colour words in the English and French phrases (in English the colour comes before the noun, whereas in French it comes after it).

6 Plenary activity: ⏱ 5–10m 📚 AT2.1 03.3
Une gomme rose

Materials

Selection of classroom objects (in different colours)

Description

Memory game to practise classroom objects with colours.

Delivery

● Divide the class into two groups. Allocate a table to each group.

● Place 8–10 classroom objects on each table. Give the groups two minutes to study the objects on their table.

● Hide the objects in two separate bags and give each group two minutes to recall the objects + colours on their table.

● Score 1 point for each correct answer.

Unit 2  Lesson 3

Context
Saying your age

National criteria
KS2 Framework: **O3.1, O3.2, O3.3, O3.4, L3.1, L3.2, L3.3**
Attainment levels: **AT1.1–2, AT2.1–2, AT3.1–2, AT4.1–2**
Language ladder levels:
  Listening: **Grade 1–2**; Reading: **Grade 1–2**;
  Speaking: **Grade 1–2**; Writing: **Grade 1–2**

Cross-curricular links
Citizenship: comparing schools around the world, families/friends/relationships
Literacy
Numeracy

Key vocabulary
Giving your age: *J'ai...ans.*

Language structures and outcomes
J'ai... ans.

---

 1 Animated story: ⏱10–15m 📖 AT1.1–2 O3.1
À l'école (2) AT3.1–2 O3.4
  L3.1

Materials
CD-ROM

Description
Watch and listen to this interactive animated story presenting the language for Lessons 3–4. You can pause and rewind the story at any point.

Delivery
● This animated story can be used for both starter and plenary activities – the whole animation can be played at the end of the unit so that pupils can gauge their improved understanding.

● At this point pupils watch the second half of the story only; the first half is in Lesson 1.

Scene 2 (classroom)

Freeze the screen on the opening scene and ask the following questions:

● Where are the children now?

● Who is in the classroom?

● What do you think the teacher is like?

● What is going to happen next?

● Play the scene through without stopping. Ask whether pupils' predictions were correct. Ask them to summarise briefly what happened.

 Language Learning Strategies

Using context to determine meaning
● The *Rigolo* animated stories are a good way to show pupils how they can use the context of the story to work out the meaning.

● By focusing on the setting (here it is the classroom) you can get pupils to predict what kind of language and events might happen. Once prepared like this, pupils can look out for the language for classroom instructions, taking the register, and so on.

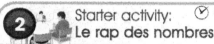 **2** Starter activity: ⏱ 5 mins 📖 AT2.1 O3.1
Le rap des nombres O3.3

Materials
n/a

Description
Starter activity practising numbers in a rap-style song.

Delivery
● Go through the rap from Unit 1, Lesson 3:

un, deux, trois,

quatre, cinq, six,

sept et huit,

neuf et DIX!

● You could ask the pupils to perform it in their groups of 6–8, or do it as a whole-class activity.

Support
● You can use the presentation from Unit 1, Lesson 5 at any time to refresh your memory of the numbers.

---

 3 Presentation: ⏱10–15 mins 📖 AT1.1 O3.2
Mon âge AT2.1 O3.4
  AT3.1 L3.1
  L3.2

Materials
CD-ROM

Description
Click on the characters to hear and see them give their age with the correct pronunciation. Use the additional features to practise sound/spelling links.

Delivery
● Select pupils to come to the board and click on a character. Madame Chanson will ask the question *Quel âge as-tu?* and the character will respond. The whole class repeats both question and answer (click on the character again if necessary, or on the Virtual Teacher, to hear dialogue again).

● Continue until all characters have been selected.

Extension
● Point at a character, and a pupil (or the whole class) must say the question and answer that would have been heard. Then click on the character to check.

● Ask a pupil to stand at the front, with their back to the board. Another pupil clicks on a character. Pupil 1 listens to the answer being given, then turns round and identifies the correct character.

● You could split the class into two groups and make this a competitive team game to see who gets the most correct answers.

Sounds

To further reinforce accurate pronunciation, and to introduce some basic reading skills:

● Point to each question/answer on the text bar and ask the class to say the phrases.

● Focus on the text on screen, click on the *Sound* icon, and click on the different highlighted sounds to hear the Virtual Teacher saying them.

● Repeat all together.

NB. If the *Sound* icon is not illuminated, that means it is not applicable for that particular phrase.

 Language Learning Strategies

Comparing languages

● Saying your age is another good way to demonstrate to pupils how similar things are said differently in French and English.

● Focus on the phrase *J'ai sept ans.* and ask pupils what it means, writing the English alongside ('I am seven years old.').

● Ask them if they remember what *J'ai* means from Lesson 1 ('I have'), *sept*, and then if they can work out what *ans* means ('years'). Write these underneath the French.

● Ask pupils if they can see what the difference is between how you say your age in French and English (in French you say 'I have seven years (old)', but in English we say 'I am seven years old').

4 Oracy activity: ⏱ 10 mins 📄 AT1.1–2 03.2 03.4
Quel âge as-tu?

Materials
CD-ROM

Description
Listen to the characters as they give their ages, then drag the correct number to the birthday cake.

Delivery
● Click on *Allez* to start the activity. Madame Chanson asks a character their age and they reply. The pupil must then drag the appropriate number candle onto the cake.

● There will be an audio/visual response to indicate whether the answer is correct or not.

● Ask different pupils to answer the questions that follow.

Extension
● Make two teams. Each team takes it in turn to answer a question and scores a point for each correct answer.

Support
● Before starting the activity, check that pupils remember the numbers at the bottom of the screen, using the question *C'est combien?*
question and scores a point for each correct answer.

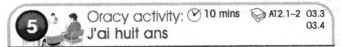

5 Oracy activity: ⏱ 10 mins 📄 AT2.1–2 03.3 03.4
J'ai huit ans

Materials
Puppets

Description
Oracy activity practising talking about your age, using puppets.

Delivery
● Hold up two of the puppets and make them ask/answer questions about each other's age (*Quel âge as-tu?/J'ai [huit] ans]*).

● According to the storyline, Jake is 7, Polly is 10 and Bof is 1 year old, although you may choose to use different ages.

● Then, make the puppets ask a few pupils at random how old they are.

● Make three groups and hand out a puppet to each group: pupils take it in turn to make a puppet ask the person to their left how old they are. When the second pupil has answered the question, they take the puppet and ask their neighbour the same question. Continue until all pupils have asked and answered a question.

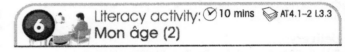

6 Literacy activity: ⏱ 10 mins 📄 AT4.1–2 L3.3
Mon âge (2)

Materials
A3 card sheets, photos (of self or siblings/cousins/friends) brought in by pupils, plain paper (for making speech bubbles), glue, scissors

Description
Literacy activity, adding speech bubbles to a photo collage.

Delivery
● Give out one card sheet and enough glue and scissors per group/table.

● Ask pupils to write out sentences (*J'ai [huit] ans.*) for each of the photos they have brought in. They must then cut out the sentence in the form of a speech bubble.

● Pupils stick their photos and speech bubbles onto the card.

● The cards can then be displayed around the room.

Extension
● Pupils could do an additional speech bubble with *Je m'appelle* [+ name].

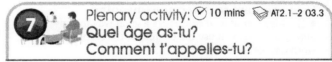

7 Plenary activity: ⏱ 10 mins 📄 AT2.1–2 03.3
Quel âge as-tu?
Comment t'appelles-tu?

Materials
Scarf or blindfold

Description
Game to practise questions and answers about age.

Delivery
● All pupils stand in a circle. Choose one pupil to stand by you in the middle. Blindfold the pupil, then point to another pupil who must silently join you in the middle.

● Pupil A then asks *Quel âge as-tu?* or *Comment t'appelles-tu?* Pupil B responds and Pupil A must identify the pupil from their voice.

● Continue until as many pupils as possible have either asked or answered a question.

Unit 2  Lesson 4

Context
Classroom instructions

National criteria
KS2 Framework: **O3.1, O3.2, O3.3, O3.4, L3.1, L3.2**
Attainment levels: **AT1.1, AT2.1, AT3.1**
Language ladder levels:
  Listening: **Grade 1**; Reading: **Grade 1**;
  Speaking: **Grade 1**

Cross-curricular links
n/a

Key vocabulary
Classroom instructions: *écoutez, regardez, lisez, asseyez-vous, levez-vous, écrivez, chantez*

Language structures and outcomes
écoutez, regardez, lisez, asseyez-vous, levez-vous, écrivez, chantez

---

 1 Starter activity: ⏱ 5 mins 📖 AT2.1 O3.3
Une course

Materials
n/a

Description
Team race game revising questions and answers for names and ages.

Delivery
● Divide the class into teams of around 10 pupils. Ask each team to line up.

● Decide which question you want to practise (*Comment t'appelles-tu?* or *Quel âge as-tu?*). The first pupil in each line turns to the pupil behind and asks the question. The second pupil replies, before turning to the pupil behind and asking the same question, and so on until the end of the line. The last pupil then runs to the front of the line and asks Pupil 1 the same question. The game ends as soon as Pupil 1 has replied.

● The winning team is the fastest, but you will need to monitor closely to ensure all questions and answers are actually said aloud!

● Repeat the game with the second target question.

Extension
● Pupils could ask both questions in the same race.

Support
● Model the race with two other more able pupils before starting.

● Accept one-word answers (e.g. *Mark* rather than *Je m'appelle Mark*; *sept* rather than *J'ai sept ans*).

 2 Presentation: ⏱ 10–15 mins 📖 AT1.1 O3.2
Asseyez-vous! AT2.1 O3.4
AT3.1 L3.1
L3.2

Materials
CD-ROM

Description
Click on the instruction icons to hear and see the correct pronunciation. Use the additional features to practise sound/spelling links, word classes and spelling.

Delivery
● Select pupils to come to the board, and click one of the icons on the left of the screen. You will hear Madame Chanson giving an instruction (with the Virtual Teacher, if activated, echoing this), then see Polly and Nathalie illustrate its

meaning. The whole class listens and repeats the order, copying the gestures of the Virtual Teacher as they do so.

● Continue in this way with all the icons. (You may wish to go through each icon twice at this stage, but there will be more opportunity for practice later in the lesson.)

● Reinforce understanding by going through the icons yourself and getting the pupils to copy Polly and Nathalie's actions.

Spelling
● For groups who have already covered the alphabet: click on an instruction icon and ask pupils to say/spell the word. Check answer by clicking on the *Spell* icon.

● To simply introduce the concept of spelling in French, click on an instruction icon, then on the *Spell* icon, and get pupils to follow the letters as they are spoken/highlighted. Repeat, this time asking the whole class to join in. Continue in the same way with all the words.

Word class
● Having selected one of the objects, ask the group if they can work out what class of word it is in English (a verb).

● Click on the *Word* icon to hear the Virtual Teacher say the word class in French.

● Repeat all together, copying the Virtual Teacher's gestures as you say the word class.

Sounds
To further reinforce accurate pronunciation, and to introduce some basic reading skills:

● Point to each instruction on the text bar and ask the class to say the words.

● Focus on the text on screen, click on the *Sound* icon, and click on the different highlighted sounds to hear the Virtual Teacher saying them.

 3 Oracy activity: ⏱ 10 mins 📖 AT1.1 O3.2
Écoutez! O3.4

Materials
CD-ROM

Description
Listen to Madame Chanson's instructions and click on the correct icon.

Delivery
● Click on *Allez* to start the activity. Mme Chanson will give an instruction and pupils must click on the correct icon on the left of the screen.

- If pupils are correct, Polly and Nathalie will do the action.
- Continue until all the instructions have been covered.

Extension
- Make two teams. Each team takes it in turn to listen then click on an icon, and scores a point for each correct answer.

Support
- Practise the phrases for each icon before starting, either by using the presentation in Activity 2, or by going over the words for the possible icons in this activity.

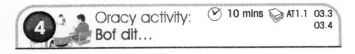

4   Oracy activity: ⏱ 10 mins   AT1.1   03.3
     Bof dit…   03.4

Materials
Bof puppet

Description
Game based on 'Simon says…', to practise classroom instructions.

Delivery
- Hold up the Bof puppet and explain the rules of the game (the same as 'Simon says…', but each correct instruction will be preceded by *Bof dit…* – the usual French game being *Jacques a dit…*).
- Begin giving instructions. Pupils must only respond if the instruction is preceded by *Bof dit…*, otherwise they are out of the game. The last pupil remaining in the game is the winner.

Extension
- In order to practise giving more polite instructions, change the rules slightly: leave out *Bof dit…*, and pupils respond only if the instruction is followed by *s'il vous plaît*.
- Ask pupils who are out of the game to stand at the front with you and help give instructions.

Support
- First, run through the target instructions by saying them and doing the actions all together.

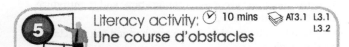

5   Literacy activity: ⏱ 10 mins   AT3.1   L3.1
     Une course d'obstacles   L3.2

Materials
CD-ROM

Description
Choose the correct instruction to help the characters get past the obstacles they meet in their path.

Delivery
- Click on *Allez* to start the activity, selecting a pupil to answer the first question. Jake and Bof will run down the corridor until they meet the first obstacle. The pupil selects the appropriate instruction for that obstacle.
- If they are correct, Jake and Bof move on to the next obstacle by clicking on the *Allez* button. If not, one of three 'lives', represented by heart icons, is lost. The game is over if all lives are lost, and can be started again by clicking on the *Jouez encore?* ✓ button.

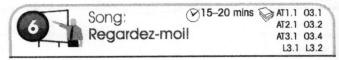

6   Song: ⏱ 15–20 mins   AT1.1   03.1
     Regardez-moi!   AT2.1   03.2
                                AT3.1   03.4
                                L3.1   L3.2

Materials
CD-ROM or Audio CD, track 08

Description
Watch and listen to the interactive karaoke song. Choose either *Practice* or *Sing* mode: the former to go through the song line by line, the latter to sing it all the way through. Switch the music and words on or off as you prefer.

Delivery
- Ask pupils to listen out for the instructions which appear in the song.
- Play the song straight through once, in *Sing* mode. Afterwards, ask pupils to tell you as many of the instructions they can remember.
- Go back and play the song in *Practice* mode, focusing on one line at a time. Repeat chorally and to check comprehension.
- When the class is comfortable with the lyrics, divide the class into two groups: one group will sing the part of Mme Chanson and the other will do the backing singers' role. In both cases, actions are obligatory!
- Swap over roles for each verse.

Extension
- Pupils, in small groups, write their own song incorporating classroom commands and actions. You could choose a well-known tune (e.g. *Frère Jacques*) and pupils fit in some new lyrics, or they could produce a rap-style song.

See the Introduction for more notes on the Song features.

7   Plenary: ⏱ 5–10 mins   AT1.1   03.3
     Levez-vous!   AT2.1   03.4

Materials
n/a

Description
Chain game to consolidate giving classroom instructions.

Delivery
- Ask pupils to stand in a circle. Start by giving one instruction; all pupils make the appropriate gesture. The pupil to your right repeats your instruction and adds another; the rest of the class again responds appropriately. The pupil to their right continues in the same way, giving three instructions this time, and so on.
- Continue in the same way until all the target instructions have been covered.
- If time allows, start again and play until each pupil has had a go at saying an instruction.

Support
- Go through each of the instructions yourself at the start of the circle, before passing on pupil to pupil.

Unit 2  Extra!

Worksheet 1A
⏱ 10–15 mins 📚 AT2.1 O3.3
AT3.1 L3.1
AT4.1 L3.2

Description
Worksheet to give further practice on classroom objects and colours.

Notes
1 Give pupils a few minutes to colour the objects in colours which have been learned in this unit. Once they have done this, ask them to look at their pictures and complete the grid accordingly.
2 Ask pupils to work in pairs for the second part. Move round the class, asking pupils to read out one or two phrases to you.

Worksheet 1B
⏱ 10–15 mins 📚 AT2.1 O3.3
AT3.1 L3.1
AT4.1 L3.3

Description
Worksheet to give further practice on classroom objects and colours.

Notes
1 Give pupils a few minutes to read Jake's sentences and colour in the objects accordingly.
2 Ask pupils to work in pairs for Activity 2, and move round the class, monitoring the activity.

Answers
1 Pupils should colour in the objects as follows: blue bag, orange pencil, red pen, pink rubber, brown ruler, yellow exercise book, blue textbook

Worksheet 2A
⏱ 10–15 mins 📚 AT2.1 O3.3
AT3.1 L3.1
AT4.1 L3.3

Description
Worksheet to give further practice on classroom objects and colours.

Notes
1 Give pupils a few minutes to complete their list of objects, then divide the class into pairs.
2 Encourage pupils to say what they have got to their partner using *J'ai un...*, rather than just read off each other's list.

Worksheet 2B
⏱ 10–15 mins 📚 AT2.1 O3.3
AT3.1 L3.1
AT4.1 L3.3

Description
Worksheet to give further practice on classroom objects and colours.

Notes
1 Give pupils a few minutes to complete this activity. If possible, move around the group and ask them to read out one of their sentences to you. Some pupils might need you to explain again which nouns you would use *bleue* with.
2 Encourage pupils to expand on the dialogue if they can, e.g. *Oui, j'ai un stylo bleu.*

Worksheet 3A
⏱ 10–15 mins 📚 AT2.1 O3.3
AT3.1 L3.1
AT4.1 L3.3

Description
Worksheet to give further practice on musical instruments and numbers.

Notes
1 Encourage pupils to read the phrases out loud as they link up numbers and pictures, e.g. *un piano.*
2 You could make a chart to log the best speed!

Worksheet 3B
⏱ 10–15 mins 📚 AT2.1 O3.3
AT3.1 L3.1
AT4.1 L3.3

Description
Worksheet to give further practice on musical instruments and numbers.

Notes
1 Encourage pupils to read the phrases aloud as they draw.
2 Pupils could make a chart to log the best speeds, and read the results out in French.

Worksheet 4A
⏱ 10–15 mins 📚 AT2.1 O3.3
AT3.1 L3.1
AT4.1 L3.3

Description
Worksheet to give further practice on saying your age.

Notes
1 Go through this activity together orally, to ensure pupils are identifying the ages correctly.
2 Monitor this activity as closely as possible, to ensure pupils are using French as much as possible!
3 Encourage pupils to write out the number word, where appropriate.

Answers
1 a J'ai un an. – *Bébé*
   b J'ai quatre ans. – *Camille*
   c J'ai six ans. – *Magali*
   d J'ai huit ans. – *David*
   e J'ai dix ans. – *Luc*

Worksheet 4B
⏱ 10–15 mins 📚 AT2.1 O3.3
AT3.1 L3.1
AT4.1 L3.3

Description
Worksheet to give further practice on saying your age.

Notes
1 Go through this activity together orally, to ensure pupils are identifying the ages correctly.
2 Monitor this activity as closely as possible, to ensure pupils are using French as much as possible!
3 Encourage pupils to write out the number word, where appropriate.

Answers
1 *Bébé* – J'ai un an.   *Camille* – J'ai quatre ans.
   Magali – J'ai six ans.   *David* – J'ai huit ans.
   Luc – J'ai dix ans.

Project work: Contact with a French school
⏱ n/a 📖 IU3.4

Description
Pupils make initial contact with a real French school.

Materials
Internet access

Delivery
● Research a suitable French school to contact. There are several ways to do this, as listed below.

● It's good to make the most of a personal connection if you can. If you have a foreign language assistant, they might be able to put you in touch with a school in their hometown. Alternatively, there might be a pupil's parent, governor, local church or business who has useful contacts. Ask other local schools in your area, in particular your primary cluster group or closest secondary school, to see if they have links you could build on with French schools or towns.

● There are various websites that help you to find a partner school, such as the British Council (www.britishcouncil.org), the Global Gateway (www.globalgateway.org) or the EU 'e-twinning' programme (www.etwinning.net).

● Try to find a class within the school whose pupils will have a roughly similar level of English, i.e. beginners. If the French children are demonstrating much better command of English than your pupils' command of French it could be demotivating.

● Once you have established a link, at this point you could organise the first communication between classes. Gather together simple introductions from all the pupils who want to take part, where they give their name and age. They could put this together with a photograph as well if you like.

● Your pupils will gradually build up mo____ __ __ ____ their partner contacts, but at this early stage it might be more interesting to gather some general information about the school, and possibly photos or even video footage of what their school looks like. Pupils can compare this with their own classroom and school.

Sound/spelling activity
⏱ 15–20 mins 📖 AT1.1 03.2 L3.2

Description
Practise listening out for and pronouncing the r sound, and then count how many times you hear this sound in the activity.

Delivery
● This sound/spelling activity focuses specifically on the r sound, one which English speakers traditionally find quite challenging.

● There are two parts to the activity: the first (Practice) allows pupils to familiarise themselves with the r sound and to practise pronouncing it in comparison to the Virtual Teacher model. The second part (Activity) is an exercise where pupils have to listen out for the r sound in a list of French words they have encountered so far in Rigolo 1.

● Select Practice and click on Next to start this part. Then click on Allez. The Virtual Teacher will say the r sound first on its own, and then as part of four words that have already been used in Units 1 and 2. For each of these, get the class to repeat the sound or word chorally several times, checking the model each time using the Encore button to see how close they are.

● Once you have finished this part, relaunch the activity and choose Activity from the selection menu to move on to test pupils' recognition of the sound. Pupils will hear 11 phrases read out. For each phrase they must work out how many times they can hear the r sound, and then click on the correct number button on the screen, between 0 (if they don't hear it at all) and

3. To show pupils how the activity works, click on the Example button. This will demonstrate an example question and its answer. Click on Allez to start the activity, and use the Encore button to repeat a phrase, if necessary. You can ask the whole class to vote on how many times they hear the sound, or ask individual pupils to step forward to choose the right number.

● When they have selected the right number, you will see the phrases appear on screen, and the letter r will highlight in time with the right part of the audio. Click on the Encore button if you want to hear the phrase again and review their answer.

● Repeat the activity again if you feel pupils need further practice.

Extension
You can continue the practice activity with more words using r if you feel that pupils have grasped this well – even words not yet covered in Rigolo. You can use the glossary in the Teacher Support area of the CD-ROM to list words beginning with r. Pupils can then hold up cards marked with the numbers, to show how many times they hear the sound.

Assessment for Units 1–2

Écoutez!

Play each audio 2–3 times or more if necessary. Pause during each activity as required.

Total marks for listening: 20. If pupils are getting 8–14/20, they are working towards level 1. If they achieve 15–20/20, they are working between levels 1–2.

Activity 1
Mark out of 10
(AT1.1; 03.2)

Answers

	(Example:)	1	2	3	4	5	6	7	8	9	10
			✓	✓			✓		✓	✓	
French	(✓)	✓			✓	✓		✓			✓

example: rose (French)
1 dragon (French)   6 dragon (English)
2 guitar (English)   7 piano (French)
3 piano (English)   8 orange (English)
4 guitare (French)   9 flute (English)
5 flûte (French)   10 orange (French)

Activity 2
Mark out of 6
(AT1.1; 03.4)

Answers
a 3 b 4 (example: c 1) d 2 e 7 f 5 g 6

1 Regardez.   5 Chantez.
2 Écrivez.   6 Asseyez-vous.
3 Levez-vous.   7 Lisez.
4 Écoutez.

Activity 3
Mark out of 4
(AT1.1–2; 03.4)

Answers
a 2 b 4 c 3 d 5 (example: e 1)

1 – Ça va?
  – Mmmm... comme ci comme ça
2 – Bonjour, Monsieur.
  – Ah, bonjour, Madame.
3 – Salut! Ça va?
  – Oui, ça va bien.
4 – Au revoir Didier!
  – Au revoir Bof!
5 – Bonjour! Ça va?
  – Oh non, ça ne va pas!

Parlez!

Pupils can work in pairs for the speaking tasks. If it is not possible to assess each pair, then assess a few pairs for each assessment block and mark the rest of the class based on the spoken work they do in class.

Total marks for speaking: 10. Pupils achieving 5/10 are working towards level 1; Pupils achieving more than 5/10 are working between levels 1–2.

Activity 1 (AT2.1; 03.2, 03.3)
5 marks

Answer
Bag A: J'ai (*example*: une trousse), une règle, un cahier, un stylo et un crayon.

Bag B: J'ai une trousse, une gomme, un livre, un stylo et un crayon.

Activity 2 (AT2.1–2; 03.3)
Sample dialogue: 5 marks

Answers
A Bonjour!
B Bonjour/Salut!
A Comment t'appelles-tu?
B Je m'appelle (Simon).
A Ça va?
B Oui, ça va./Non, ça ne va pas.
A Quel âge as-tu?
B J'ai (huit) ans.
A Au revoir!
B Au revoir!

Lisez!

Total marks for reading: 20. If pupils are getting 8–14/20, they are working towards level 1. If they achieve 15–20/20, they are working between levels 1–2.

Activity 1 (AT3.1; L3.1)
Mark out of 10

Answers
a un dragon b un garçon c un piano d une fille e une trompette f une règle g un tambour h un sac i un stylo j une guitare k une flûte à bec

Activity 2 (AT 3.1–2; L3.1)
Mark out of 10; 2 for each correct answer

Answers
(*example*: J'ai huit ans.)

a J'ai **une trousse** jaune.
b J'ai **neuf** ans.
c J'ai **une gomme** orange.
d J'ai **un cahier** rouge.
e J'ai **dix** ans.

Écrivez!

For the writing tasks, the copying of words can be approximate.

Total marks for writing: 20. Pupils achieving 8–14/20 are working towards level 1. Pupils achieving 15 (or more) out of 20 are working between levels 1–2.

Activity 1 (AT4.1; L3.3)

Activity 2 (AT4.2; L3.3)
Mark out of 10; 2 marks per answer

Answers
a Bonjour!/Salut!
b Ça va?/Oui, ça va bien.
c Comment t'appelles-tu?/Je m'appelle Luc.
d Quel âge as-tu?/J'ai neuf ans.
e Au revoir, Monsieur!/Au revoir, Madame!

 **Unit 3: Mon corps**

National criteria

KS2 Framework objectives

O3.1 Listen and respond to simple rhymes, stories and songs
O3.2 Recognise and respond to sound patterns and words
O3.3 Perform simple communicative tasks using single words, phrases and short sentences
O3.4 Listen attentively and understand instructions, everyday classroom language and praise words
L3.1 Recognise some familiar words in written form
L3.2 Make links between some phonemes, rhymes and spellings, and read aloud familiar words
L3.3 Experiment with the writing of simple words

QCA Scheme of Work

Unit 1   Je parle français
Unit 2   Je me présente
Unit 3   En famille
Unit 9   Les sports

Language ladder levels

Listening: Breakthrough, Grade 1–2
Reading: Breakthrough, Grade 1–2
Speaking: Breakthrough, Grade 1–2
Writing: Breakthrough, Grade 1–2

5–14 guideline strands   Levels A–C

Listening		**Reading**	
Listening for information and instructions	A, C	Reading for information and instructions	A, C
Listening and reacting to others	A, B, C	Reading aloud	A, C
Speaking		**Writing**	
Speaking to convey information	A, C	Writing to exchange information and ideas	A, C
Speaking and interacting with others	B, C	Writing to establish and maintain personal contact	A, C
Speaking about experiences, feelings and opinions	A, B	Writing imaginatively/to entertain	n/a

Unit objectives

- identify parts of the body
- describe eyes and hair
- recognise days of the week
- give basic character descriptions

Key language

- parts of the body: *les yeux* (eyes), *le nez* (nose), *la bouche* (mouth), *les oreilles* (ears), *les cheveux* (hair), *la jambe* (leg), *le bras* (arm), *la tête* (head)
- colours: *vert* (green), *rouge* (red), *marron* (brown), *jaune* (yellow), *bleu* (blue)
- adjectives: *long* (long), *court* (short)
- days of the week: *lundi, mardi, mercredi, jeudi, vendredi, samedi, dimanche*
- adjectives describing character: *Je suis… grand(e), petit(e), timide, bavard(e), drôle, sympa*

Grammar and skills

- gender of different nouns
- the definite article
- simple word order
- simple facial and character descriptions
- simple adjectival agreement (for more able pupils)

Unit outcomes

Most children will be able to:

- use spoken French to identify parts of the body
- recognise and copy out the days of the week
- begin to recognise, read and pronounce sounds of combinations of letters, words and set phrases

Some children will also be able to:

- write and say phrases from memory, with clear pronunciation and meaning
- describe hair and eyes with a limited range of adjectives in simple phrases
- describe character with one-word adjectives
- appreciate simple adjectival agreement (for more able pupils only)

Unit 3  Lesson 1

Lesson summary

Context
Introducing parts of the body

National criteria
KS2 Framework: **O3.1, O3.2, O3.3, O3.4, L3.1, L3.2**
Attainment levels: **AT1.1, AT2.1, AT 2.2, AT3.1**
Language ladder levels:
　Listening: **Grade 1**; Reading: **Grade 1**;
　Speaking: **Grade 1**

Cross-curricular links
Science

Key vocabulary
Parts of the body: *les yeux* (eyes), *le nez* (nose), *la bouche* (mouth), *les oreilles* (ears), *les cheveux* (hair), *la jambe* (leg), *le bras* (arm), *la tête* (head)

Language structures and outcomes
As above

---

 1 Starter activity: ⏱ 5–10 mins 📖 AT1.1 03.4
Bof dit...

Materials
Bof puppet

Description
Revision of classroom instructions

Delivery
● Revise the target instructions by saying them and doing the actions all together.

● Hold up the Bof puppet and remind pupils of the rules, which are the same as 'Simon says...' but each correct instruction will be preceded by *Bof dit...* – the usual French game being *Jacques a dit...*

● Begin giving instructions. Pupils respond only if the instruction is preceded by *Bof dit...*, otherwise they are out of the game. The last pupil remaining in the game is the winner.

● You can use the Virtual Teacher at any time to refresh your memory of the target expressions.

 2 Animated story: ⏱ 10–15m 📖 AT1.1 03.1
Le miroir magique (1) AT2.1 03.4
AT3.1 L3.1

Materials
CD-ROM

Description
Watch and listen to this interactive animated story, which presents the language for Lessons 1 and 2. You can pause and rewind the story at any point.

Delivery
● This animated story can be used for both starter and plenary activities – the whole animation can be played at the end of the unit so that pupils can gauge their improved understanding.

● At this point pupils watch the first half of the story only; the second half is in Lesson 3.

Scene 1 (Polly and Jake in château corridor)

Play the scene, then pause the screen and ask pupils to describe what is happening. Where are the children? How are they feeling? (Why? How can we tell how they're feeling?) What are they doing? What's going to happen?

Play the scene through, without stopping. Ask whether pupils' predictions were correct. Ask them to summarise briefly what happened.

Scene 2 (by the mirror)

Repeat as for Scene 1. Also ask the class if they can tell you how the characters are saying 'Look!' to each other. Ask more confident groups to listen for the words for 'hair', 'eyes',

'nose', 'ears' and 'mouth'. Play the scene again for pupils to check their answers.

 3 Presentation: ⏱ 10–15 mins 📖 AT1.1 03.2
Le corps AT2.1 03.4
AT3.1 L3.1
L3.2

Materials
CD-ROM

Description
Click on the icons for different parts of the cavalier's body to hear and see the correct pronunciation of these body parts. Use the additional features to practise sound/spelling links, word classes and spelling.

Delivery
● Start by asking pupils if they know, or can remember from the animation, the word for any of the following in French: 'head', 'eyes', 'ears', 'arm', 'leg', 'nose', 'mouth' and 'hair'. Ask the class to listen carefully during this activity to see if they were right.

● Select pupils to come in turn to the whiteboard and click on a body part, choosing from a selection of those mentioned above. The whole class then listens and repeats the word, pointing to the relevant part of their own body. The appropriate part of the cavalier's body is animated as the body parts are selected.

● Click on the Virtual Teacher to listen again. Repeat chorally, copying the Virtual Teacher's gestures as you say the words. Continue until all parts of the body have been selected.

Extension
● Choose another set of pupils to click on the body parts in turn. Point at each body part, and ask the class what they will hear. Click to see if they were right.

● Ask a few pupils to stand at the front, with their backs to the board.

● Another pupil clicks on a part of the body to trigger the Virtual Teacher audio. Without turning round, pupils point to the relevant part of their body. The rest of the class tells them if they are correct or not.

● Repeat with different groups of pupils.

Spelling
● You can practise spelling using the language in this presentation. See the Introduction for notes on how to use this feature of the Language Presentation

Sounds
● This is a good opportunity to practise sound/spelling links. See the Introduction for notes on how to use this feature of the Language Presentation.

Word class
● This is a good opportunity to practise word classes. See the Introduction for notes on how to use this feature of the Language Presentation.

Knowledge About Language

Gender
● As in previous units, in this lesson the notion of gender can be examined with pupils.

● This is the first time pupils will have seen the definite article *le/la/les*. As with *un/une*, the masculine nouns are positioned on the left and the feminine on the top right. The plural nouns are on the bottom right.

● Draw pupils' attention to the three groups of nouns and ask them to point out the patterns with the articles. Then, with the text bar on, see if they can guess what the word for 'the' is in French (*le/la/les*).

● If you have explored this, remind them how you have seen that nouns in French are in different groups for *un* or *une*. Explain that this is the same rule with *le* and *la*, and that *les* is for more than one word, or a plural.

4 Oracy activity: Qu'est-ce qui manque?
⏲ 10 mins 📖 AT1.1 03.3

Materials
CD-ROM

Description
Click on *Allez*. A part of the body is indicated with a flashing arrow. Say what part of the body it is. Click on the audio check button in the speech bubble to check the answer, if necessary.

Delivery
● Click (or invite a pupil to click) on the *Allez* button. You will see the portrait of a cavalier with missing body parts, and hear the question *Qu'est-ce que c'est?* A flashing arrow will indicate a part of the body alongside the portrait.

● Ask the class to answer the question by saying the missing part of the body.

● Click on the audio check button in the speech bubble to hear the correct answer.

● If the class answered correctly, click on the tick. If their answer was wrong, click on the cross.

● Click on the *Allez* button again to go on to the next body part.

Extension
Split the activity into two parts, each with four body parts, in order to do the activity as a team game and see who gets the most correct answers.

Support
Go through the eight different body parts with pupils before they start the activity.

5 Song: Écoutez Jake
⏲ 15–20 mins 📖 AT1.2 03.1 / AT2.2 03.2 / AT3.2 03.4 / L3.1 / L3.2

Materials
CD-ROM or Audio CD, track 09

Description
Watch and listen to the interactive song practising parts of the body. Choose either *Practice* or *Sing* mode: the former to go through the song line by line, the latter to sing it all the way through. Switch the music and words on or off as you prefer.

Delivery
● Ask pupils to listen out for all the different actions which appear in the song.

● Play the song once right the way through in *Sing* mode. Afterwards, ask pupils to tell you as many of the actions as they can remember.

● Play the song through again, this time asking pupils to note down the number of any action they see/hear. Focus on one verse at a time. Go through the lyrics, stopping after each line to repeat chorally and to check comprehension.

● Check through pupils' answers about the different actions. Write a numbered list of their suggestions on the board.

● Go back and play the song in *Practice* mode, focusing on one line at a time. Repeat chorally and to check comprehension.

● Play the song through again: all join in with singing and actions.

Extension
● Split the class into five groups and assign a verse to each group. Each group must perform their verse. You could ask each group to represent a country, and have a 'Eurovision Song Contest'-style vote to decide on the best performance.

See the Introduction for more notes on the Song features.

6 Plenary: Qu'est-ce que c'est?
⏲ 5–10 mins 📖 AT1.1 03.2 / AT2.1 03.3

Materials
Unit 3 Flashcards 1–8 (Parts of the body)

Description
Oracy activity practising parts of the body, using realia or flashcards.

Delivery
● Hold up a flashcard and ask *Qu'est-ce que c'est?* Say one of the parts of the body already learned in a slightly questioning tone (e.g. *C'est la bouche?*).

● The class responds *Oui* or *Non* according to whether your statement is true or false.

● Go through all the items in the same way.

● If time allows, invite a few pupils to make similar statements that the other pupils must respond to.

Extension
● Hold up a flashcard and ask *Qu'est-ce que c'est?* The first pupil to respond correctly comes to the front of the class and chooses another card, which they then hold up and ask *Qu'est-ce que c'est?* Continue in the same way with all the cards.

● Alternatively, stick all the parts of the body flashcards on the board. Give the class one minute to study the board. Ask pupils to turn away/close their eyes while you remove one or two cards. Ask *Qu'est-ce qui manque?* Pupils say which card(s) is/are missing.

Unit 3  Lesson 2

Lesson summary

Context
Describing eyes and hair appearance

National criteria
KS2 Framework: **O3.2, O3.3, O3.4, L3.1, L3.2, L3.3**
Attainment levels: **AT1.2, AT2.1–2, AT3.2, AT4.2**
Language ladder levels:
  Listening: **Grade 1–2;** Reading: **Grade 1–2;**
  Speaking: **Grade 1–2;** Writing: **Grade 1–2**

Cross-curricular links
Science, art, literacy

Key vocabulary
Parts of the body: *les yeux* (eyes), *les cheveux* (hair)
Colours: *vert* (green), *rouge* (red), *marron* (brown), *jaune* (yellow), *bleu* (blue)
Adjectives: *long* (long), *court* (short)

Language structures and outcomes
J'ai les cheveux/les yeux + [adjective]

1 **Starter activity:** ⏱ 5–10 mins 📖 AT2.1 O3.3 O3.4
Les couleurs

Materials
Unit 2 Flashcards 9–14 (colours)

Description
Game based on 'Kim's Game', to practise colours.

Delivery
● Stick the colour flashcards on the board. Quickly go through the colours with the class.

● Ask the class to close their eyes (*Fermez les yeux!*) and remove one or two colours whilst they do so. Ask the class to look (*Regardez!*) and tell you which colour(s) are missing.

● Repeat a few times, until pupils seem comfortable with the colours.

2 **Presentation:** ⏱ 10 mins 📖 AT1.2 O3.2 AT2.2 O3.4 AT3.2 L3.1 L3.2
J'ai les cheveux longs

Materials
CD-ROM

Description
Click on the ghosts, each of which has one defining physical characteristic, to hear and see the correct pronunciation of that body part. Use the additional features to practise sound/spelling links.

Delivery
● Invite pupils to come to the whiteboard and click on the ghosts one by one, then encourage the class to repeat what they hear and to point to the relevant part of their own body. Ensure that they imitate the intonation as accurately as possible.

● Continue until all ghosts have been selected. You may wish to repeat the activity with a different set of pupils.

● Use the Virtual Teacher at any time to compare intonation.

Extension
● Ask a pupil to stand at the front, with their back to the board.

● Another pupil clicks on a ghost to trigger the Virtual Teacher audio and animation.

● The pupil at the front then turns round and points to the ghost corresponding to the description they have just heard.

Sounds
To further reinforce accurate pronunciation, and to introduce some basic reading skills:

● Point to each phrase on the text bar and ask the class to repeat.

● Focus on the text on screen, click on the *Sound* icon, and click on the different highlighted sounds to hear the Virtual Teacher saying them.

● Repeat all together.

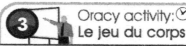
Language Learning Strategies

Comparing languages
● This is another opportunity (as in Unit 2, Lesson 2) to look at the different word order between French and English when using adjectives, i.e. in French the adjective comes after the noun.

---

3 **Oracy activity:** ⏱ 10–15 mins 📖 AT1.2 O3.2 O3.4
Le jeu du corps

Materials
CD-ROM

Description
Click on *Allez* to hear the audio of a ghost describing its defining physical characteristic. Then, judging from the appearance of the three different ghosts on screen, pupils choose the correct ghost.

Delivery
● Ask a pupil to click on the *Allez* button.

● You will see three ghosts (contestants) on a game show podium and will hear one audio description. Pupils decide which ghost matches the description and click on the ghost.

● If their choice is correct, the ghost will confirm its description. The Virtual Teacher will tell pupils if the answer was incorrect and they can try again using the *Encore* button.

Extension
● Turn the activity into a team game by forming two groups; each has three 'lives'. Invite pupils, in turn, from each group to click on a character, and keep scores of the correct answers.

Support
● Play each description twice using the *Encore* button before asking pupils to respond.

4 Oracy activity: ⏱ 10 mins 📚 AT1.2 O3.3
Tu es comment? AT2.2

Materials
Unit 3 Flashcards 9–13 (Eyes and hair)

Description
Pairwork/Role-play activity practising self-descriptions (talking about hair and eyes), using flashcard prompts.

Delivery
● Hold up the 'hair' flashcard and describe your hair (*J'ai les cheveux longs/courts*). Hold up the 'eyes' flashcard and describe your eye colour (*J'ai les yeux bleus/verts/marron*). Hold up one of the two flashcards and ask a pupil *Tu es comment?* They then describe their hair/eyes according to the flashcard. Repeat a few times with different pupils, helping with vocabulary where necessary.

● Alternatively, make groups of 6–8 pupils. One pupil in each group turns to the pupil on their left and asks *Tu es comment?* The second pupil describes their hair or eyes (or, preferably, both). They then turn to the person on their left and ask the same question.

● Continue until all pupils have had a chance to ask and answer the question.

Support
● Get pupils to identify the noun first, and then expand with the rest of the phrase, e.g. *les cheveux – J'ai les cheveux courts*.
● Pupils could say the phrase without *j'ai* if necessary.

5 Literacy activity: ⏱ 10–15m 📚 AT3.2 L3.1
Les visages L3.2

Materials
CD-ROM

Description
Read the descriptions given, then select the correct hair or eyes to complete the series of portraits.

Delivery
● Ask a pupil to click on *Allez* to start the activity. A description will appear under the portrait, e.g. *J'ai les cheveux longs*. The pupil selects, from the side of the screen, the correct hair/eyes to fit the description, and drags it/them to the portrait.

● If the selection is correct, the portrait will become animated. If the answer is incorrect, a 'life' will be lost and the hair/eyes will automatically be returned to the side of the screen.

● The pupils have three 'lives' – the game is over if all lives are lost, and can be started again by clicking on the *Jouez encore?* ✔ button.

● Invite a different pupil to come to the board for each portrait. Repeat as above until all portraits have been covered.

Extension
Play a second time as a team game: each team takes it in turn to answer a question, and scores a point if correct.

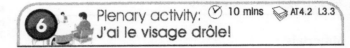

6 Plenary activity: ⏱ 10 mins 📚 AT4.2 L3.3
J'ai le visage drôle!

Materials
Paper and coloured crayons

Description
Plenary activity, drawing and describing funny pictures of people/ghosts/monsters. Pictures can then be displayed in the classroom.

Delivery
● Give out paper and pens. Give pupils five minutes to draw a character, e.g. a person or an alien/monster/ghost.

● Ask pupils to stop drawing and to write a first-person description of their character underneath the picture beginning *J'ai…* Give help with vocabulary and spelling as necessary.

Support
● Write the phrases on the board, with a choice of adjectives, so that pupils can copy them.

Unit 3    Lesson 3

Context
Days of the week

National criteria
KS2 Framework: **O3.1, O3.2, O3.3, O3.4, L3.1, L3.2**
Attainment levels: **AT1.1, AT2.1, AT3.1**
Language ladder levels:
  Listening: **Grade 1–2**; Reading: **Grade 1–2**;
  Speaking: **Grade 1**

Cross-curricular links
n/a

Key vocabulary
Days of the week: *lundi, mardi, mercredi, jeudi, vendredi, samedi, dimanche*

Language structures and outcomes
C'est quel jour (aujourd'hui)? C'est…

 1 Starter activity: ⏱ 5–10 mins 📖 AT2.1 O3.3
Ça va?

Materials
Character puppets

Description
Revision role-play game using puppets/basic props.

Delivery
● Quickly go through the target expressions.

● Divide the class into groups of three and ask each pupil in the group to take on the role of Jake, Polly or Bof. Give them two minutes to prepare a mini role-play with the three characters, using as many of the target expressions as possible.

● Choose two or three groups to come out to the front and perform their role with the puppets.

Support
You can use the Virtual Teacher from Unit 1 at any time to refresh your memory of the target expressions.

 2 Animated story: ⏱ 10 mins 📖 AT1.1 O3.1
Le miroir magique (2) AT2.1 O3.4
AT3.1 L3.1

Materials
CD-ROM

Description
Watch and listen to this interactive animated story presenting the language for Lessons 3–4. You can pause and rewind the story at any point.

Delivery
● This animated story can be used for both starter and plenary activities – the whole animation can be played at the end of the unit so that pupils can gauge their improved understanding.

● At this point pupils watch the second half of the story only; the first half is in Lesson 1.

Scene 3 (Polly, Jake and Nathalie in château corridor)

● Ask pupils for a quick recap of the first two scenes, and play once through to refresh their memories.

● Freeze the screen on the opening frame of the third scene and ask the following questions: What's going to happen now? Who do they think is behind the curtain? (Try to wait until pupils notice the shape in the curtain!)

Extension
● Play the animation through without the sound and ask pupils to think what the characters might be saying to each other (encourage answers in French). Write some of their

suggestions on the board and play the animation again with the sound on.

● Recap what happened and tick off any correct suggestions on the board.

 3 Presentation: ⏱ 10-15 mins 📖 AT1.1 O3.2
Les jours AT2.1 O3.4
AT3.1 L3.1
L3.2

Materials
CD-ROM

Description
Click on the different calendar squares to hear and see the correct pronunciation of the days of the week. Use the additional features to practise sound/spelling links **and spelling**.

Delivery
● Focus pupils on the classroom scene and ask them what they think is on the board (timetable/days of the week).

● Select pupils to come to the board and click on a day, in chronological order. The whole class then listens and repeats the word, counting out the days on their hands, i.e. *lundi* = 1 thumb up, *mardi* = thumb and index finger, etc.

● Continue until all the days have been selected. You will probably need to repeat the activity a couple of times at least, to reinforce learning.

Extension
● Ask a few pupils to stand at the front with their backs to the board. Another pupil clicks on a day to trigger the Virtual Teacher audio.

● The pupils race to be the first to click on the day they have just heard. Repeat with different groups of pupils. Get pupils to record themselves, and then compare their pronunciation with the original.

Spelling
● For groups who have already covered the alphabet: Point to a day and ask pupils to say/spell the word. Check answer by clicking on the word then on the *Spell* icon.

● To simply introduce the concept of spelling in French, click on a day, then on the *Spell* icon, and point to the letters as the Virtual Teacher says them. Repeat, this time asking the whole class to join in. Continue in the same way with all the words.

Sounds
To further reinforce accurate pronunciation, and to introduce some basic reading skills:

● Point to each day on the text bar and ask the class to say the word.

• Focus on the text on screen, click on the *Sound* icon, and click on the different highlighted sounds to hear the Virtual Teacher saying them.

• Repeat altogether.

4 Oracy activity: ⏱10–15 mins 📚 AT1.1 03.2
AT2.1 03.3
C'est quel jour?

Materials
CD-ROM

Description
Look at the day indicated. Say the correct day aloud, in French. Click on the audio check button in Bof's speech bubble to check the answer, if necessary.

Delivery
• Click on the *Allez* button to hear Polly asking *C'est quel jour?* ('What day is it?'). Ask the class to say the day that is highlighted at the bottom of the screen, then click on the audio check button in Bof's bubble to hear the day being said.

• If the class answered correctly, click on the tick. If their answer was wrong, click on the cross. Repeat for all the days. Click on the audio check button in Bof's bubble to play the answer again.

Extension
• Encourage the class to repeat all the days in sequence, adding the new day each time. This will help reinforce the pattern of the days of the week.

• Alternatively, make two teams. Each team takes it in turn to answer a question and scores a point for each correct answer.

Support
• Go through each day once, seeing the answers, before getting pupils to answer.

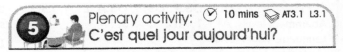

5 Plenary activity: ⏱ 10 mins 📚 AT3.1 L3.1
C'est quel jour aujourd'hui?

Materials
Cards with days of the week written on (enough sets for each group).

Description
Plenary activity practising days of the week; race against the clock.

Delivery
• Quickly go through the days of the week, orally, all together.

• Split the class into groups of seven pupils (or as near as possible). Give each group a set of 'days of the week' cards. Each pupil takes a card but doesn't look at it yet.

• When you give a signal, each group lines up in the correct order of the days and say the days aloud (again, in correct order). The fastest group wins the game.

Extension
• Set up game as above. This time, pupils memorise their day before handing their card back to you. They then line up as above, but do the activity entirely orally and from memory.

Support
• Stick the cards in sequence on the board before starting, to remind pupils of what they look like. You could even keep this sequence on the board during the game.

Lesson summary

Context
Character descriptions

National criteria
KS2 Framework: O3.2, O3.3, O3.4, L3.1, L3.2, L3.3
Attainment levels: AT1.1–2, AT2.1–2, AT3.2, AT4.2
Language ladder levels:
Listening: **Grade 2**, Speaking: **Grade 1–2**,
Reading: **Grade 2**, Writing: **Grade 2**

Cross-curricular links
Literacy

Key vocabulary
Adjectives describing character: *Je suis... grand(e)*, *petit(e)*,
timide, *bavard(e)*, *drôle*, *sympa*

Language structures and outcomes
Je suis... [+ adjective]

---

1 Starter activity: Dans la salle de classe
⏱ 10 mins AT1.1 O3.2 / AT2.1 O3.3

Materials
Unit 2 Flashcards 1–8 (Classroom objects), timer

Description
Team drawing game to revise classroom objects.

Delivery
● Use the flashcards to quickly revise target words, if necessary.

● Form two teams. Invite a pupil from Team A to come to the front. Show them a card. They must then draw the object on the board for their team to guess in less than 30 seconds. The team gets 2 points if they correctly guess and say the French word. Team B may win 1 point for a correct guess if Team A is unsuccessful. Repeat for Team B.

● Continue, selecting different pupils to be the 'artist' each time, until all the words have been covered.

Support
● You can use the Virtual Teacher (from Unit 2) to refresh pupils' memory of the target expressions.

2 Presentation: Les portraits
⏱ 10–15 mins AT1.2 O3.2 / AT2.2 O3.4 / AT3.2 L3.1 / L3.2

Materials
CD-ROM

Description
Click on the portraits to hear and see the correct pronunciation of descriptions of people. Use the additional features to practise sound/spelling links, word classes and spelling.

Delivery
● Choose pupils to come up, in turn, and click on a portrait.

● The whole group repeats the word and copies the Virtual Teacher's gestures, if activated. Click on *Continuez* to return to the portrait gallery and select another portrait, or on *Encore* to repeat the current one.

● When each portrait has been covered a couple of times, make two teams. Ask each team (in turn) to say the phrase when you point to a character. Click on the picture to check whether the answer is correct, and give a point for each correct answer.

Extension
● Point to one of the portraits and ask the class to stand up and give the description whilst doing the Virtual Teacher model gesture for that character. Click on the character to check if they were right. Ask them to repeat the sentence.

● Go through all the portraits in the same way.

Spelling
● For groups who have already done the alphabet: Point to a portrait and ask pupils to say/spell the word. Check answer by clicking on the word then on the *Spell* icon.

● To simply introduce the concept of spelling in French, click on a portrait, then on the *Spell* icon, and point to the letters as the Virtual Teacher says them. Repeat, asking the whole class to join in. Continue in the same way with all the words.

Sounds
To further reinforce accurate pronunciation, and to introduce some basic reading skills:
● Point to the words on the text bar and ask the class to repeat.

● Focus on the text on screen, click on the *Sound* icon, and click on the different highlighted sounds to hear the Virtual Teacher saying them.

● Repeat all together.

NB. If the *Sound* icon is not illuminated, that means it is not applicable for that particular word.

Word class
● This is a good opportunity to practise word classes. See the Introduction for notes on how to use this feature of the Language Presentation.

 Knowledge About Language

Genders and agreements
● If you feel your pupils are up to it, in the Presentation activity above click on the portrait for *bavard*. With the text bar on, ask pupils if they can spot the difference between the two phrases (one of them has an *e* at the end of *bavard*).

● Repeat this for *grand* and *petit*. Then ask if they can see a pattern here (the adjectives have an *e* at the end when they are describing a woman).

● Tell pupils they will see more of this as they progress.

③ Oracy activity: C'est qui? ⏱ 15 mins 📚 AT1.1 03.2 03.4

Materials
CD-ROM

Description
Click on *Allez* to hear the audio of a character in the painting describe what they are like. Click on the corresponding character to see them become animated.

Delivery
● Ask a pupil to click on the *Allez* button. The whole painting comes to life, and you will hear one of the characters describe themselves. The pupil clicks on the character they believe just described themselves.

● If the pupil answered correctly, the character will become animated and confirm their description. In the case of an incorrect answer, the Virtual Teacher will invite the pupil to try again.

● Repeat each character a couple of times.

Extension
● Turn this activity into a team game by forming two groups, inviting pupils, in turn, from each group to click on a character. Keep scores of the correct answers.

Support
● Play each scenario twice using the *Encore* button before asking pupils to respond.

④ Oracy activity: Tu es comment? ⏱ 10–15 mins 📚 AT2.2 03.3 AT3.2 L3.1

Materials
Puppets, Unit 4 Flashcards 9–14 (Character descriptions).

Description
Oracy activity using puppets and flashcards to practise describing oneself.

Delivery
● Quickly go through the target adjectives.

● Stick the word and picture cards face down on the board together in pairs. Take one of the puppets, and remove a pair of the cards. Prompt the class to ask *Tu es comment?* Make the puppet give the answer on the card, e.g. *Je suis [timide.]* in a shy/booming/small, etc. voice to emphasise the characteristic.

● Invite pupils to come to the front, choose a puppet, and take a pair of cards. The rest of the class asks *Tu es comment?* and the pupil responds as per the pair of cards selected.

Extension
● Make three copies of the flashcards and form three groups. Place the cards face down on a table in the middle of the group and give each group a puppet. Play as above – this version gives more pupils the opportunity to have a go.

Support
● Pupils can give the adjectives only, i.e. without using the *Je suis…* phrase, although you should add this to their answer to reinforce its importance, e.g. *Oui, bravo, je suis timide*, and so on.

⑤ Literacy activity: Je suis drôle ⏱ 10–15m 📚 AT3.2 L3.1 L3.2

Materials
CD-ROM

Description
Drag the sentences in speech bubbles to the appropriate character.

Delivery
● Ask a pupil to click on *Allez* to start the activity. The characters will, one at a time, be given an empty speech bubble. Pupils must drag three words from a selection at the bottom of the screen into the bubble to make a sentence describing that character.

● If the sentence is correct and appropriate, the character will become animated and the Virtual Teacher will congratulate the pupil.

● In the case of an incorrect or incomplete answer, the Virtual Teacher will invite the pupil to have another go.

Extension
● Play a second time as a team game: each team takes it in turn to make a sentence and scores a point if correct.

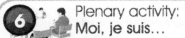

⑥ Plenary activity: Moi, je suis… ⏱ 10 mins 📚 AT2.2 03.3 AT3.2 L3.1 AT4.2 L3.3

Materials
Paper and pens, cloth bag

Description
Plenary literacy activity, to consolidate describing characteristics in a game of charades.

Delivery
● Give out paper and pens. Put class into groups of six. Give pupils a couple of minutes to write out one target sentence each, e.g *Je suis [timide]*.

● Put all the papers into a bag.

● Make two teams. In turns, a pupil from each team comes to the front, takes a paper, and has one minute (maximum) to act out the description, without speaking or noises. Their team must guess the correct description to win 2 points. If the answer is incorrect, the opposing team has one chance to say the correct sentence for a bonus point.

● Continue until as many pupils as possible have had a turn.

Support
● You can use the Virtual Teacher on the CD-ROM at any time to refresh your memory of the target expressions.

Unit 3

⏱ 10–15 mins 📚 AT2.1 O3.3
AT3.1 L3.1
AT4.1 L3.2

Worksheet 1A

Description
Worksheet to give further practice on parts of the body.

Notes
1 Pupils can discuss Activity 1 in pairs.
2 This activity can be done in pairs again, or individually.

Answers
a	jambe	c	yeux	e	oreilles
b	nez	d	bouche	f	bras

⏱ 10–15 mins 📚 AT2.1 O3.3
AT3.1 L3.1
AT4.1 L3.2

Worksheet 1B

Description
Worksheet to give further practice on parts of the body

Notes
1 Pupils can discuss Activity 1 in pairs.
2 This activity can be done in pairs again, or individually.

Answers
a	les yeux	c	le nez	e	le bras
b	les oreilles	d	la bouche	f	la jambe

⏱ 10–15 mins 📚 AT2.2 O3.3
AT3.2 L3.1
L3.2

Worksheet 2A

Description
Worksheet to give further practice on parts of the body and numbers.

Notes
1 Read each speech bubble together, before giving pupils a couple of minutes to complete the picture. Check their answers before moving on to the next one.
2 If time allows, pupils could copy out the relevant sentences underneath their picture.

⏱ 10–15 mins 📚 AT2.2 O3.3
AT3.2 L3.1
AT4.1 L3.2 L3.3

Worksheet 2B

Description
Worksheet to give further practice on parts of the body and numbers.

Notes
1 Go through Activity 1 orally together, to elicit suggestions before pupils write/draw.
2 More confident pupils could add one or two more descriptions to their dictation!

Answers
1 a J'ai cinq jambes.
  b J'ai les cheveux courts.
  c J'ai une jambe.

⏱ 10–15 mins 📚 AT2.1 O3.3
AT3.1 L3.1
AT4.1 L3.2 L3.3

Worksheet 3A

Description
Worksheet to give further practice on days of the week.

Notes
1 Encourage pupils to say the days aloud as they find them.
2 Pupils could draw a little picture of an activity they do on a certain day (e.g. football, swimming costume) to help them remember the days.
3 They could also write down their favourite day with a little picture of what they do on that day.

Answers

M	A	R	D	I	J	E	U	D	I	M	O
B	M	E	R	C	R	E	D	I	S	O	N
L	U	N	D	I	W	S	A	M	E	D	I
D	I	M	A	N	C	H	E	J	O	L	I
P	V	E	N	D	R	E	D	I	B	O	N

⏱ 10–15 mins 📚 AT2.1 O3.3
AT3.1 L3.1
AT4.1 L3.2 L3.3

Worksheet 3B

Description
Worksheet to give further practice on days of the week.

Notes
1 Encourage pupils to say the days aloud as they complete them.
2 Pupils could draw a little picture of an activity they do on a certain day (e.g. football, swimming costume) to help them remember the days.
3 They could also write down their favourite day with a little picture of what they do on that day.

Answers
1	a	dimanche	e	mercredi
	b	vendredi	f	lundi
	c	samedi	g	jeudi
	d	mardi		

⏱ 10–15 mins 📚 AT2.2 O3.3
AT3.2 L3.1
AT4.2 L3.2 L3.3

Worksheet 4A

Description
Worksheet to give further practice of introductions and descriptions.

Notes
1 Encourage pupils to read the sentences aloud.
2 Pupils could work in pairs and ask each other *Tu es comment?* to elicit the answers.

⏱ 10–15 mins 📚 AT2.1 O3.3
AT3.1 L3.1
AT4.1 L3.2 L3.3

Worksheet 4B

Description
Worksheet to give further practice introductions and descriptions.

Notes
1 Encourage pupils to read the sentences aloud.
2 Pupils could work in pairs and ask each other *Tu es comment?* to elicit the answers.

Project work: Famous French people

⏱ 20–30 mins 📚 AT4.1–2
L3.3
IU3.3

Description
Pupils find pictures of French celebrities and imagine them describing themselves.

Materials
French lifestyle magazines, internet access.

Delivery
● Prepare a selection of pages or cuttings from some French lifestyle magazines like *Paris-Match* or *Marie Claire*, or similar websites (e.g. www.parismatch.com) or with pictures of French (or international) celebrities. Write their name and age on the back.

● Try to choose pictures where the celebrities have clearly got traits pupils can describe using the language from Unit 3, i.e. blue, brown or green eyes; short or long hair; tall, short, funny, kind, talkative or shy.

● Provide the cuttings in a pile, and divide pupils into small groups of two or three, with one or two pictures each. Pupils should stick the pictures into their books or onto a sheet of paper, then draw in one or more speech bubbles by their mouths saying *Je m'appelle…*, *J'ai… ans*, and any phrases from *J'ai les yeux…*, *J'ai les cheveux…* and *Je suis…* that are appropriate.

● Pupils can complete this activity using a word processor or Microsoft PowerPoint if you prefer.

● Once complete, you can create a display of the results, or collate a presentation of all the pictures.

Support
● Write a list of the relevant phrases on the board for pupils to select from and copy for their chosen celebrities.

Rigolo 1 — Unit 4: Les animaux

National criteria

KS2 Framework objectives

O3.1	Listen and respond to simple rhymes, stories and songs
O3.2	Recognise and respond to sound patterns and words
O3.3	Perform simple communicative tasks using single words, phrases and short sentences
O3.4	Listen attentively and understand instructions, everyday classroom language and praise words
L3.1	Recognise some familiar words in written form
L3.2	Make links between some phonemes, rhymes and spellings, and read aloud familiar words
L3.3	Experiment with the writing of simple words

QCA Scheme of Work

Unit 1	Je parle français
Unit 2	Je me présente
Unit 3	En famille
Unit 4	Les animaux

Language ladder levels

Listening:	Breakthrough, Grade 1–2
Reading:	Breakthrough, Grade 1–2
Speaking:	Breakthrough, Grade 1–2
Writing:	Breakthrough, Grade 1–2

5–14 guideline strands   Levels A–C

Listening
Listening for information and instructions	A, C
Listening and reacting to others	A, B, C

Speaking
Speaking to convey information	A, C
Speaking and interacting with others	B, C
Speaking about experiences, feelings and opinions	A, B

Reading
Reading for information and instructions	A, C
Reading aloud	A, C

Writing
Writing to exchange information and ideas	A, C
Writing to establish and maintain personal contact	A, C
Writing imaginatively/to entertain	n/a

Unit objectives

- identify animals and pets
- recognise and use numbers 11–20
- give someone's name
- describe someone

Key language

- animals: *un chien* (dog), *un chat* (cat), *une tortue* (tortoise), *un lapin* (rabbit), *un oiseau* (bird), *une souris* (mouse), *un dragon* (dragon)
- numbers 11–20: *onze, douze, treize, quatorze, quinze, seize, dix-sept, dix-huit, dix-neuf, vingt*
- *il/elle s'appelle...* (s/he's called...)
- adjectives describing character: *grand(e)* (tall), *petit(e)* (small), *drôle* (funny), *sévère* (strict), *timide* (shy)

Grammar and skills

- gender of different nouns
- recognise negative form
- count numbers 11–20
- give names and descriptions in the third person (he/she)

Unit outcomes

Most children will be able to:

- use spoken French to identify different animals
- recognise and use numbers 11–20 orally and in writing
- reply when asked someone's name
- describe someone using set phrases
- begin to recognise, read and pronounce sounds of combinations of letters, words and set phrases

Some children will also be able to:

- write and say phrases from memory, with clear pronunciation and meaning
- describe character with one-word adjectives
- appreciate simple adjectival agreement (for more able pupils only)

Unit 4  Lesson 1

Context
Animals and pets

National criteria
KS2 Framework: **O3.1, O3.2, O3.3, O3.4, L3.1, L3.2**
Attainment levels: **AT1.1–2, AT2.1–2, AT3.1–2**
Language ladder levels:
  Listening: **Grade 1–2**; Speaking: **Grade 1–2**;
  Reading: **Grade 1–2**

Cross-curricular links
Science

Numeracy

Key vocabulary
Animals: *un chien* (dog), *un chat* (cat), *une tortue* (tortoise), *un lapin* (rabbit), *un oiseau* (bird), *une souris* (mouse), *un dragon* (dragon)

Language structures and outcomes
Tu as [un chien]? (Do you have a dog?)
J'ai [un chien.] (I have a [dog.]), *Je n'ai pas d'animal.* (I don't have a pet.)

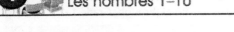
1 Starter activity: ⏱ 5 mins 📚 AT2.1 O3.3
Les nombres 1–10

Materials
n/a

Description
Pupils choose a number between 1 and 10, then replace this number with 'Bof' when saying the numbers in sequence.

Delivery
● Ask the class to choose a number between 1 and 10. This number will now be replaced with the word 'Bof!' in the game.

● The class should be standing. Go round the class, each pupil saying a number in the correct sequence. When a pupil has to say 'Bof!', they must sit down. When number 10 is reached, go back to 1, and continue until only one pupil is left standing.

● You can change the 'Bof!' number a few times, to keep pupils on their guard!

Support
● If you feel pupils need revision, go through the numbers 1 to 10 before starting, or at any time during the game.

2 Animated story: ⏱ 10 mins 📚 AT1.2 O3.1
La famille Chanson (1) AT3.2 O3.4

Materials
CD-ROM

Description
Watch and listen to this interactive animated story, set in the Chanson family's house, presenting the language for Lessons 1 and 2 (animals and numbers up to 20). You can pause and rewind the story at any point.

Delivery
● This animated story can be used for both starter and plenary activities – the whole animation can be played at the end of the unit so that pupils can gauge their improved understanding.

● At this point pupils watch the first half of the story only; the second half is in Lesson 3.

Scene 1 (Exterior of the Chansons' house) and Scene 2 (Close-up of the house exterior)

Freeze the screen on the opening scene and ask the following questions:

● Who lives in the house?
● What animals do they have?
● How many animals?

Note pupils' answers on the board. Play the scene through without stopping. Ask whether their predictions were correct. Ask pupils to briefly summarise what happened.

3 Presentation: ⏱ 5–10 mins 📚 AT1.1–2 O3.2
Tu as un animal? AT2.1–2 O3.4
AT3.1–2 L3.1
L3.2

Materials
CD-ROM

Description
Click on an animal or symbol to hear and see the correct pronunciation. Use the additional features to practise sound/spelling links, word classes and spelling.

Delivery
● Ask pupils to come in turn to the whiteboard and click on an animal. The class repeats the word and the Virtual Teacher's gesture each time, to reinforce learning.

● Click on the *Replay* button to listen again. Repeat chorally, copying the Virtual Teacher's gestures as you say the words.

● Continue until all animals have been selected. Having presented the animals, you can then use them in the phrase *J'ai un chien* (etc.), by clicking on the relevant character standing closest to the animal in question.

● Finally, click on the 'no cats/dogs' sign to teach the phrase *Je n'ai pas d'animal.* ('I don't have a pet').

Extension
● Ask a few pupils to stand at the front, with their backs to the board. Another pupil clicks on an animal or character to trigger the Virtual Teacher audio. The pupils turn round and point to the relevant image on the board. Repeat with different groups of pupils.

Spelling
● For groups who have already done the alphabet: Point to an animal and ask pupils to say/spell the word. Check answer by clicking on the word, then on the *Spell* icon.

● To simply introduce the concept of spelling in French, click on an animal, then on the *Spell* icon, and point to the letters as the Virtual Teacher says them. Repeat, this time asking the whole class to join in. Continue in the same way with all the words.

Word class

- Focus on a word and ask the group what class of word it is (noun).
- Click on the *Word* icon, then on the image in question to hear the Virtual Teacher say the word class.
- Repeat all together, copying the Virtual Teacher's gestures as you say the word class.

Sounds

To further reinforce accurate pronunciation, and to introduce some basic reading skills:

- Point to each word on the text bar and ask the class to say the word.
- Focus on the text on screen, click on the *Sound* icon, and click on the different highlighted sounds to hear the Virtual Teacher saying them.
- Repeat all together.

NB. If the *Sound* icon is not illuminated, that means it is not applicable for that particular word.

Knowledge About Language

Genders

- Once again the animals are positioned according to gender, with the five masculine ones on the left of the screen and the two feminine to the right, making this a good way to revisit the notion of gender groups.

Negative forms

- The phrase *Je n'ai pas d'animal.* is the first negative formation pupils will have encountered.
- Having presented this in Activity 3 above, extract the phrases *J'ai* and *Je n'ai pas* and ask pupils which one means 'I have' and which one means 'I don't have'.
- Ask pupils how they change 'I have' to mean the opposite in English (they add 'don't'). Show them how in French you add the *ne... pas* phrase to do the same thing. They can look out for other negative phrases like this throughout *Rigolo*.

4 Oracy activity: ⏲ 10 mins   📖 AT1.2   03.2
Les animaux   03.4

Materials
CD-ROM

Description

Listen to the characters and click on the correct pet or symbol.

Delivery

- Click on *Allez* to start (or invite a pupil to start) the activity. You will hear one of the characters saying which pet(s) they have and asking where they are.
- Pupils click on the animals to identify them.

Extension

- Make two teams. Each team takes it in turn to answer a question and scores a point for each correct answer.

Support

- Go through the animals with pupils before they start the activity.

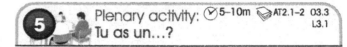

5 Plenary activity: 🕐 5–10m   📖 AT2.1–2   03.3
Tu as un...?   L3.1

Materials
Unit 4 Flashcards 1–7 (Animals & pets)

Description
Oracy plenary activity to practise saying which pets you have, using flashcards.

Delivery

- Quickly go through the flashcards to check pupils remember the words.
- Stick the picture flashcards onto the board, with or without the word card as you prefer.
- Model *J'ai* [*un chien*], pointing to the relevant flashcard at the same time.
- Shake your head and shrug your shoulders to model *Je n'ai pas d'animal.*
- Invite pupils to come to the front, point to a card, and make a sentence.

Extension

- Stick all flashcards on the board.
- Give the class one minute to study the board.
- Ask the pupils to turn away/close their eyes while you remove one or two cards. Ask *Qu'est-ce qui manque?*
- Pupils must say which card(s) is/are missing.

Support

- Get pupils simply to identify the nouns rather than use the *J'ai...* phrase. They can add this for a bonus point if they can.
- Put the word cards on the board to act as a prompt, either grouped in pairs with the picture, or in a separate group so they have to match these first.

Unit 4 Lesson 2

Context
Numbers 11–20, and animals

National criteria
KS2 Framework: **O3.1, O3.2, O3.3, O3.4, L3.1, L3.2, L3.3**
Attainment levels: **AT1.1–2, AT2.1–2, AT3.1–2. AT4.1–2**
Language ladder levels:
  Listening: **Grade 1–2**; Speaking: **Grade 1–2**;
  Reading: **Grade 1–2**; Writing: **Grade 1–2**

Cross-curricular links
Literacy, numeracy

Key vocabulary
Numbers 11–20: *onze, douze, treize, quatorze, quinze, seize, dix-sept, dix-huit, dix-neuf, vingt*

Language structures and outcomes
Onze chats, etc.

---

1 Starter activity: ⏲ 5 mins 📚 AT2.1-2 O3.3
J'ai un dragon

Materials
Unit 4 Flashcards 1–7 (Animals & pets), puppets

Description
Use animal flashcards and puppets to revise pets.

Delivery
- Quickly go through the flashcards to revise vocabulary.
- Hold up a puppet and a flashcard, and make the puppet say a sentence, e.g. *J'ai [un chien]*. Invite a few pupils to come up and do the same with different puppets and flashcards.
- See Lesson 1, Activity 5 for more ideas.

2 Presentation: ⏲ c.10 mins 📚 AT1.2 O3.2 / AT2.2 O3.4 / AT3.2 L3.1 / L3.2
Les nombres 11–20

Materials
CD-ROM

Description
Click on a number to hear and see the correct pronunciation. Use the additional features to practise sound/spelling links **and spelling.**

Delivery
- Invite pupils to click on a number.
- The corresponding numbers of birds will remain on the perches and the Virtual Teacher will say the number.
- Chorally repeat the number, illustrating (as the Virtual Teacher) with your fingers. Ensure that pupils imitate the intonation as accurately as possible.
- Continue until all numbers have been selected. You may wish to repeat the activity with a different set of pupils.
- Use the Virtual Teacher at any time to compare intonation.

Extension
- Ask a couple of pupils to stand near the board.
- Other pupils in the class call out numbers, one at a time, and the pupils try to be the first to click on that number.
- Correct selections will be confirmed as the Virtual Teacher speaks.

Spelling
- For groups who have already done the alphabet: Point to an number and ask pupils to say/spell the word. Check answer by clicking on the word then on the *Spell* icon.

- To simply introduce the concept of spelling in French, click on a number, then on the *Spell* icon, and point to the letters as the Virtual Teacher says them. Repeat, this time asking the whole class to join in. Continue in the same way with all the words.

Sounds
To further reinforce accurate pronunciation, and to introduce some basic reading skills:
- Point to each number on screen and ask the class to repeat.
- Focus on the number on screen, click on the *Sound* icon, and click on the different highlighted sounds to hear the Virtual Teacher saying them.
- Repeat all together.

3 Oracy activity: ⏲ c.10 mins 📚 AT1.1 O3.2 / AT2.1 O3.3 / O3.4
Les nombres de onze à vingt

Materials
CD-ROM

Description
Listen to the question. Count the animals aloud and click on them to count them off. Then click on the total number at the bottom of the screen.

Delivery
- Click on *Allez* to start the activity. You will hear the Virtual Teacher asking how many of a certain type of animal are in the picture. Pupils should count silently and then give their total.
- Get a pupil to count the animals by clicking on each one as they count it. The rest of the class should count along with them. The pupil then clicks on the appropriate number.
- If the pupil selects the correct number, there will be celebratory animation and audio, otherwise they will be invited to have another go.

Extension
- Make this activity into a team game by forming two groups. Invite pupils, in turn, from each group to count the animals, and keep scores of the correct answers.

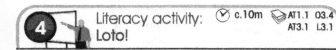

4 Literacy activity: ⏱ c.10m 📖 AT1.1 03.4 AT3.1 L3.1
Loto!

Materials
CD-ROM

Description
Play bingo in teams, either using completed cards, or filling your own cards in on screen or using a printed grid. Then mark off the word on your card if you see the object appear on-screen. The first player or team with all their words marked off wins.

Delivery
There are three ways of playing the bingo game:

● *Ready to go*: the computer automatically completes two grids for each team. Team members mark off phrases on their grid as pictures appear on-screen.

● *Make your own*: as above, but teams complete their grids with their choice of phrases on-screen.

● *Print your own* as *Ready to go*, but print off blank *Loto* grids from the CD-ROM, which pupils fill with their choice of animals and numbers from those listed on-screen.

● When you are ready to start the game, call up a member of each team to click on the card.

● Click on *Allez* to make each item appear. When pupils hear a phrase from their grid, they must either click on the relevant square, or mark the square off on their printed grid.

● When the first on-screen grid is complete, there will be a celebratory animation.

● If playing with printed grids, then the first player to fill their grid calls out *Gagné!*

● You can play the game again if time allows.

Support
● You can play with or without sound by clicking on the *Audio on/Audio off* button on the taskbar at the bottom. With sound on, pupils will hear each phrase spoken as it appears.

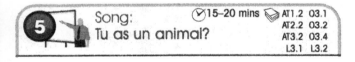

5 Song: ⏱ 15–20 mins 📖 AT1.2 03.1
Tu as un animal? AT2.2 03.2
AT3.2 03.4
L3.1 L3.2

Materials
CD-ROM or Audio CD, track 10; Unit 4 Flashcards 1–7 (Animals & pets)

Description
Watch and listen to the interactive song practising animals, numbers and questions. Choose either *Practice* or *Sing* mode: the former to go through the song line by line, the latter to sing it all the way through. Switch the music and words on or off as you prefer.

Delivery
● Using the flashcards, quickly recap the animal words.

● Stick the cards onto the board and ask pupils to note down in which order they appear in the song as they listen.

● Play the song once right the way through in *Sing* mode.

● Check through pupils' answers.

● Write the following numbers on the board: 16, 11, 20, 18, 12, 15.

● Play the song through again, this time asking pupils to note down the numbers in the order they appear in the song.

● Go through their answers at the end of the song. Match up the numbers with the animals.

● Go back and play the song in *Practice* mode, focusing on one verse at a time. Repeat chorally and check comprehension.

● Play the verse through again, all joining in with singing and actions.

● Continue in the same way with all the verses.

Extension
● Split the class into six groups and assign a verse to each group (or three groups, two verses per group).

● Each group must perform their verse.

● Alternatively, assign the part of Jake to one half of the class and the part of Nathalie to the other half.

● You could ask each group to represent a country, and have a Eurovision Song Contest-style vote to decide on the best performance!

See the Introduction for more notes on the Song features.

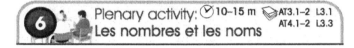

6 Plenary activity: ⏱ 10–15 m 📖 AT3.1–2 L3.1
Les nombres et les noms AT4.1–2 L3.3

Materials
Paper, pencils and coloured crayons

Description
Plenary literacy activity, in which pupils combine French numbers and nouns learned so far to make a number wall chart for the classroom.

Delivery
● Either prepare a list of numbers + nouns on the board (e.g. *un dragon, deux filles, trois trompettes*, etc., up to number 20) or ask pupils to choose their own combination.

● Pupils then draw/write out their number + noun on a piece of A4 card or paper.

● When everyone has finished, the papers can be taped together to make a wall display.

NB. if preferred, this chart could be produced on computer, with pupils using clip-art for visuals.

Support
● Write two lists of all the numbers, and all the relevant nouns in plural form. Pupils can combine as they like.

Unit 4  Lesson 3

Context
Give someone's name

National criteria
KS2 Framework: O3.1, O3.2, O3.3, O3.4, L3.1, L3.2
Attainment levels: AT1.1–2, AT2.1–2, AT3.2
Language ladder levels:
  Listening: **Grade 1–2**; Speaking: **Grade 1–2**;
  Reading: **Grade 1–2**

Cross-curricular links
Numeracy

Key vocabulary
Il/Elle s'appelle... (S/he's called...)

Language structures and outcomes
Il/Elle s'appelle... (S/he's called...)

---

1 Starter activity: ⏱ 5 mins 📖 AT1.1–2 O3.3 AT2.1–2 O3.4
Il y a combien?

Materials
Duplicated mini-flashcards of animals (Unit 4 Flashcards 1–7 (Animals & pets))

Description
Display a number of mini-flashcards on the board; pupils say how many there are.

Delivery
● Place a number of mini-flashcards on the board and ask the class: *Il y a combien [de chats]?*

● Pupils reply *Il y a [dix] chats*, etc.

Extension
● Make this into a quick team game and award a point for each correct answer.

Support
● Pupils give the number plus animal name only, rather than using the *il y a* phrase.

2 Animated story: ⏱ 10 mins 📖 AT1.2 O3.1 AT3.2 O3.4
La famille Chanson (2)

Materials
CD-ROM

Description
Watch and listen to this interactive animated story presenting the language for Lessons 3–4. You can pause and rewind the story at any point.

Delivery
● This animated story can be used for both starter and plenary activities – the whole animation can be played at the end of the unit so that pupils can gauge their improved understanding.

● At this point pupils watch the second half of the story only; the first half is in Lesson 1.

Scene 3 – Inside the Chansons' house

Freeze the screen on the opening scene and ask the following questions:

● Who lives in the house (recap)?

● What is the family like?

● Can they name any animals/objects on the screen?

Play the scene through without stopping. Ask whether pupils' predictions were correct. Ask pupils to briefly summarise what happened.

Extension
● Play the animation through without the sound and ask pupils to think what the characters might be saying to each other. Encourage answers in French.

● Write some of their suggestions on the board and play the animation again with the sound on.

● Recap what happened and tick off any correct suggestions on the board.

3 Presentation: ⏱ 5–10 mins 📖 AT1.2 O3.2 AT2.2 O3.4 AT3.2 L3.1 L3.2
Il s'appelle comment?

Materials
CD-ROM

Description
Click on a character to hear them being introduced in the third person. Use the additional features to practise sound/spelling links.

Delivery
● Ask pupils to click on each character in turn; the class repeats the sentence each time.

● You will probably need to repeat the activity at least a couple of times to reinforce learning.

Extension
● Point to (without touching) a character and ask pupils to introduce them using the model sentences just heard.

● Click on the character to hear the Virtual Teacher presentation and compare with pupils' answers.

● Ask pupils to record themselves, then compare their pronunciation with the original.

Sounds
To further reinforce accurate pronunciation, and to introduce some basic reading skills:

● Point to a sentence on the text bar and ask the class to read it aloud.

● Focus on the text on screen, click on the *Sound* icon, and click on the different highlighted sounds to hear the Virtual Teacher saying them.

● Repeat all together.

4 Plenary activity: ⏱ 5 mins 📖 AT1.1–2 O3.3
Il s'appelle Mark   AT2.1–2 O3.4

Materials
n/a

Description
Oracy plenary activity practising naming pupils in class.

Delivery
● Stand with the pupils in a circle.

● Start by pointing at the pupil on your left, asking the class *Il s'appelle comment?/Elle s'appelle comment?* (You can miss out the question if you prefer.)

● Everyone chorally repeats *Il s'appelle Chris* (etc.) or *Elle s'appelle Becca*, as appropriate.

● Then move on to the next pupil, repeating their name chorally, until you have gone round the whole circle.

Extension
● Divide the class into two teams, standing in two different circles. Repeat the game as above. The first team to get round the whole of their circle wins. Monitor the teams to make sure they are playing the game properly!

● As above, but each pupil has to give the name in turn, moving round clockwise until it comes back to the next pupil in sequence.

Unit 4    Lesson 4

Context
Describing someone

National criteria
KS2 Framework: **O3.2, O3.3, O3.4, L3.1, L3.2, L3.3**
Attainment levels: **AT1.2, AT2.1–2, AT3.2, AT4.2**
Language ladder levels:
  Listening: **Grade 2**; Speaking: **Grade 1–2**;
  Reading: **Grade 2**; Writing: **Grade 2**

Cross-curricular links
Literacy

Key vocabulary
Adjectives describing character: *grand(e)* (tall), *petit(e)*
(small), *drôle* (funny), *sévère* (strict), *timide* (shy)

Language structures and outcomes
Il/Elle est... (S/he's ...)

1 Starter activity: ⏱ 5 mins 📖 AT2.1–2 O3.3
Il s'appelle...

Materials
Puppets of *Rigolo* characters

Description
Pupils choose a puppet representing a *Rigolo* character, and
introduce them using *Il/Elle s'appelle* [+ name].

Delivery
● Model the structure using one or two puppets to refresh
pupils' memories.

● Pass the puppets round the class and ask pupils to introduce
them in the same way.

Extension
● Go round the class asking pupils to introduce the person to
their left in the same way.

2 Presentation: ⏱ 10 mins 📖 AT1.2 O3.2
Il est comment?   AT2.2 O3.4
Elle est comment?   AT3.2 L3.1
                             L3.2

Materials
CD-ROM

Description
Click on a character to hear and see the correct pronunciation
of their description in the third person. Use the additional
features to practise sound/spelling links, word classes and
spelling.

Delivery
● Start the activity. Ask pupils to come up and click on each
character in turn.

● The class repeats the sentence and the Virtual Teacher's
gesture each time.

● When each character has been covered a couple of times,
make two teams. Ask each team, in turn, to say the phrase
when you point to a character.

● Click on the picture to check whether the answer is correct,
and give a point for each right answer.

Extension
● Ask a few pupils to stand at the front, with their backs to
the board.

● Another pupil clicks on a character to trigger the Virtual
Teacher audio. The pupils turn round and point to the
relevant character on the board.

● Repeat with different groups of pupils.

Spelling
● For groups who have already done the alphabet: Point to a
character and ask pupils to say/spell the word. Check answer
by clicking on the word then on the *Spell* icon.

● To simply introduce the concept of spelling in French, click
on a character, then on the *Spell* icon, and point to the letters
as the Virtual Teacher says them. Repeat, this time asking the
whole class to join in. Continue in the same way with all the
words.

Sounds
To further reinforce accurate pronunciation, and to introduce
some basic reading skills:

● Point to the words on the text bar and ask the class to
repeat.

● Focus on the text on screen, click on the *Sound* icon, and
click on the different highlighted sounds to hear the Virtual
Teacher saying them.

● Repeat all together.

NB. If the *Sound* icon is not illuminated, that means it is not
applicable for that particular word.

Word class
● Focus on a word and ask the group what class of word it is.

● Click on the *Word* icon, then on the image in question to
hear the Virtual Teacher say the word class.

● Repeat all together, copying the Virtual Teacher's gestures as
you say the word class.

 Knowledge About Language

Genders and adjectives
● If in Unit 3 you pointed out to pupils the different
spellings of adjectives for men and women, you can
revise this concept with the Presentation above.

● This time, focus on either the words *grand/grande*
and *petit/petite*. Encourage pupils to find both words for
'tall', and to point out the difference. Do the same for
'short'.

● Ask pupils if they can work out a pattern from this
(when describing women or girls, you add an 'e' to the
adjectives).

3 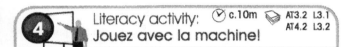 Oracy activity: ⏱ 10 mins 📚 AT1.2 O3.2
Les personnages   AT2.2 O3.3

Materials
CD-ROM

Description
Pupils identify the characters that are being described by clicking on them.

Delivery
● Click on *Allez* to start the activity. You will hear one of the people being described on screen. Encourage the class to repeat the description they have just heard. Pupils must then click on the person they think is being described.

● If the pupil answered correctly, the character will become animated and the Virtual Teacher will congratulate the pupils. In the case of an incorrect answer, the Virtual Teacher will invite the pupil to try again.

Extension
● Make two teams. Each team takes it in turn to answer a question and scores a point for each correct answer.

Support
● Play each scenario twice using the *Encore* button before asking pupils to respond.

4 Literacy activity: ⏱ c.10m 📚 AT3.2 L3.1
Jouez avec la machine!   AT4.2 L3.2

Materials
CD-ROM

Description
Drag words from a selection on screen into the machine to make sentences using *Il/Elle s'appelle* [+ name], and *Il/Elle est* [+ adjective]. Then click on the *Fini* button to see these animated accordingly.

Delivery
● Invite two pupils to the board. They select words from the screen and drag them to the gaps in the sentences. The two sentences must agree, i.e. if they have selected a boy's name, they must also select the masculine form (where applicable) of the adjective to go in the second sentence.

● When a correct sentence is composed, the character described will appear out of the machine.

● In the case of an incorrect sentence being composed, the machine 'malfunctions', and the pupils will be invited to try again.

Extension
● This is a good opportunity to touch lightly on the agreement of adjectives.

● Ask why pupils think some of the sentences are incorrect – demonstrate one, if necessary! See if they have already spotted any patterns in words changing according to whether we are talking about a male or female character.

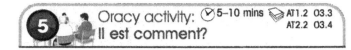 **5** Oracy activity: ⏱ 5–10 mins 📚 AT1.2 O3.3
Il est comment?   AT2.2 O3.4

Materials
Unit 4 Flashcards 8–14 (Character descriptions), puppets

Description
Oracy activity using flashcards and puppets to revise third person descriptions.

Delivery
● Quickly go through the target adjectives.

● Hold up a flashcard or a puppet and ask *Il/Elle est comment?* to elicit descriptions from the class.

Extension
● Stick all flashcards on the board and prop up the puppets.

● Describe one of the characters, or ask a pupil to describe one, and ask a pupil to go up and point to the puppet or card being described.

Support
● Instead of leaving each question open, give pupils options for each question, e.g. *Il est grand ou il est petit? Il est sévère ou il est sympa?*

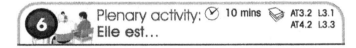 **6** Plenary activity: ⏱ 10 mins 📚 AT3.2 L3.1
Elle est...   AT4.2 L3.3

Materials
Sets of individual word cards (*il, elle, est* + adjectives covered so far).

Description
Plenary literacy activity, in which pupils build sentences to describe someone in the third person, using individual word cards.

Delivery
● Give out a set of cards to each table/group.

● Allow five minutes for each group to make as many different sentences as possible using the cards.

● Pupils write out the different sentences so they can compare with the other groups at the end.

Support
● Write out a few model sentences on the board as reminders for pupils of how to construct the sentences.

Unit 4  Extra!

⏱ 10–15 mins 📖 AT2.1 O3.3
Worksheets 1A & 1B AT2.2

Description
Worksheet to give further practice on saying what pets pupils have, by way of a class survey.

Notes
Model the question/answer dialogue with a couple of pupils before asking the class to begin their survey: *Tu as un animal? Oui, j'ai un chien./Non, je n'ai pas d'animal.*

⏱ 10–15 mins 📖 AT2.1 L3.1
Worksheet 2A AT4.1 L3.3

Description
Worksheet to give further practice on pets and numbers up to 20.

Notes
1 & 2 Quickly go through the animals, using Unit 4 Flashcards (1–8), before pupils begin the activities. Encourage them to say the animal words as they're doing these activities.

3 Again, quickly revise the numbers up to 20 and encourage pupils to say the numbers aloud as they do the activity.

Answers
1 dog – *un chien*; cat – *un chat*; bird – *un oiseau*; dragon – *un dragon*; tortoise – *une tortue*; rabbit – *un lapin*; mouse – *une souris*

2	**a** un chien	**c** un oiseau	**e** une souris
	b un chat	**d** une tortue	**f** un lapin

3	**a** *onze*	**c** *douze*
	b *seize*	**d** *vingt*

⏱ 10–15 mins 📖 AT2.2 O3.3
Worksheet 3A AT3.1 L3.1 AT4.1 L3.2 L3.3

Description
Worksheet to give further practice on using *Il/Elle s'appelle…*

Notes
1 Model the target language by standing behind a few pupils in turn, to elicit *Il/Elle s'appelle…*

2 Go through the answers to Activity 1 before setting up the pairs for Activity 2. Alternatively, put pupils who complete Activity 1 quickly into pairs whilst allowing slower children a little more time.

Answers
1	**a** Il s'appelle M. Mills.	**f** Elle s'appelle Mme
	b Elle s'appelle Mme Mills.	Chanson.
	c Elle s'appelle Polly.	**g** Il s'appelle M. Chanson.
	d Il s'appelle Jake.	**h** Elle s'appelle Nathalie.
	e Il s'appelle Bof.	**i** Il s'appelle Olivier.

⏱ 10–15 mins 📖 AT2.2 O3.3
Worksheet 3B AT3.1 L3.1 AT4.1 L3.2 L3.3

Description
Worksheet to give further practice on using *Il/Elle s'appelle…*

Notes
1 Model the target language by standing behind a few pupils in turn, to elicit *Il/Elle s'appelle…*

2 Go through the answers to Activity 1 before setting up the pairs for Activity 2. Alternatively, put pupils who complete Activity 1 quickly into pairs whilst allowing less able pupils a little more time.

Answers
1	**a** Il s'appelle Jake.	**d** Elle s'appelle Polly.
	b Il s'appelle M. Chanson.	**e** Elle s'appelle Nathalie.
	c Elle s'appelle Mme Moulin.	**f** Il s'appelle Olivier.

⏱ 10–15 mins 📖 AT3.1 L3.1
Worksheet 2B AT4.1 L3.3

Description
Worksheet to give further practice on pets and numbers up to 20.

Notes
1 Quickly go through the animals, using Unit 4 Flashcards 1–8, before pupils begin the activity. Encourage them to say the animal words as they're doing the activity.

2 Again, quickly revise the numbers up to 20 and encourage pupils to say the numbers aloud as they do exercises 2 and 3.

Answers
1	**a** lapin	**d** oiseau	**f** chat
	b souris	**e** chien	**g** tortue
	c dragon		

2	onze	quinze	dix-huit
	douze	seize	dix-neuf
	treize	dix-sept	vingt

3	quinze	vingt	onze
	quatorze	dix-neuf	treize
	dix-huit	seize	douze

Worksheet 4A

⏱ 10–15 mins 📖 AT3.2 O3.3
Worksheet 4A AT4.2 L3.1 L3.2 L3.3

Description
Worksheet to give further practice on third person descriptions using *Il/Elle est* [+ adjective].

Notes
1 & 2 Model the target language using a puppet. Do one female and one male example.

3 Ask pupils to listen carefully to each other's pronunciation and help where they can as they read out their sentences in Activity 3.

⏱ 10–15 mins 📖 AT3.2 O3.3
Worksheet 4B AT4.2 L3.1 L3.2 L3.3

Description
Worksheet to give further practice on third person descriptions using *Il/Elle est* [+ adjective].

Notes
1 Model the target language using a puppet. Do one female and one male example.

2 Ask pupils to listen carefully to each other's pronunciation and help where they can as they read out their sentences in Activity 2.

⏱ 20–30 mins 📖 AT4.1–2 L3.3

Project work: Pets

Description
Pupils bring in photos of their pets and write descriptions of them.

Materials
Photographs of pupils' pets, A4 blank paper

Delivery
● The lesson before, ask pupils to bring in photographs of their pets. If a pupil doesn't have a pet, they can bring in a photo – either printed or electronic – of an imaginary pet, or of a celebrity with their pet instead.

● Write a list of pet words encountered in Unit 4 on the board, adding other likely words that might come up, such as *un cheval* (horse), *un poisson* (fish), *un cochon d'Inde* (guinea pig), *un hamster* (hamster).

● Ask pupils either to stick their printed photos onto a sheet of blank paper, or to copy their pictures into a word processor document or Microsoft PowerPoint presentation.

● Pupils should write captions underneath. These can vary from simply *J'ai un/une...* to a description of the pet. If you are adding descriptions, pupils can either write these in speech bubbles as *J'ai...* or *Je suis...* phrases, or using *il* or *elle* instead. Although the gender should match that of the noun, it is easier to get pupils to choose the right pronoun for their actual pet instead!

● Create a wall display of the results, or collate a PowerPoint presentation, using audio clips of the pupils if you like, to show in assembly.

Support
● Write a full list of the relevant phrases on the board for pupils to choose from and copy for their pets.

⏱ 15–20 mins 📖 AT1.1 O3.2 L3.2

Sound/spelling activity

Description
Practise listening out for and pronouncing the *é* and *ou* sounds. Then identify the words when you hear them read out, and which words use the sounds.

Delivery
● This sound/spelling activity focuses specifically on the *é* and *ou* sounds.

● There are two parts to the activity: the first (*Practice*) allows pupils to familiarise themselves with the two sounds and to practise pronouncing them in comparison to the Virtual Teacher model. The second part (*Activities*) contains two exercises: *Activity 1* where pupils have to identify the correct word read out from a list of French words they have encountered in *Rigolo 1* already; and *Activity 2*, where pupils have to recognise and select the five words containing the sound *é* from a given list, and then the five that contain *ou*.

● Select *Practice* and click on *Next* to start this part. Then click on *Allez*. The Virtual Teacher will say the *é* sound first on its own, and then as part of three words that have already been met in Units 1-4. For each of these, get the class to repeat the sound or word chorally several times, checking the model each time using the *Encore* button to see how close they are.

● Once you have finished this part, relaunch the activity and choose *Activities* from the selection menu to move on to test pupils' recognition of these sounds. In *Activity 1*, they will see 10 words on the board, and hear them read out in a random

order. They must click on the right word when they hear it spoken before the time runs out! Click on *Allez* to start the activity, and use the *Encore* button to repeat a word, if necessary. Once pupils have completed each answer, you can use the *Encore* button to hear the word again, and to review their answer.

● Finally, in *Activity 2*, pupils must look at the words in the list, and say them carefully to themselves, or out loud. They must then click on the five words in the list that use the *é* sound, followed by the five using *ou*.

● Repeat the activity again if you feel pupils need further practice.

Extension
● You can continue the practice activity with more words using these sounds if you feel that pupils have grasped this well – even words not yet covered in *Rigolo*. Pupils can then hold up cards marked with the sounds, to show when they hear the appropriate one.

Assessment for Units 3–4

Ecoutez!

Play the recording 2–3 times or more if necessary. Pause the recording during each activity as required.

Total marks for listening: 20. If pupils are getting 8–14/20, they are working towards level 1. If they achieve 15–20/20, they are working between levels 1–2.

Activity 1 (AT1.1; O3.2)
Mark out of 5

Answers
numbers ticked: (*example*: 11), 12, 15, 17, 18, 20

> TRANSCRIPT
> (*example*: numéro onze)
> numéro 12
> numéro 15
> numéro 17
> numéro 18
> numero 20

Activity 2 (AT1.1–2; O3.4)
Mark out of 5

Answers
(*example*: 12 dogs), 13 birds, 14 tortoises, 16 cats, 17 rabbits, 20 mice

> TRANSCRIPT
> (*example*: Il y a douze chiens.)
> 1 Il y a seize chats.
> 2 Il y a dix-sept lapins.
> 3 Il y a vingt souris.
> 4 Il y a quatorze tortues.
> 5 Il y a treize oiseaux.

Activity 3 (AT1-2; O3.2, O3.4)
Mark out of 10

Answers
(*example*: Il s'appelle M. Chanson)
1 Il est grand.
2 Il est timide.
3 Il est sympa.
4 Elle s'appelle Mme Moulin.
5 Elle est petite.
6 Elle est sévère.
7 Elle est bavarde.
8 Elle s'appelle Polly.
9 Elle est petite.
10 Elle est drôle.

(*example*: Il s'appelle Monsieur Chanson.)
1 Il est grand.
2 Il est timide.
3 Il est sympa.
4 Elle s'appelle Madame Moulin.
5 Elle est petite.
6 Elle est sévère.
7 Elle est bavarde.
8 Elle s'appelle Polly.
9 Elle est petite.
10 Elle est drôle.

Parlez!

Pupils can work in pairs for the speaking tasks. If it is not possible to assess each pair, then assess a few pairs for each assessment block and mark the rest of the class based on the spoken work they do in class.

Total marks for speaking: 10. Pupils achieving 5/10 are working towards level 1; Pupils achieving more than 5/10 are working between levels 1–2.

Activity 1   (AT2.1; O3.2, O3.3)
5 marks

Answers
(*example*: J'ai un lapin.)
J'ai une tortue.
J'ai un chat.
J'ai un chien.
J'ai une souris.
J'ai un oiseau.
Je n'ai pas d'animal.

Activity 2   (AT2.2; O3.3)
5 marks

Answers
Je m'appelle Charlotte.
J'ai les cheveux longs.
Je suis petite.
Je suis bavarde.
J'ai un chat.

Je m'appelle Luc.
J'ai les cheveux courts.
Je suis grand.
Je suis drôle.
J'ai un lapin.

Lisez!

Total marks for reading 20: Pupils achieving 8–14 are working towards level 1. Pupils achieving 15 or more are working between levels 1–2.

Activity 1   (AT3.1, L3.1)
Mark out of 7

Answers
dimanche 7, mardi 2, vendredi 5, mercredi 3, jeudi 4, samedi 6, lundi 1

Activity 2   (AT3.1; L3.2)
Mark out of 6

Answers
petit/souris, les yeux/les cheveux, vingt/lapin, sympa/chat *or* ça va?, long/marron, (*example*: le nez/écoutez!), le bras/chat *or* ça va?

Activity 3   (AT3.1–2; L3.1)
Mark out of 7

Answers
(*example*: 1e) 2g 3h 4f 5a 6d 7b 8c

Écrivez!

For the writing tasks, the copying of words can be approximate.

Total marks for writing: 20. Pupils achieving 8–14/20 are working towards level 1. Pupils achieving 15 or more out of 20 are working between levels 1–2.

Activity 1   (AT4.1; L3.3)
Mark out of 8

Answers
labels as follows: hair = les cheveux, head = la tête, arm = le bras, leg = la jambe, ears = les oreilles, eyes = les yeux, nose = le nez, mouth = la bouche

Activity 2   (AT4/1–2, L3.3)
Mark out of 6

Answers
picture a: (*example*: Elle s'appelle Sarah.) Elle est petite. Elle est bavarde.
picture b: Il s'appelle Thomas. Il est petit.
picture c: Elle s'appelle Émilie. Elle est grande.

Activity 3   (AT4.2, L3.3)
Mark out of 6

Pupil's own answers based on language from ex 2, e.g.
Il s'appelle David Beckham. Il est grand. Il est sympa.

National criteria

KS2 Framework objectives

O3.1 Listen and respond to simple rhymes, stories and songs
O3.2 Recognise and respond to sound patterns and words
O3.3 Perform simple communicative tasks using single words, phrases and short sentences
O3.4 Listen attentively and understand instructions, everyday classroom language and praise words
L3.1 Recognise some familiar words in written form
L3.2 Make links between some phonemes, rhymes and spellings, and read aloud familiar words
L3.3 Experiment with the writing of simple words

QCA Scheme of Work

Unit 2 Je me présente
Unit 3 En famille

Language ladder levels

Listening:	Breakthrough, Grade 1–2
Reading:	Breakthrough, Grade 1–2
Speaking:	Breakthrough, Grade 1–2
Writing:	Breakthrough, Grade 1–2

5–14 guideline strands   Levels A–C

Listening		**Reading**	
Listening for information and instructions	A, C	Reading for information and instructions	A, C
Listening and reacting to others	A, B, C	Reading aloud	A, C

Speaking		**Writing**	
Speaking to convey information	A, C	Writing to exchange information and ideas	A, C
Speaking and interacting with others	B, C	Writing to establish and maintain personal contact	A, C
Speaking about experiences, feelings and opinions	A, B	Writing imaginatively/to entertain	n/a

Unit objectives

- identify family members
- recognise and spell with letters of the alphabet
- list household items
- use basic prepositions *sur* and *dans* to describe position

Key language

- family members: *ma mère* (mother), *mon père* (father), *mon frère* (brother), *ma sœur* (sister), *mes parents* (my parents)
- letters of the alphabet a–z, plus some accented letters
- household objects: *le CD* (CD), *le lecteur de CD* (CD player), *l'ordinateur* (computer), *le jeu vidéo* (video game), *le DVD* (DVD), *la machine* (machine), *la chaise* (chair), *la table* (table)
- prepositions: *dans* (in), *sur* (on)

Grammar and skills

- gender of different family members and nouns
- spell words using the French alphabet

- describe position using basic prepositions *sur* and *dans* and familiar language

Unit outcomes

Most children will be able to:

- use spoken French to identify family members, using *mon/ma/mes*
- recognise and use French alphabet, not necessarily including accented letters
- recognise the meaning of prepositions *dans* and *sur* in sentences

Some children will also be able to:

- write and say phrases from memory, with clear pronunciation and meaning
- use all letters of alphabet, including accented letters where appropriate
- create phrases and sentences using prepositions to describe position

Unit 5  Lesson 1

Context
Identify members of your family

National criteria
KS2 Framework: **O3.1, O3.2, O3.3, O3.4, L3.1, L3.2**
Attainment levels: **AT1.1–2, AT2.1, AT3.1–2**
Language ladder levels:
  Listening: **Grade 1–2**; Speaking: **Grade 1**;
  Reading: **Grade 1–2**

Cross-curricular links
n/a

Key vocabulary
Family members: *ma mère* (mother); *mon père* (father),
mon frère (brother), *ma sœur* (sister), *mes parents* (my
parents)

Language structures and outcomes
As above

---

 1 Starter activity: ⏱ 5 mins 📖 AT1.1 O3.3
Ça va? AT2.1 O3.4

Materials
n/a

Description
Pupils orally practise asking and answering the question 'How
are you?'

Delivery
● Ask a few pupils at random how they are (*Ça va?*). Once
they have answered, they ask the person to their right the
same question.

● Continue round the room until everyone has
asked/answered the question.

Support
● Model possible questions and answers (e.g. *Ça va bien./Ça
ne va pas.*) using puppets before starting to ask pupils if they
need a reminder.

---

 2 Animated story: ⏱ 10 mins 📖 AT1.2 O3.1
Voici ma famille (1) AT3.2 O3.4
L3.1

Materials
CD-ROM

Description
Watch and listen to this interactive animated story based in the
Château Rigolo presenting the language for Lessons 1 and 2
(family vocabulary and possessive pronouns). You can pause
and rewind the story at any point.

Delivery
● This animated story can be used for both starter and
plenary activities – the whole animation can be played at the
end of the unit so that pupils can gauge their improved
understanding.

● At this point pupils watch the first half of the story only; the
second half is in Lesson 3.

Scene 1 (Doorway/Corridor of Château Rigolo)

● Freeze the screen on the opening scene with Nathalie and
Olivier, and ask *Comment s'appellent-ils?* ('What are their
names?') to elicit and refresh *Il/Elle s'appelle...*

● Ask pupils to note any numbers they hear (10, 3).

● Play the scene through. Check if pupils heard the numbers.

Extension
● Later in the lesson, once pupils have covered the key words,
you could play the animation through and ask them to note
which 'family' words are featured.

---

 3 Presentation: ⏱ 5–10 mins 📖 AT1.1 O3.2
Ma famille AT2.1 O3.4
AT3.1 L3.1
L3.2

Materials
CD-ROM, Unit 5 Flashcards 9–13 (Family)

Description
Click on the small screen images of the Mills family. Jake and
Polly introduce the family members using possessive
adjectives. Use the additional features to practise
sound/spelling links, word classes and spelling.

Delivery
● Click on the small screen images of each of the Mills family
members, one by one, and Jake or Polly will present the
relevant phrase.

● Click on the Virtual Teacher to listen again – repeat chorally,
copying the Virtual Teacher's gestures as you say the words.

● The class repeats what they hear each time, to reinforce
learning.

● Click on each of the small screen images as many times as
necessary to listen to the audio again, and give pupils enough
opportunity to repeat the words.

Extension
● Place family member flashcards on a table at the front. Ask
a few pupils to stand with their backs to the board. Click on
one of the family members on-screen to hear them being
introduced; pupils try to be the first to hold up the
appropriate card. Repeat with different groups of pupils.

Spelling
● For groups who have already done the alphabet: Point to a
family member and ask pupils to say/spell the words. Check
their answer by clicking on the word, and then on the *Spell*
icon.

● To simply introduce the concept of spelling in French, click
on a family member, then on the *Spell* icon, and point to the
letters as the Virtual Teacher says them. Repeat, this time
asking the whole class to join in. Continue in the same way
with all the words.

Word class

- Focus on a word and ask the group what class of word it is (a noun).
- Click on the *Word* icon, then on the image in question to hear the Virtual Teacher say the word class.
- Repeat all together, copying the Virtual Teacher's gestures as you say the word class.

Sounds

To further reinforce accurate pronunciation, and to introduce some basic reading skills:

- Point to each word on the text bar and ask the class to say the word.
- Focus on the text on screen, click on the *Sound* icon, and click on the different highlighted sounds to hear the Virtual Teacher saying them.
- Repeat all together.

NB. If the *Sound* icon is not illuminated, that means it is not applicable for that particular word.

Knowledge About Language

Genders

- This is another point where you can revisit the concept of genders with pupils.
- Using the Presentation above, point to either the picture of Mr Mills, Jake or Bof with the text bar on, and ask pupils what the phrase means. Ask them which word means 'my' (*mon*).
- Then point to either the picture of Polly or Mrs Mills and do the same – this time the word for 'my' is *ma*. Do likewise for the picture of Mr and Mrs Mills together (*mes*).
- Ask pupils if they can work out why there are three different words for 'my' in French. This relates to the gender groups for masculine and feminine that have already been highlighted in previous units.
- You can extend this activity by listing nouns of different genders from previous units and asking pupils if they can work out which words for 'my' are used with them.

Oracy activity: ⏲ c.10 mins 📖 AT1.1 O3.2 / AT2.1 O3.3
Où est mon père?

Materials
CD-ROM

Description
Listen to Jake and Polly asking where someone is, and correctly identify the person by clicking on their picture.

Delivery
- Click on *Allez* to start (or invite a pupil to start) the activity. You will hear one of the four kids asking where one of their family is. Pupils must identify the person by clicking on them.

- Jake or Polly will confirm the identity when a correct choice is made.

Extension
- Make two teams. Each team takes it in turn to answer a question and scores a point for each correct answer.

Literacy activity: ⏲ c.10 mins 📖 AT3.1 L3.1 / L3.2
C'est ma mère

Materials
CD-ROM

Description
Drag the correct label to each picture in Polly, Jake and Nathalie's photo album.

Delivery
- Invite a pupil to click on *Allez* to start the activity. You will see Polly, Jake or Nathalie looking at their photo album.
- Pupils select the label which matches the photo they're looking at and drag it into position.
- When the label is correct, it will remain in place. If not, it will bounce back to the bottom of the screen.
- Continue until all six sentences have been covered. Repeat, if time allows, to allow more pupils to have a turn.

Extension
- Make teams: each team scores a point for a correct answer. Encourage teams to say the answer aloud.

Support
- Work through each screen, asking pupils to give the correct answer orally before finding the correct written phrase.

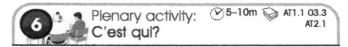

Plenary activity: ⏲ 5–10m 📖 AT1.1 O3.3 / AT2.1
C'est qui?

Materials
Puppets, Unit 5 Flashcards 9–13 (Family)

Description
Pupils practise using family vocabulary and possessive adjectives using puppets and/or flashcards.

Delivery
- Display the flashcards on the board.
- Hold up a puppet of Jake or Polly.
- Point to a flashcard on the board and say *C'est [ma mère]*. Repeat with another card, encouraging the class to say it with you.
- Repeat again, this time keeping quiet so the class can make the sentence without your help.
- Invite pupils up to the front. Give them a puppet. Point to a card and ask them to make a sentence.
- Repeat with as many pupils as possible in the time available.

Extension
- Stick all flashcards on the board.
- Give the class one minute to study the board.
- Ask the pupils to turn away/close their eyes while you remove one or two cards. Ask *Qui manque?*
- Pupils must say who is missing.

Unit 5  Lesson 2

Lesson summary

Context	Cross-curricular links
The alphabet	Literacy

National criteria
KS2 Framework: **O3.1, O3.2, O3.3, O3.4, L3.1, L3.2**
Attainment levels: **AT1.1, AT2.1, AT3.1**
Language ladder levels:
  Listening: **Grade 1**; Speaking: **Grade 1**;
  Reading: **Grade 1**

Key vocabulary
Letters of the alphabet

Language structures and outcomes
Ça s'écrit... (it's spelt...)

---

 1 Starter activity: ⏱ 5 mins 📖 AT2.1 O3.3 O3.4
Qu'est-ce que c'est?

Materials
Units 1–4 Flashcards (nouns only)

Description
Pupils identify objects covered so far using flashcard prompts.

Delivery
● Quickly go through flashcards to revise vocabulary.

● Hold up the cards in turn and ask *Qu'est-ce que c'est?* ('What is it?').

● Elicit answers from pupils.

● You may wish to use the Virtual Teacher from relevant presentations, to encourage pupils to concentrate on pronunciation.

Extension
● Stick the cards on the board. Ask pupils to close their eyes.

● Remove a card and ask them to identify the missing card.

---

2 Presentation: ⏱ c.10 mins 📖 AT1.1 O3.2 / AT2.1 O3.4 / AT3.1 L3.1 / L3.2
L'alphabet

Materials
CD-ROM

Description
Click on the letters of the alphabet to hear how they sound, or to hear the whole alphabet read out in sequence.

Delivery
● Click on all the letters once each, in order, and repeat chorally. Do this for the whole alphabet. Repeat as many times as you feel necessary.

● Once you feel confident that pupils have grasped the letters, pick on random letters out of sequence to test pupils' memory further.

● Finally you can run through the whole sequence at once using the '*L'alphabet*' button, repeating chorally.

Extension
● Go around the class. Each pupil says a letter of the alphabet in the correct order.

● Use the Virtual Teacher when a pupil gets stuck: encourage him/her to repeat the letter after the Virtual Teacher.

● 'Alphabet Tennis': Split class into two or four groups. Each group has three 'lives' and must, in turn, say the letters of the alphabet in order. The group loses a 'life' if they get stuck.

● 'Accents': at a later stage, or with groups who are already comfortable with the main letters of the alphabet, you may wish to focus on the accented letters. Once you have practised them a couple of times, make two teams. Each team scores a point for correctly identifying the letter/accent (check with the Virtual Teacher if necessary).

---

 3 Oracy activity: ⏱ c.10 mins 📖 AT1.1 O3.2 O3.4
Ça s'écrit...

Materials
CD-ROM

Description
Listen to the audio prompts and select the correct letters in order, to complete the words on screen.

Delivery
● Click on *Allez* to start the activity. Pupils will be invited to click on a letter from the first word. When a pupil clicks on this letter, it will go into the appropriate blank space in the middle of the screen.

● Invite different pupils to come up to select each letter.

● When a word is complete, the whole word will be heard and the appropriate picture displayed.

● Encourage pupils to guess the word before its spelling is complete.

Extension
● Make two teams. Each team takes it in turn to spell a word (do two words each). The team with the most 'lives' left is the winner!

---

 4 Song: ⏱ 15–20 mins 📖 AT1.1 O3.1 / AT2.1 O3.2 / AT3.1 O3.4 / L3.1 L3.2
Chantez l'alphabet!

Materials
CD-ROM or Audio CD, track 11; cards/pieces of paper with individual letters

Description
Watch and listen to the interactive song practising the letters of the alphabet. Choose either *Practice* or *Sing* mode: the former to go through the song line by line, the latter to sing it all the way through. Switch the music and words on or off as you prefer.

52

Delivery
● Hand out one card/letter to each pupil (hand out two to some pupils if you have fewer than 26 in your class).

● Play the song through and ask pupils to stand up, then to sit down quickly when they hear 'their' letter. For a less chaotic activity, just ask pupils to wave the paper in the air when their letter is sung!

● Ask pupils to group themselves according to how the letters are grouped in the song, e.g. pupils with letters 'a', 'b', 'c' and 'd' will form one group.

● Play the song again. This time, each group is responsible for singing along with their line/letters, with individual pupils holding up their letter when it is sung.

● Go through the song again as a whole-class activity, with or without the audio.

Extension
● Divide the class into groups of 6–8 pupils.

● **Each group performs its own version of the alphabet song.** More adventurous groups could make their own Alphabet Rap.

● **The other groups can award points to see which version was the best.**

See the Introduction for more notes on the Song features

5 Plenary activity:
Le jeu du pendu
5–10m AT2.1 O3.2
AT3.1 O3.3
L3.1
L3.2

Materials
Whiteboard/pens, possibly noun flashcards from units to date

Description
French version of 'Hangman', in which pupils practise the alphabet and revise nouns covered so far.

Delivery
● Choose a noun that pupils have already learned. Draw dashes on the board, one for each letter of that word.

● Pupils call out letters randomly, one by one. If the letter is part of the chosen word, write it in the appropriate space. Otherwise, draw one line of the 'Hangman' for each incorrect suggestion.

● The object of the game is to discover the word before the 'Hangman' is complete.

● Ask a volunteer to say and spell the revealed word, or do this chorally.

● You could then invite a pupil to choose a word and lead the activity at the board, with your help as required.

Support
● Use the picture flashcards as prompts if pupils can't think of any words.

● Stick to words without accents at first.

Unit 5   Lesson 3

Lesson summary

Context
Household items

National criteria
KS2 Framework: **O3.1, O3.2, O3.3, O3.4, L3.1, L3.2, L3.3**
Attainment levels: **AT1.1–2, AT2.1, AT3.1–2, AT4.1**
Language ladder levels:
  Listening: **Grade 1–2**; Speaking: **Grade 1**;
  Reading: **Grade 1–2**; Writing: **Grade 1**

Cross-curricular links
Literacy

Key vocabulary
Household objects: *le CD* (CD), *le lecteur de CD* (CD player),
l'ordinateur (computer), *le jeu vidéo* (video game), *le DVD*
(DVD), *la machine* (machine), *la table* (table), *la chaise*
(chair)

Language structures and outcomes
As above

---

 1 Starter activity: ⏲ 5 mins 📖 AT1.1 O3.4
Dictée   AT3.1 L3.1
                                        AT4.1 L3.3

Materials
n/a

Description
'Dictate' words, letter by letter, for pupils to write down.

Delivery
● Select around five nouns you have covered so far with your
class.

● One by one, spell out each word. Pupils write down the
letters as you say them.

● Go through all the words on your list, without saying the
actual words.

● Write the first word on the board. Ask the class to say the
word, then spell it chorally.

● Continue in the same way with all the words.

Extension
● Make this into a quick team game and award a point for
each correct answer.

Support
● Before starting, run through the alphabet song or the
alphabet presentation in Lesson 2 to refresh pupils' memory.

2 Animated story: ⏲ 10 mins 📖 AT1.2 O3.1
Voici ma famille (2)   AT3.2 O3.4
                                         L3.1

Materials
CD-ROM, Unit 5 Flashcards 1–8 (Household items)

Description
Watch and listen to this interactive animated story presenting
the language for Lessons 3–4 (household objects and
prepositions). You can pause and rewind the story at any
point.

Delivery
● This animated story can be used for both starter and
plenary activities – the whole animation can be played at the
end of the unit so that pupils can gauge their improved
understanding.

● At this point pupils watch the second half of the story only;
the first half is in Lesson 1.

Scene 2: Jake & Olivier in the tower room
● Freeze the screen on the opening scene with Jake and
Olivier and ask *Comment s'appellent-ils?* ('What are their
names?') to elicit and refresh *Il s'appelle...*

● Stick flashcards on the board for the objects in the room.
Label each card.

● Ask pupils to note the order in which these objects are
talked about in the film (CD, CD player, video game, table,
DVDs, computer, machine).

● Play the scene through. Check answers for above. Accept
answers in English at this stage, but encourage pupils to try
and remember the French words if possible.

● Rearrange the flashcards in the correct order and replay the
scene straight through.

 3 Presentation: ⏲ c.10 mins 📖 AT1.1 O3.2
Qu'est-ce que c'est?   AT2.1 O3.4
                                          AT3.1 L3.1
                                          L3.2

Materials
CD-ROM

Description
Click on an object to hear and see the correct pronunciation.
Use the additional features to practise sound/spelling links,
word classes and spelling.

Delivery
● Chorally repeat the Virtual Teacher's question *Qu'est-ce que
c'est?* ('What is it?').

● Repeat the answers in the same way, using *C'est...*

● Go through all the objects as above.

● Repeat a couple of times to reinforce the vocabulary,
encouraging pupils to give the answer before hearing the
Virtual Teacher for a second time.

Extension
● Have a team game: two points for each correct answer, one
point for a bonus question answered incorrectly by the other
team.

● Point to, without touching, an object and ask pupils to say
what it is, using the model sentences they have just heard.

● Click on the object to hear the Virtual Teacher presentation
and compare with pupils' answers.

Spelling
● For groups who have already done the alphabet: Point to an
object and ask pupils to say/spell the word. Check answer by
clicking on the word then on the *Spell* icon.

● To simply introduce the concept of spelling in French, click
on an object, then on the *Spell* icon, and point to the letters as

the Virtual Teacher says them. Repeat, this time asking the whole class to join in. Continue in the same way with all the words.

Sounds

To further reinforce accurate pronunciation, and to introduce some basic reading skills:

● Point to a word on the text bar and ask the class to read it aloud.

● Focus on the text on screen, click on the *Sound* icon, and click on the different highlighted sounds to hear the Virtual Teacher saying them.

● Repeat all together.

NB. If the *Sound* icon is not illuminated, that means it is not applicable for that particular word.

Word class

● Focus on a word and ask the group what class of word it is.

● Click on the *Word* icon, then on the image in question to hear the Virtual Teacher say the word class.

● Repeat all together, copying the Virtual Teacher's gestures as you say the word class.

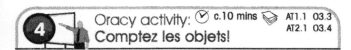

4 Oracy activity: ⊘ c.10 mins 📖 AT1.1 03.3 / AT2.1 03.4
Comptez les objets!

Materials
CD-ROM

Description
Click on *Allez*. Answer the questions by identifying the correct number of objects on the screen.

Delivery
● Click on *Allez* to start the activity. You will hear the audio asking how many items (e.g. how many CDs) are in the picture.

● Pupils count the designated items and click on the correct number at the bottom of the screen.

● The pictures will become animated when a correct choice is made, and the Virtual Teacher will confirm the answer, or pupils will be invited to have another try.

● Click on *Allez* to proceed to the next question.

● Click on *Jouez encore?* ✔ to play again.

Extension
Make two teams. Each team takes it in turn to answer a question and scores a point for each correct answer.

Support
Play the audio for each item twice using the *Encore* button before asking pupils to respond.

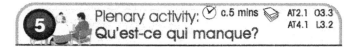

5 Plenary activity: ⊘ c.5 mins 📖 AT2.1 03.3 / AT4.1 L3.2
Qu'est-ce qui manque?

Materials
Unit 2 Flashcards 1–8 (Classroom objects) and Unit 5 Flashcards 1–8 (Household items), and/or realia representing these words

Description
Pupils revise household and classroom objects playing a version of 'Kim's game' with flashcards or realia.

Delivery
● Display the flashcards/realia that you wish to revise. Quickly go through the words with the class. Give them another 30 seconds to study the objects.

● Ask pupils to close their eyes, or cover the cards/objects whilst you remove one or two items.

● Tell them to look again (*Regardez*) and ask what is missing (*Qu'est-ce qui manque?*).

● Repeat a few times to cover as many words as possible.

Extension
● As a variation, you could ask one or two pupils to leave the room whilst the rest of the class remove an object. Call the pupils back into the room and continue as above.

● Once pupils have identified the missing object, ask *Comment ça s'écrit?* and ask pupils to spell the word.

Unit 5  Lesson 4

Lesson summary

Context
Using basic prepositions *sur* and *dans* to describe position

National criteria
KS2 Framework: **O3.2, O3.3, O3.4, L3.1, L3.2, L3.3**
Attainment levels: **AT1.2, AT2.1–2, AT3.1–2, AT4.1–2**
Language ladder levels:
  Listening: **Grade 2**; Speaking: **Grade 1–2**;
  Reading: **Grade 1–2**; Writing: **Grade 1–2**

Cross-curricular links
Literacy

Key vocabulary
dans (in); *sur* (on)

Language structures and outcomes
Le CD [etc.] *est dans le sac* [etc.], *Le DVD* [etc.] *est sur la chaise* [etc.]

---

 1 Starter activity: ⏱ 5 mins 📚 AT2.1 O3.3 / AT4.1 L3.2
C'est un…

Materials
Unit 5 Flashcards 1–8 (Household items)

Description
Hold up flashcards from the unit to elicit the vocabulary from pupils.

Delivery
● Hold up the flashcards, one by one. Ask *Qu'est-ce que c'est?* ('What is it?') and model the first answer, for example *C'est [un lecteur de CD]* ('It's a CD player').

● Go through all the flashcards in the same way, eliciting the same type of response from pupils.

Extension
● Add *Ça s'écrit* + spelling to give further alphabet practice.

---

 2 Presentation: ⏱ c.10 mins 📚 AT1.2 O3.2 / AT2.2 O3.4 / AT3.2 L3.1 / L3.2
Dans et sur

Materials
CD-ROM

Description
Click on an object to hear its position described, using the prepositions *sur* or *dans*.

Delivery
● Firstly click on the two arrows (on the empty chair and in the empty rucksack) illustrating *sur* and *dans*, before moving on to the objects scattered around the room to hear their position described in sentences using the prepositions *sur* ('on') or *dans* ('in').

● Ask different pupils to come to the board and click on the objects one by one. Chorally repeat the sentences, copying the Virtual Teacher's gestures to illustrate the prepositions each time.

Extension
● Ask a few pupils to stand at the front, with their backs to the board.

● Another pupil clicks on an object to trigger the Virtual Teacher audio. The pupils turn round and point to the relevant object, in the relevant place on the board.

● Repeat with different groups of pupils.

---

 3 Oracy activity: ⏱ c.10 mins 📚 AT1.2 O3.2 / O3.4
Rangez les objets

Materials
CD-ROM

Description
Listen to the audio prompts and choose the correct position for each object.

Delivery
● Click on *Allez* to start the activity. You will hear a sentence in which the position of one of the objects is described. Pupils respond by choosing the correct item displayed at the bottom of the screen, and dragging it to the position described.

● Repeat a couple of times with different pupils for each sentence, to ensure maximal exposure to the language.

Extension
● Make two teams. Each team takes it in turn to choose an object, and a point is awarded for each correct answer.

Support
● Play each scenario twice using the *Encore* button before asking pupils to respond.

---

 4 Oracy activity: ⏱ 5–10 mins 📚 AT1.2 O3.3 / AT2.2 O3.4
Où est le… ?

Materials
Various flashcards, puppets

Description
Pupils hide an object/flashcard in the classroom and guide another pupil to find it by indicating its whereabouts using prepositions.

Delivery
● Hold up the card or object you will be hiding so the class can see, and check they all remember the word!

● Ask one or two pupils to leave the room.

● Ask the rest of the class to tell you where to hide the object, using *dans* ('in') or *sur* ('on') and other known classroom objects.

● Call the pupil(s) back in. They ask *Où est le/la... ?* ('Where's the... ?').

● The class reply in French, and pupils race to find the object.

● Repeat a couple of times with different objects.

Support
● Model the questions and answers that pupils will use before starting the game.

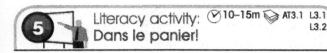

5 Literacy activity: ⏱10–15m 📖 AT3.1 L3.1 L3.2
Dans le panier!

Materials
CD-ROM

Description
Drag and drop words from Mme Moulin's washing line into one of three washing baskets labelled *les nombres* ('numbers'), *les personnes* ('people'), or *les objets* ('objects').

Delivery
● Invite a pupil to begin the game by clicking on *Allez* – the washing line will start to move.

● Pupils drag and drop the words into the most appropriate basket before the word disappears off screen.

● The three word groups/baskets are labelled *les nombres* ['numbers'], *les personnes* ['people'], or *les objets* ['objects']. Pupils must put all the words into the appropriate baskets.

Extension
● Make teams: each team plays a game right through, until it has sorted all the words.

● The first team to complete is the winner.

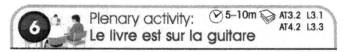

6 Plenary activity: ⏱5–10m 📖 AT3.2 L3.1 AT4.2 L3.3
Le livre est sur la guitare

Materials
Whiteboard/pens

Description
Pupils complete sentences to describe the position of objects in a picture.

Delivery
● Draw simple illustrations alongside the phrases used in Activity 4: *Le CD est dans le lecteur de CD*; *Le livre est sur la guitare*; *L'ordinateur est dans le sac*; *Le jeu vidéo est sur la table*; *Le lecteur de CD est sur la chaise*; *Le DVD est dans le piano*.

● In each sentence blank out a couple of words (alternate nouns and prepositions).

● As a whole-class activity, go through each sentence and complete them. Encourage pupils to reuse the gestures for the prepositions to further reinforce learning.

● If pupils are having difficulty remembering the position of the objects, display the screen from the game to remind them.

Support
● With less confident groups you could write the missing words above or below the sentences, to make the sentence completion easier.

Unit 5  Extra!

Worksheet 1A
🕑 10–15 mins 📖 AT2.1 O3.3
AT4.1 L3.1
L3.2 L3.3

Description
Worksheet to give further practice on nouns and spelling.

Notes
1 Quickly recap the alphabet chorally before handing out the worksheets. Encourage pupils to say the letters aloud as they are doing Activity 1.
2 Move round the class to offer help where necessary for Activity 2 and to ensure pupils are spelling words in French!

Answers
1 a chat   c guitare   e tortue
   b crayon   d dix   f nez

Worksheet 1B
🕑 10–15 mins 📖 AT2.1 O3.3
AT4.1 L3.1
L3.2 L3.3

Description
Worksheet to give further practice on nouns and spelling.

Notes
1 Quickly recap the alphabet chorally before handing out the worksheets. Encourage pupils to say the letters out loud as they are doing Activity 1.
2 Move round the class to offer help where necessary for Activity 2 and to ensure pupils are spelling words in French!
3 Pair up pupils who have completed Activities 1 and 2 to do Activity 3 together.

Answers
1 a chat   c guitare   e tortue
   b crayon   d dix   f nez

Worksheet 2A
🕑 10–15 mins 📖 AT2.1 L3.1
AT3.1 L3.2
AT4.1 L3.3

Description
Worksheet to give further practice on family words and possessive adjectives.

Notes
1 Pupils may need help completing the sentences: you could do Activity 1 as a whole-class activity, then give pupils a couple of minutes to match speech bubbles and characters.
2 Activity 2 could be done in small groups.

Answers
1 Olivier – a C'est ma sœur.   Nathalie – d C'est ma mère.
Polly – b C'est mon frère.   Jake – e C'est mon père.
Jake – c C'est mon dragon.

Worksheet 2B
🕑 10–15 mins 📖 AT2.2 L3.1
AT3.2 L3.2
AT4.2 L3.3

Description
Worksheet to give further practice on family words and possessive adjectives.

Notes
1 You may wish to go through Activity 1 orally, before giving pupils a few minutes to write out the sentences and pair up the speech bubbles and characters.
2 Activity 2 could be done in small groups.

Answers
1 Jake – C'est mon dragon.
Nathalie – C'est ma mère.
Polly – C'est mon frère.
Jake – C'est mon père.
Olivier – C'est ma sœur.

Worksheet 3A
🕑 10–15 mins 📖 AT2.1 L3.1
AT3.1 L3.2
AT4.1

Description
Worksheet to give further practice on household objects and spelling.

Notes
1 Give pupils a couple of minutes to study the picture, then go through the answers together if you think they need extra support.
2 Move around the class and give help where required.
3 Give pupils five minutes to complete Activity 3 then go over the answers orally together.

Answers
1 l'ordinateur
le DVD
le lecteur de CD

3 *laptop computer* – l'ordinateur
DVD – le DVD
music CD – le CD
computer game – le jeu vidéo
Mme Moulin's machine – la machine
CD player – le lecteur de CD

Worksheet 3B
🕑 10–15 mins 📖 AT2.1 L3.1
AT3.1 L3.2
AT4.1 L3.3

Description
Worksheet to give further practice on household objects and spelling.

Notes
1 If necessary, give pupils a couple of minutes to study the picture and the word list, then go through the answers orally together.
2 Move around the class to give help where required and to ensure the activity is being conducted in French!

Answers
1 *laptop computer* – l'ordinateur
DVD – le DVD
music CD – le CD
computer game – le jeu vidéo
Mme Moulin's machine – la machine
CD player – le lecteur de CD
piano – le piano

Worksheet 4A
🕑 10–15 mins 📖 AT3.1–2 L3.1

Description
Worksheet to give further practice on household objects and prepositions.

Notes
1 Give pupils a few minutes to do Activity 1, then go through the answers together.

2 If time allows, go round the class and ask pupils to say aloud one of the objects they ticked in Activity 2.

Answers

1 a CD in piano   c CD on the table
  b CD in the bag   d CD on Mme Moulin's machine

⊘ 10–15 mins ⊗ AT3.2 L3.1
                    AT4.1 L3.3

Worksheet 4B

Description
Worksheet to give further practice on household objects and prepositions.

Notes
1 Give pupils a couple of minutes to do Activity 1, then go through the answers together.

2 If time allows, go round the class and ask pupils to say aloud one of the items they chose in Activity 2.

Answers
1 a Le DVD est dans le piano.
  b Le jeu vidéo est dans le sac.
  c L'ordinateur est sur la table.
  d Le CD est sur la machine.

⊘ 10–15 mins ⊗ AT2.2 03.3
                    AT3.2 L3.1
                    AT4.2 L3.3

Project work:
Alphabet chart

Description
Pupils create a chart of the letters of the alphabet, where they can list new vocabulary.

Materials
Units 1–5 Flashcards, large sheet of paper

Delivery
● Prepare a large sheet (or sheets) of blank paper, onto which you can fit the 26 letters of the alphabet, with space for several words underneath each letter.

● Stick the chart on the wall and explain to pupils that you will be gathering new vocabulary here as you learn it in French.

● Give each pupil one or several flashcards (with word cards if they need the support) from the language covered in *Rigolo* so far, depending on numbers, and ask them to find the words in French. They are then responsible for writing or copying these words, and drawing pictures if you like, under the right letter on the alphabet chart.

● Each time you learn new language in subsequent units, get pupils to add the new words to the alphabet chart.

Support
● Provide pupils with copies of the words to stick on the chart instead of writing, if you prefer.

Extension
● You can use the chart as the basis for quick language tests in future: as a quick starter or plenary activity ask pupils to study the chart for a few minutes and remember all the words beginning with a certain letter. Then hide the chart and show them the corresponding picture flashcards, and ask them to write down the right words in French.

Rigolo 1 — Unit 6: Bon anniversaire!

National criteria

KS2 Framework objectives

O3.1	Listen and respond to simple rhymes, stories and songs
O3.2	Recognise and respond to sound patterns and words
O3.3	Perform simple communicative tasks using single words, phrases and short sentences
O3.4	Listen attentively and understand instructions, everyday classroom language and praise words
L3.1	Recognise some familiar words in written form
L3.2	Make links between some phonemes, rhymes and spellings, and read aloud familiar words
L3.3	Experiment with the writing of simple words

QCA Scheme of Work

Unit 1	Je parle français
Unit 2	Je me présente
Unit 3	En famille
Unit 8	Qu'est-ce que tu veux?

Language ladder levels

Listening:	Breakthrough, Grade 1–2
Reading:	Breakthrough, Grade 1–2
Speaking:	Breakthrough, Grade 1–2
Writing:	Breakthrough, Grade 1–2

5–14 guideline strands
Levels A–C

Listening		Reading	
Listening for information and instructions	A, C	Reading for information and instructions	A, C
Listening and reacting to others	A, B, C	Reading aloud	A, C

Speaking		Writing	
Speaking to convey information	A, C	Writing to exchange information and ideas	A, C
Speaking and interacting with others	B, C	Writing to establish and maintain personal contact	A, C
Speaking about experiences, feelings and opinions	A, B, C	Writing imaginatively/to entertain	n/a

Unit objectives

- recognise and ask for snacks
- give basic opinions about food
- use numbers 21–31
- recognise and use the months
- form dates

Key language

- snacks: *une pomme* (an apple), *une banane* (a banana), *un jus d'orange* (an orange juice), *un sandwich* (a sandwich), *une pizza* (a pizza), *un gâteau* (a cake)
- simple opinions (about food): *C'est délicieux!* (It's delicious.), *C'est bon!* (It tastes nice.), *Ce n'est pas bon!* (It doesn't taste nice.), *C'est mauvais!* (It tastes bad.)
- numbers 21–31
- months: *janvier* (January), *février* (February), *mars* (March), *avril* (April), *mai* (May), *juin* (June), *juillet* (July), *août* (August), *septembre* (September), *octobre* (October), *novembre* (November), *décembre* (December)
- dates: *le...* [*mars*, etc.] (the... [March, etc.])

Grammar and skills

- gender of different nouns for food
- understand and reply to questions on food wanted
- count numbers up to 31
- use numbers up to 31 together with months to form dates

Unit outcomes

Most children will be able to:

- understand when they are being asked what they want
- use spoken French to identify various snacks
- recognise and count numbers 1–31
- recognise French months and combine with numbers to form dates

Some children will also be able to:

- have short question and answer dialogue asking others what they want and replying to same question
- form dates using a short phrase, e.g. *c'est le 5 mars*

60

Unit 6 Lesson 1

Context
Recognise and ask for various snacks

National criteria
KS2 Framework: **O3.1, O3.2, O3.4, L3.1, L3.2, L3.3**
Attainment levels: **AT1.1–2, AT2.1, AT3.1–2, AT4.1**
Language ladder levels:
  Listening: **Grade 1–2**; Speaking: **Grade 1**;
  Reading: **Grade 1–2**; Writing: **Grade 1**

Cross-curricular links
n/a

Key vocabulary
Snacks: *une pomme* (an apple), *une banane* (a banana), *un jus d'orange* (an orange juice), *un sandwich* (a sandwich), *une pizza* (a pizza), *un gâteau* (a cake)

Language structures and outcomes
Qu'est-ce que tu veux? (What would you like?); *Je voudrais [une pomme,* etc.] (I'd like [an apple], etc.)

1 Starter activity: L'alphabet — 5 mins — AT1.1 03.1 / AT2.1 03.2 / AT3.1 03.4 / L3.1 L3.2

Materials
CD-ROM (Unit 5 Song)

Description
Pupils sing the song *Chantez l'alphabet* to revise the letters of the alphabet.

Delivery
● Quickly recap the alphabet chorally.

● The whole class sings the song, following the text on screen.

Support
● You can use *Practice* mode to go through the alphabet song line by line rather than in its entirety.

See the Introduction for more notes on the Song features.

2 Animated story: Le pique-nique (1) — 5–10 m — AT1.2 03.1 / AT3.2 03.4 / L3.1

Materials
CD-ROM

Description
● Watch and listen to this interactive animated story, based on a picnic, presenting the language for Lessons 1 and 2 (food vocabulary and some related adjectives).

● You can pause and rewind the story at any point.

Delivery
● This animated story can be used for both starter and plenary activities – the whole animation can be played at the end of the unit so that pupils can gauge their improved understanding.

● At this point pupils watch the first half of the story only; the second half is in Lesson 3.

Scene 1: Children in the meadow

● Freeze the screen on the opening scene and ask *Comment s'appellent-ils?* ('What are their names?') to elicit and refresh *Il/Elle s'appelle...*

● Ask pupils what the children are doing (going for a picnic) and ask for predictions about the food and drink they will have. Write suggestions on the board, or stick up flashcards/pictures if possible.

● Play the scene, asking pupils to take note of the food and drink. Compare their predictions with the actual food and drink in the animated story.

Extension
● Later on, in Lesson 2 of this unit, once pupils have covered the key words, play the animation through and ask them to note how each of the food items is described.

3 Presentation: La nourriture — c.10 mins — AT1.1 03.2 / AT2.1 03.4 / AT3.1 L3.1 / L3.2

Materials
CD-ROM

Description
Click on the food items to hear and see the correct pronunciation. Use the additional features to practise sound/spelling links, word classes and spelling.

Delivery
● Invite pupils to click on the food items, one by one. The Virtual Teacher will say the word for the item. Pupils repeat the word and mime eating or drinking that food, as appropriate.

● The class repeat what they hear each time, using appropriate gestures to reinforce learning.

● Invite a different set of pupils up to the board to click on a food item. Bof will then request something to eat/drink, and the item will fly to him.

● Again, the whole class repeat and make appropriate gestures to help reinforce the words.

Spelling
● For groups who are familiar with the alphabet: click on a food item and ask the children to say/spell the word. Check answer by clicking on the word then on the *Spell* icon.

● To simply introduce the concept of spelling in French, click on a food item, then on the *Spell* icon, and point to the letters as the Virtual Teacher says them. Repeat, this time asking the whole class to join in. Continue in the same way with all the words.

Word class
● Focus on one of the food items and ask the group what type of word it is.

● Click on the *Word* icon, then on the image in question to hear the Virtual Teacher say the word class.

● Repeat all together, copying the Virtual Teacher's gestures as you say the word class.

Sounds

To further reinforce accurate pronunciation, and to introduce some basic reading skills:

● Point to each word on the text bar and ask the class to say the word.

● Focus on the text on screen, click on the *Sound* icon, and click on the different highlighted sounds to hear the Virtual Teacher saying them.

● Repeat all together.

NB. If the *Sound* icon is not illuminated, that means it is not applicable for that particular word.

Knowledge About Language

Genders

● Once again, another good opportunity here to reinforce genders, with masculine food items grouped on the left, and feminine on the right.

● As pupils have by now encountered the indefinite article (*un/une*), the definite article (*le/la*) and possessive adjectives (*mon/ma*), you could use this to point out the correlation between the three.

● For example, ask pupils what *une banane* means ('a banana'), and write on the board. Then ask if they can think how to say 'the banana' (*la banane*), writing this underneath. Follow suit with 'my banana' (*ma banane*) as well.

4 Oracy activity: ⏱ c.10 mins 📚 AT1.1–2 03.2
Qu'est-ce que tu veux? 03.4

Materials
CD-ROM

Description
Listen to the food Bof asks for, and drag the correct item to his plate to feed him.

Delivery
● Click on *Allez* to start, or invite a pupil to start, the activity. You will hear the picnic basket asking Bof what he wants to eat/drink. Bof replies, and pupils select the requested food items and drag them to his plate.

● If their selection is correct, Bof will eat and drink then thank the pupils.

● If their selection is wrong, the Virtual Teacher will invite pupils to have another try.

Extension
● Make two teams. Each team takes it in turn to answer a question and scores a point for each correct answer. Deduct a point if they get it wrong.

5 Literacy activity: ⏱ c.10 mins 📚 AT1.2 03.4
Je voudrais un gâteau AT3.1 L3.1

Materials
CD-ROM

Description
Look at Polly and Bof's requests for food and drink in their thought bubbles. Read the options at the bottom of the screen. Drag the correct word to their plate.

Delivery
● Invite a pupil to begin the game by clicking on *Allez*.

● Each character's thought bubble shows what they would like to eat.

● Pupils drag the appropriately labelled box(es) to make the right food item appear on the character's plate.

● Repeat each request a couple of times to reinforce learning and to give as many pupils as possible a chance to participate.

Extension
● Divide the class into two teams. Each team takes it in turn to drag the appropriate word and scores a point for each correct answer. A 'life' is lost for each incorrect answer.

Support
● Before asking pupils to select the right written word, check their understanding by asking them *Qu'est-ce qu'il/elle veut?* ('What does he/she want?'), so that everyone is sure of the right word.

6 Plenary activity: ⏱ 5 mins 📚 AT2.1 03.2
Le jeu du pendu AT3.1 L3.1
AT4.1 L3.2
L3.3

Materials
Whiteboard/pens, possibly Unit 6 Flashcards 1–6 (Food and drink)

Description
French version of 'Hangman', in which pupils practise the alphabet, and revise food and drink vocabulary covered so far.

Delivery
● Choose a food item that the pupils have already learned. Draw dashes on the board, one for each letter of the chosen word.

● Pupils call out letters randomly, one by one. If the letter is part of the chosen word, write it in the appropriate space. Otherwise, draw one line of the 'hangman' for each incorrect suggestion.

● The object of the game is to discover the word before the 'hangman' is complete.

● Ask a volunteer to say and spell the revealed word, or do this chorally.

● You could then invite a pupil to choose a word and lead the activity at the board, with your help as required.

Support
● Use the flashcards as prompts if pupils can't think of any words.

Unit 6  Lesson 2

Context
Giving opinions about food

National criteria
KS2 Framework: O3.2, O3.3, O3.4, L3.1, L3.2, L3.3
Attainment levels: AT1.1, AT2.1–2, AT3.1–2, AT4.1–2
Language ladder levels:
  Listening: **Grade 1**; Speaking: **Grade 1–2**;
  Reading: **Grade 1–2**; Writing: **Grade 1–2**

Cross-curricular links
Literacy

Key vocabulary
Simple opinions about food: *C'est délicieux!* (It's delicious),
C'est bon! (It tastes nice), *Ce n'est pas bon!* (It doesn't
taste nice), *C'est mauvais!* (It tastes bad)

Language structures and outcomes
C'est + adjective

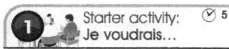

1 Starter activity: Je voudrais...   ⏱ 5 mins   AT1.1 03.3 / AT2.1 03.4

Materials
Unit 6 Flashcards 1–6 (Food and drink)

Description
Pupils respond to requests for food and drink by selecting the
appropriate flashcard.

Delivery
● Stick the flashcards on the board.

● Say *Je voudrais* [*une pomme.*] and ask a pupil to come and
point to the correct card.

● Continue with all vocabulary. You could ask pupils to say *Je
voudrais...* instead of leading the whole activity yourself.

● You may wish to use the Virtual Teacher in the presentation
from Lesson 1 to encourage pupils to concentrate on
pronunciation.

Extension
● Make two–four teams. A pupil from each team stands by the
board and races to be the first to touch the correct card. Score
a point for each win.

Support
● Use a puppet to say the *Je voudrais* phrases, then work
through the flashcards on the board with pupils, asking
yes/no questions to help them identify each one: e.g. *C'est un
gâteau, oui ou non?*

2 Presentation: C'est délicieux!   ⏱ c.10 mins   AT1.1 03.2 / AT2.1 03.4 / AT3.1 L3.1 / L3.2

Materials
CD-ROM

Description
Click on the food and drink items to hear Bof's opinion of
them items as he eats/drinks. Use the additional features to
practise sound/spelling links, and word classes.

Delivery
● Invite pupils to click on the food items, one by one. Bof will
eat or drink the item and then respond by saying whether the
item was good or not.

● Go through each item a couple of times, repeating the words
after Bof and copying the Virtual Teacher's gestures.

Extension
● Point to an item. Ask pupils to guess from the thumbs
up/thumbs down above it what Bof will say. Click on the item
to compare pupils' answers.

Sounds
● This is a good opportunity to practise sound/spelling links.
See the Introduction for notes on how to use this
feature of the Language Presentation.

Word class
● This is a good opportunity to practise word classes. See
the Introduction for notes on how to use this
feature of the Language Presentation.

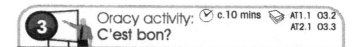

3 Oracy activity: C'est bon?   ⏱ c.10 mins   AT1.1 03.2 / AT2.1 03.3

Materials
CD-ROM

Description
Look at the food being presented, and Bof's reaction to it.
Listen to the options in the question. Give your answer aloud,
in French.

If necessary, check the answer before marking by clicking on
the audio check button in Bof's speech bubble.

Delivery
● Click on *Allez* to start the activity. An item of food appears
from inside the picnic basket, and the audio suggests two
possible opinions of the food.

● Pupils say what they think the food is like before you click
on the audio check button in Bof's bubble to hear what he
says.

● If their selection is correct, click on the tick. If their answer
is wrong, click on the cross.

Extension
● Make two teams. Each team takes it in turn to answer a
question and scores a point for each correct answer.

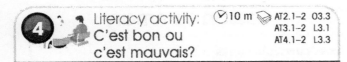

4 Literacy activity: ⏱10 m 📖 AT2.1–2 O3.3 / AT3.1–2 L3.1 / AT4.1–2 L3.3
C'est bon ou c'est mauvais?

Materials
Several copies of the Unit 6 Flashcards 1–6 (food items); real food items; cards with different opinions from the lesson written on them.

Description
Pupils give their opinions on various food items.

Delivery
● Divide the class into several groups. Give each group a pile of the food flashcards, along with the cards with the four different opinions.

● Ask groups to discuss between themselves whether they like the food or not, using the target language.

● Based on the most common result in their group, pupils position the flashcards in groups, under the heading of the different opinions.

● One member of each group reports back to the class, using the target phrase of e.g. *Une pomme – c'est délicieux*, and so on.

Extension
● Ask pupils to write sentences for each food item, to summarise their opinions.

Support
● Pupils don't have to say the words in a complete phrase. They can just write the food item and the opinion separately.

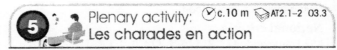

5 Plenary activity: ⏱c.10 m 📖AT2.1–2 O3.3
Les charades en action

Materials
Cards or papers: on each one is a food item and a short descriptive phrase (e.g. *Une pizza – c'est mauvais*). Or Unit 6 Flashcards 1–6 (Food and drink).

Description
Pupils act out the food item and the description for their team-mates to guess the words.

Delivery
● Prepare the prompt cards (see Materials, above).

● Make two teams. Pupils from each team take it in turn to mime (no speaking or noises!) a food item and an appropriate reaction, so their team can correctly guess the words on the card.

● Award two points for correct answers within 30 seconds, one point for up to one minute. Offer a bonus point to the other team if answer not given after one minute.

Support
● Use Flashcards 1–6 instead of miming the food item.

Unit 6  Lesson 3

Lesson summary

Context Numbers 21–31	**Cross-curricular links** Numeracy

National criteria
KS2 Framework: **O3.1, O3.2, O3.3, O3.4, L3.1, L3.2, L3.3**
Attainment levels: **AT1.1–2, AT2.1, AT3.1–2, AT4.1**
Language ladder levels:
  Listening: **Grade 1–2;** Speaking: **Grade 1;**
  Reading: **Grade 1–2;** Writing: **Grade 1**
	Key vocabulary
	Numbers 21–31
	
	Language structures and outcomes
	As above

---

① Starter activity: ⏱ 5 mins 📖 AT1.1–2 03.3 AT2.1 03.4
Les nombres

Materials
n/a

Description
Pupils solve simple additions to practise numbers up to 20.

Delivery
● Quickly recap numbers 1–20 chorally.

● Write two numbers on the board, totalling no more than 20, and ask *Ça fait combien, [deux] plus [dix]?*

● Repeat a few times to give as much practice as possible.

Extension
● You may wish to select a few pupils to ask the questions instead of you!

② Animated story: ⏱ 10–15 m 📖 AT1.2 03.1 AT3.2 03.4 L3.1
Le pique-nique (2)

Materials
CD-ROM, Unit 6 Flashcards 1–6 (Food and drink), or pictures of these

Description
Watch and listen to this interactive animated story presenting the language for Lessons 3–4 (dates and birthdays). You can pause and rewind the story at any point.

Delivery
● This animated story can be used for both starter and plenary activities – the whole animation can be played at the end of the unit so that pupils can gauge their improved understanding.

● At this point pupils watch the second half of the story only; the first half is in Lesson 1.

Scene 2: Children and Bof by the river

● Freeze the screen on the opening scene and ask *Comment s'appellent-ils?* ('What are their names?') to elicit and refresh *Il/Elle s'appelle...*

● Freeze the screen on Bof arriving with the birthday cake. Ask pupils what he's carrying, and what they think is going to happen in this scene.

● Play the scene through and compare predictions with what actually happened.

③ Presentation: ⏱ c.10 mins 📖 AT1.1 03.2 AT2.1 03.4 AT3.1 L3.1 L3.2
Les nombres 21–31

Materials
CD-ROM

Description
Click on the stepping stones to help Jake cross the river and hear a presentation of the numbers 21–31. Use the additional features to practise sound/spelling links and spelling.

Delivery
● Start the activity. Invite pupils to click on the stepping stones, in numerical order. The Virtual Teacher will say the number and pupils repeat.

● Then encourage pupils to click on the other stones in any order as many times as necessary to listen to the Virtual Teacher saying the numbers again.

● Once the initial presentation is complete, take a few minutes to go through the numbers again in order. Pupils repeat the numbers each time.

Spelling
● For groups who have already done the alphabet: Point to a number and ask the children to say/spell the word. Check answer by clicking on the word then on the *Spell* icon.

● To simply introduce the concept of spelling in French, click on a number, then on the *Spell* icon, and point to the letters as the Virtual Teacher says them. Repeat, this time asking the whole class to join in. Continue in the same way with all the numbers.

Sounds
To further reinforce accurate pronunciation, and to introduce some basic reading skills:

● Point to each number on the text bar and ask the class to say the word.

● Focus on the text on screen, click on the *Sound* icon, and click on the different highlighted sounds to hear the Virtual Teacher saying them.

● Repeat all together.

NB. If the *Sound* icon is not illuminated, that means it is not applicable for that particular word.

4 Oracy activity: ⏱ c.10 mins 📚 AT1.1 03.3 / AT2.1 03.4
Comptez et sautez!

Materials
CD-ROM

Description
Help Jake to cross the river! Read the numbers on the stepping stones. Say them aloud in French.

If necessary, check the answer before marking by clicking on the audio check button in Jake's speech bubble.

Delivery
● Click on *Allez* to start the activity. A number will appear next to a stone. Pupils must read out the number on that stone.

● Click on the audio check button in Jake's bubble to hear the correct number in French. If the pupil's answer was correct, click on the ✔ button and Jake will progress across the river. If the answer was incorrect, click on the ✘ button: he loses a 'life' and remains on the previous stones.

● Continue until pupils have answered all the numbers correctly without losing all their 'lives', and Jake will successfully get to the other side of the river.

Extension
● Make two teams. Each team takes it in turn to read out a number and scores a point for each correct answer.

Support
● Go through the numbers orally before starting the activity itself.

5 Plenary activity: ⏱ c.10 mins 📚 AT1.1 03.4 / AT3.1 L3.1 / AT4.1 L3.3
Loto!

Materials
Blank Loto cards

Description
A bingo game to practise the numbers further.

Delivery
● Group pupils in pairs or on their own, and distribute a blank bingo card to each of them.

● Ask them to fill the spaces on the card with any number between 1 and 31. Ensure that they write these in numeral and word form.

● Stand at the front of the class and read out random numbers from this range in French. Pupils cross off numbers which are on their card, until one pupil or pair has crossed them all out.

● The first pupil or pair to complete their grid is the winner and calls out *Gagné!*

● The winner comes to the front and reads out the numbers on their card to confirm that the checked-off numbers are correct.

Support
● Pupils could write the numbers down as numerals only, and just listen for the French.

Unit 6  Lesson 4

Context
Months of the year

National criteria
KS2 Framework: **O3.1, O3.2, O3.3, O3.4, L3.1, L3.2**
Attainment levels: **AT1.1–2, AT2.1–2, AT3.1–2**
Language ladder levels:
  Listening: **Grade 1–2**; Speaking: **Grade 1–2**;
  Reading: **Grade 1–2**

Cross-curricular links
Numeracy

Key vocabulary
Months: *janvier* (January), *février* (February), *mars* (March),
avril (April), *mai* (May), *juin* (June), *juillet* (July), *août*
(August), *septembre* (September), *octobre* (October),
novembre (November), *décembre* (December)

Language structures and outcomes
n/a

---

 1 Starter activity: ⏱ 5 mins 📖 AT1.1–2 O3.3
Les nombres AT2.1 O3.4

Materials
n/a

Description
Pupils solve simple additions to practise numbers up to 31.

Delivery
● Quickly recap numbers 1–31 chorally.
● Write two numbers on the board, totalling no more than 31,
and ask *Ça fait combien, [deux] plus [dix]?*'
● Repeat a few times to give as much practice as possible.

Extension
● You may wish to select a few pupils to ask the questions
instead of you!

 2 Presentation: ⏱ c.10 mins 📖 AT1.1 O3.2
Les mois AT2.1 O3.4
AT3.1 L3.1
L3.2

Materials
CD-ROM

Description
Click on the panels to hear and see a presentation of the
months of the year. Use the additional features to practise
sound/spelling links **and spelling**.

Delivery
● Invite pupils to click on the month panels one by one, in
order. The image will become animated and the relevant
audio will be played.
● Go through the whole year in this way. Repeat a couple of
times in order to reinforce learning. Then click on the months
in random order to reinforce each month separately.

Spelling
● For groups who have already done the alphabet: Point to a
month and ask the children to say/spell the word. Check
answer by clicking on the word then on the *Spell* icon.
● To simply introduce the concept of spelling in French, click on
a month, then on the *Spell* icon, and point to the letters as the
Virtual Teacher says them. Repeat, this time asking the whole
class to join in. Continue in the same way with all the months.

Sounds
To further reinforce accurate pronunciation, and to introduce
some basic reading skills:
● Point to each month on the text bar and ask the class to say
the word.

● Focus on the text on screen, click on the *Sound* icon, and
click on the different highlighted sounds to hear the Virtual
Teacher saying them.
● Repeat all together.
NB. If the *Sound* icon is not illuminated, that means it is not
applicable for that particular word.

 3 Literacy activity: ⏱ 10 mins 📖 AT3.1 L3.1
Janvier, février, mars

Materials
Copies of Unit 6 Flashcard 7 (Months of the year)

Description
Matching activity with month flashcards.

Delivery
● Divide the class into several teams.
● Photocopy the picture flashcards enough times so there is
one set for each team, and likewise a set of all the word cards.
Shuffle these yourself.
● Ask pupils to cut up the picture cards and to shuffle them
into a random order.
● Give pupils a shuffled set of word cards, then set them in a
race to match up the picture and word cards as fast as
possible. The first team to do this correctly wins.

Extension
● Hand out the word cards only, and ask pupils to put these in
order without the support of the picture cards.

 4 Song: ⏱ 10–15 mins 📖 AT1.2 O3.1
Combien de jours? AT2.2 O3.2
AT3.2 O3.4
L3.1

Materials
CD-ROM or Audio CD, track 12; Unit 6 Flashcard 7 (Months
of the year)

Description
Watch and listen to the interactive song practising the months
of the year. Choose either *Practice* or *Sing* mode: the former to
go through the song line by line, the latter to sing it all the
way through. Switch the music and words on or off as you
prefer.

Delivery

● Hand out one month flashcard to each pupil.

● Play the song through, and ask pupils just to listen out for 'their' month.

● Play the song again, this time asking pupils to stand up, then quickly sit down again when they hear their month. For a less chaotic activity, just ask pupils to wave the card in the air when their month is sung!

● Ask pupils to group themselves according to how the months are grouped in the song, e.g. pupils with *janvier, fèvrier* and *mars* will form one group.

● Play the song again. This time each group is responsible for singing along with their line/months, individual pupils holding up their month when it is sung.

● Go through song again as a whole-class activity, with or without the audio.

Extension

● Divide the class into groups of 6–8 pupils.

● **Each group performs its own version of the song.**

● **The other groups can award points to see which version was the best!**

See the Introduction for more notes on the Song features.

5 Plenary activity: ⏱ c.5 mins 📚 AT2.1 O3.3 AT3.1 L3.1
Tous les mois

Materials

Unit 6 Flashcard 7 (Months of the year)

Description

Pupils revise the months with a game using flashcards.

Delivery

● Give each pupil a card with a month on.

● Pupils must not show their card to others, but must memorise it before handing it back to you.

● The objective is for pupils to form a line of months in the correct order. To do this, they are allowed to move around, saying only their month in French, and must position themselves correctly in the line.

Extension

● You could make this a team race, with each group of 12 forming a separate line.

Unit 6  Lesson 5

Context
Dates and birthdays

National criteria
KS2 Framework: O3.1, O3.2, O3.3, O3.4, L3.1, L3.2, L3.3
Attainment levels: AT1.2, AT2.12, AT3.1–2, AT4.1
Language ladder levels:
  Listening: **Grade 2**; Speaking: **Grade 2**;
  Reading: **Grade 1–2**; Writing: **Grade 1**

Cross-curricular links
Numeracy

Key vocabulary
Dates: *le...* [*mars*, etc.] (the... March, etc.)

Language structures and outcomes
C'est quand, ton anniversaire? (When's your birthday?)
[*C'est*] le... ([It's] the...)

1 Starter activity: Chantez!
⏱ 5 mins 📖 AT1.2 O3.1 / AT2.2 O3.2 / AT3.2 O3.4 / L3.1 L3.2

Materials
CD-ROM (Unit 6 – Song) or Audio CD, track 12

Description
Sing Unit 6 Lesson 4 Song *Combien de jours?* again, to revise months of the year.

Delivery
● Quickly recap the months chorally.
● The whole class sings the song, following the text on screen.

Support
● Go through the song slowly in *Practice* mode before singing it all the way through.
See the Introduction for more notes on the Song features.

2 Presentation: C'est quand, ton anniversaire?
⏱ c.10 mins 📖 AT1.2 O3.2 / AT2.2 O3.4 / AT3.2 L3.1 / L3.2

Materials
CD-ROM

Description
Click on the balloons to hear and see the characters say the date of their birthday. Use the additional features to practise sound/spelling links.

Delivery
● Invite pupils to click on the balloons, one by one. The character will say when their birthday is, which will be the date on that balloon. Pupils should repeat the date.
● Once a date has been heard, point again to the same balloon. Ask pupils to say the date aloud, and click on the balloon to compare their answer with the Virtual Teacher pronunciation.

Extension
● Say a date which appears on the screen. Ask a pupil to click on the correct balloon – the audio response will confirm whether or not they were right.
● You could play a team game in the same way, awarding a point for each correct answer.

Sounds
● This is a good opportunity to practise sound/spelling links. See page ix of the Introduction for notes on how to use this feature of the Language Presentation.

3 Oracy activity: Les anniversaires
⏱ c.10 mins 📖 AT1.2 O3.2 / O3.4

Materials
CD-ROM

Description
Pupils listen to the audio prompts and then click on the correct balloon.

Delivery
● Click on *Allez* to start the activity. You will hear each character giving the date of their birthday.
● Pupils respond by clicking on the balloon with the correct date on it.
● In the case of an incorrect choice, the Virtual Teacher will invite the pupil to try again.

Extension
● Make two teams. Each team takes it in turn to click on the balloons, and a point is awarded for each correct answer.

Support
● Play each audio exchange twice using the *Encore* button before asking pupils to respond.

4 Literacy activity: Quelle est la date?
⏱ c.10 mins 📖 AT1.2 O3.1 / AT2.2 O3.2 / AT3.2 O3.4 / L3.1 L3.2

Materials
CD-ROM

Description
Play bingo in teams, either using completed cards, or filling in your own cards on screen, or using a printed grid. Then mark off the date on your card if you hear it.

Delivery
There are three ways of playing the bingo game:
● *Ready to go*: the computer automatically completes two grids for each team. Team members mark off the dates on their grid as they hear them.
● *Make your own*: as above, but teams complete their grids with their choice of phrases on-screen.

● *Print your own*: as *Ready to go*, but print off blank *Loto* grids from the CD-ROM, which pupils fill in with their choice of dates from those listed on-screen.

● When you are ready to start the game, call up a member of each team to click on the card.

● Click on *Allez* to hear each date. When pupils hear a date from their grid, they either click on the relevant square, or mark the square off on their printed grid.

● When the first on-screen grid is complete, there will be a celebratory animation.

● If playing with printed grids, then the first player to complete their grid calls out *Gagné!*

Support

● You can play with or without sound by clicking on the *Audio on/Audio off* button on the taskbar at the bottom. With sound on, pupils will hear each date spoken as it appears.

Oracy activity: ⏱ c.5–10m 📑 AT1.2–2 03.3 / AT4.1 L3.3
Une enquête

Materials

Blank paper (or pre-printed, questionnaire-style grids with spaces for five names and birthday dates)

Description

Pupils conduct a survey on their classmates' birthdays to revise dates.

Delivery

● Give each pupil a piece of paper/grid.

● Allow five minutes for pupils to ask up to five classmates when their birthday is (*C'est quand, ton anniversaire?/C'est le…*). They note down the person's name, and the date in French.

Extension

● You could ask pupils to group together in months, according to when their birthday is, using only French to communicate with each other.

Support

● You can use the Virtual Teacher on the CD-ROM at any time to refresh your memory of the target expressions.

6 Plenary activity: ⏱ c.5–10m 📑 AT2.1 03.3 / AT3.1 L3.1 / AT4.1 L3.3
Mon anniversaire

Materials

Small pieces of blank paper, cloth bag

Description

Pupils read out dates and guess whose birthday they refer to.

Delivery

● Hand out the paper and ask pupils to write down the date of their birthday (in French!).

● Collect the papers and place in cloth bag.

● Invite individual pupils to the front. They take a paper from the bag, without looking, and read out the date. They have a maximum of three guesses to identify correctly whose birthday it is. Try and get pupils to use the French phrase *C'est…* when guessing the name.

Unit 6  Extra!

Worksheet 1A
🕐 10–15 mins 📚 AT3.1 L3.1 L3.3

Description
Worksheet to give further practice on food vocabulary.

Notes
1 If necessary, give pupils a minute or two to complete one drawing at a time, then say the answer together. Alternatively, give pupils 5–10 minutes to complete all four drawings, then go through all the answers together.

Answers
1 a une pizza   c un jus d'orange
   b une pomme   d une banane

Worksheet 1B
🕐 10–15 mins 📚 AT3.1 L3.1 L3.3

Description
Worksheet to give further practice on food vocabulary.

Notes
1 If necessary, give pupils a minute or two to complete one drawing at a time, then say the answer together. Alternatively, give pupils 5–10 minutes to complete all six drawings, then go through all the answers together.

2 Move around the class to provide help where needed for Activity 2.

Answers
1 a une pizza   d un jus d'orange
   b un gâteau   e une banane
   c une pomme   f un sandwich

Worksheet 2A
🕐 10–15 mins 📚 AT2.1 L3.1 AT3.1 L3.2

Description
Worksheet to give further practice on food vocabulary and opinions of food.

Notes
1 Give pupils a few minutes to do Activity 1 and check/read through the answers together at the end.

2 Move around the class to provide help where needed for Activity 2.

Worksheet 2B
🕐 10–15 mins 📚 AT2.2 O3.3 AT3.2 L3.1 AT4.1–2 L3.2 L3.3

Description
Worksheet to give further practice on food vocabulary and opinions of food.

Notes
1 Give pupils a few minutes to do Activity 1 and check/read through the answers together at the end.

2 & 3 Move around the class to provide help where needed.

Answers
1 a C'est délicieux. (*C'est bon* would also be acceptable.)
   b C'est mauvais. (*Ce n'est pas bon* would also be acceptable.)
   c C'est bon. (*C'est délicieux* would also be acceptable.)
   d Ce n'est pas bon. (*C'est mauvais* would also be acceptable.)

Worksheet 3A
🕐 10–15 mins 📚 AT2.1 O3.3 AT3.1 L3.1 L3.2

Description
Worksheet to give further practice on months, numbers, and nouns.

Notes
1 If necessary, read out the words together to check pupils' comprehension before asking them to work through the activity.

2 Move around to listen to pupils' answers to Activity 2.

Answers
1 a pomme   c rouge   e trente
   b vingt-deux   d gâteau   f vingt-neuf

Worksheet 3B
🕐 10–15 mins 📚 AT2.1 O3.3 AT3.1 L3.1 AT4.1 L3.2 L3.3

Description
Worksheet to give further practice on months, numbers, and nouns.

Notes
1 If necessary, read out the words together to check pupils' comprehension before asking them to work through the activity.

2 Move around to listen to pupils' answers to Activity 2.

Answers
1 a pomme   e trente   h trente
   b vingt-deux   f vingt-cinq   i bouche
   c banane   g bras   j ordinateur
   d gâteau

Worksheet 4A
🕐 10–15 mins 📚 AT2.2 O3.3 AT3.1 L3.1 AT4.1–2 L3.3

Description
Worksheet to give further practice on giving information about yourself.

Notes
1 Go round the class, asking each pupil to introduce themselves verbally, using the model from the worksheet, before they complete Activity 1.

2 Move around to listen to pupils' answers.

3 Pupils can just write the name of the person, and their birthday date as fully as possible in French.

Worksheet 4B
🕐 10–15 mins 📚 AT2.2 O3.3 AT3.2 L3.1 AT4.2 L3.3

Description
Worksheet to give further practice on giving information about yourself.

Notes
1 Go round the class, asking each pupil to introduce themselves verbally, using the model from the worksheet, before they complete Activity 1.

2 Move around to listen to pupils' answers to Activity 2.

3 Pupils fill in the details on the identity card for a friend or family member. They could also write out full sentences, e.g. *Il/Elle s'appelle* [+ name].

30 mins AT3.1
AT4.2
L3.3

Project work: French name days

Description
Pupils find the date of their name day in France.

Materials
List of French name days

Delivery
● Before the lesson, prepare a list of the French name days and dates. You can easily find this on the internet using Google or another search engine.

● Explain to pupils that in France each date is the day of a saint with a different name, meaning that French children traditionally have a "name day" as well as a birthday.

● Give pupils a list of the names and dates, and ask them to find their own name and date. The list is mainly based on Christian, traditional names, so not all of your class will find their names in the list. If this is the case, then give them another name to find instead.

● Pupils write up their results using the sentence *Ma fête, c'est le...* You can create a wall display with pictures of pupils and speech bubbles giving their birthday and name day.

● In subsequent lessons, start by checking the date in French with pupils, then asking *C'est la fête de qui aujourd'hui?* ('Whose name day is it today?')

15–20 mins AT1.1 O3.2
L3.2

Sound/spelling activity

Description
Practise listening out for and pronouncing the *eu* and *on* sounds. Then identify the words when you hear them read out, and which words use the sounds.

Delivery
● This sound/spelling activity focuses specifically on the *eu* and *on* sounds.

● There are two parts to the activity: the first (*Practice*) allows pupils to familiarise themselves with the two sounds and to compare their pronunciation with the Virtual Teacher model. The second part (*Activities*) contains two exercises: *Activity 1* is an exercise where pupils have to click on a button if they hear the *eu* sound in a list of words; and *Activity 2*, where pupils do the same with the *on* sound instead.

● Select *Practice* and click on *Next* to start this part. Then click on *Allez*. The Virtual Teacher will say the *eu* sound first on its own, and then as part of three words that have already been used in the units to date. For each of these, get the class to repeat the sound or word chorally several times, checking the model each time using the *Encore* button to see how close they are.

● Once you have finished this part, relaunch the activity and choose *Activities* from the selection menu to move on to test pupils' recognition of these sounds. To show pupils how the activity works, click on the *Example* button. This will demonstrate an example question and its answer. Click on *Allez* to start *Activity 1*. Pupils will hear one of 20 words read out in random order, and must click on the *eu* button before the timer runs out if they hear this sound in the word. If they do not hear the sound, they should click on the red cross. Pupils score a point when they correctly identify a word

containing the *eu* sound within the time allowed. You can click on *Encore* to hear the word again, and to restart the timer. Once they have completed each answer, you can use the *Encore* button to hear the word again, in order to review their understanding.

● Finally, in *Activity 2*, pupils must do the same as above, this time listening out for words using the *on* sound.

● Repeat the activity again if you feel pupils need further practice.

Extension
● You can continue the practice activity with more words using these sounds if you feel that pupils have grasped this well, even words not yet covered in *Rigolo*. Pupils can then hold up cards marked with the sounds to show when they hear the appropriate one.

Assessment for Units 5-6

Ecoutez!

Play the recording 2–3 times or more if necessary. Pause the recording during each activity as necessary.

Total marks for listening: 20. If pupils are getting 8–14/20, they are working towards level 1. If they achieve 15–20/20, they are working between levels 1–2.

Activity 1   (AT1.1; O3.2)
Mark out of 5

Answers
a3 b4 (*example*: c1) d5 e2

1 C-H-A-I-S-E
2 D-V-D
3 C-D
4 M-A-C-H-I-N-E
5 T-A-B-L-E

Activity 2   (AT1.1; O3.2)
Mark out of 8

Answers
a1 b7 c6 d2 e5 f3 g4 h8

1 C'est l'ordinateur... oui, l'ordinateur.
2 C'est le CD... le CD.
3 C'est la machine... la machine.
4 C'est la chaise... la chaise.
5 C'est le lecteur de CD... oui, le lecteur de CD.
6 C'est le DVD... le DVD.
7 C'est le jeu vidéo... oui, le jeu vidéo.
8 C'est la table... la table.

Activity 3   (AT1.2; O3.4)
Mark out of 7

Answers
(*example*: 23 février)
1 30 avril
2 25 décembre
3 22 octobre
4 1 mai
5 29 janvier
6 21 mars
7 28 juin

TRANSCRIPT

(*example*: C'est quand ton anniversaire? C'est le 23 février... le 23 février.)

1 – C'est quand ton anniversaire?
– C'est le 30 avril... le 30 avril.
2 – C'est quand ton anniversaire?
– C'est le 25 décembre... le 25 décembre.
3 – C'est quand ton anniversaire?
– C'est le 22 octobre... le 22 octobre.
4 – C'est quand ton anniversaire?
– C'est le premier mai... le premier mai.
5 – C'est quand ton anniversaire?
– C'est le 29 janvier... le 29 janvier.
6 – C'est quand ton anniversaire?
– C'est le 21 mars... le 21 mars .
7 – C'est quand ton anniversaire?
– C'est le 28 juin... le 28 juin.

Parlez!

Pupils can work in pairs for the speaking tasks. If it is not possible to assess each pair, then assess a few pairs for each assessment block and mark the rest of the class based on the spoken work they do in class.

Total marks for speaking: 10. Pupils achieving 5/10 are working towards level 1; pupils achieving more than 5/10 are working between levels 1–2.

Activity 1   (AT2.1, O3.3)
5 marks

Answers
(*example*: Je voudrais une pomme.)
Je voudrais un gâteau.
Je voudrais une pizza.
Je voudrais une banane.
Je voudrais un jus d'orange
Je voudrais un sandwich.

Extra! *This part can be awarded extra marks at your discretion.*

Activity 2   (AT2.1–2 O3.3)
5 marks

Answers
(*example*: C'est le vingt-deux mars.)
C'est le vingt-cinq juin.
C'est le vingt-neuf septembre.
C'est le vingt-quatre août.
C'est le vingt-sept janvier.
C'est le vingt-trois novembre.
C'est le vingt et un décembre.
C'est le vingt-six avril.
C'est le vingt-huit juillet.

Lisez!

Total marks for reading: 20. Pupils achieving 8–14/20 are working towards level 1. Pupils achieving 15 or more out of 20 are working between levels 1–2.

Activity 1   (AT3.1, L3.1)
Mark out of 10

Answers
21 vingt et un; 22 vingt-deux; (*example*: 23 vingt-trois);
24 vingt-quatre; 25 vingt-cinq; 26 vingt-six; 27 vingt-sept;
28 vingt-huit; 29 vingt-neuf; 30 trente; 31 trente et un

Activity 2   (AT3.1, L3.1, L3.2)
Mark out of 10; 2 for each correct answer

Answers
(*example*: ✗) a ✔ b ✔ c ✗ d ✔ e ✔

Écrivez!

For the writing tasks, the copying of words can be approximate.

Total marks for writing: 20. Pupils achieving 8–14/20 are working towards level 1. Pupils achieving 15 or more out of 20 are working between levels 1–2.

Activity 1   (AT4.1, L3.3)
Mark out of 5

Answers
mother – ma mère, father – mon père, brother – mon frère, sister – ma sœur, cat – mon chat

Activity 2   (AT4.1–2, L3.3)
Mark out of 5

Answers
(*example*: **a** un gâteau)
b une pizza
c une banane
d un jus d'orange
e un sandwich
f une pomme

Activity 3   (AT4.1–2, L3.3)
Mark out of 10; 2 for each correct answer

Answers
Accept either of the two answers given:
(*example*: **a** Ce n'est pas bon.)
b C'est bon./C'est délicieux.
c Ce n'est pas bon./C'est mauvais.
d C'est bon./C'est délicieux.
e C'est bon./C'est délicieux.
f Ce n'est pas bon./C'est mauvais.

Rigolo 1

Unit 7: Encore!

National criteria

KS2 Framework objectives

O4.1	Memorise and present a short spoken text
O4.2	Listen for specific words and phrases
O4.3	Listen for sounds, rhyme and rhythm
O4.4	Ask and answer questions on several topics
L4.1	Read and understand a range of familiar written phrases
L4.2	Follow a short familiar text, listening and reading at the same time
L4.3	Read some familiar words and phrases aloud and pronounce them accurately
L4.4	Write simple words and phrases using a model and some words from memory
IU4.4	Learn about ways of travelling to the country/countries

QCA Scheme of Work

Unit 2	Je me présente
Unit 3	En famille
Unit 4	Les animaux
Unit 6	Le monde

Language ladder levels

Listening:	Breakthrough, Grade 1–3
Reading:	Breakthrough, Grade 1–3
Speaking:	Breakthrough, Grade 1–2
Writing:	Breakthrough, Grade 1–3

5–14 guideline strands   Levels A–C

Listening		**Reading**	
Listening for information and instructions	A, C	Reading for information and instructions	A, C
Listening and reacting to others	A–C	Reading aloud	A, C

Speaking		**Writing**	
Speaking to convey information	A, C	Writing to exchange information and ideas	A, C
Speaking and interacting with others	B, C	Writing to establish and maintain personal contact	A, C
Speaking about experiences, feelings and opinions	A, B	Writing imaginatively/to entertain	n/a

Unit objectives

- revise ways to describe people, using *avoir* and *être* phrases
- describe people's nationality

Key language

- descriptive vocabulary: *il/elle a* (he/she has)… *les cheveux courts/longs* (short/long hair), *les yeux bleus,* etc. (blue eyes, etc.), *un chien* (a dog), *un frère/une sœur* (brother/sister); *il/elle a sept ans* (he/she is seven years old),
- nationalities: *français(e)* (French), *canadien(ne)* (Canadian), *britannique* (British)
- character adjectives: *intelligent(e)* (clever), *sportif/sportive* (sporty), *sévère* (strict)

Grammar and skills

- revision of a variety of *avoir* phrases
- use *être* phrases with adjectives
- recognise and the use third person singular (*il/elle*) with both *avoir* and *être*
- recognise different adjective endings

Unit outcomes

Most children will be able to:

- use a variety of expressions to describe people in third person singular
- recognise different nationalities

Some children will also be able to:

- use and recognise different adjective endings, both singular and plural

Unit 7  Lesson 1

Context
Revision of ways to describe people

National criteria
KS2 Framework: **O4.1, O4.2, O4.3, O4.4, L4.1,
L4.2, L4.3**
Attainment levels: **AT1.2–3, AT2.2, AT3.2–3**
Language ladder levels:
  Listening: **Grade 2–3;** Speaking: **Grade 2;**
  Reading: **Grade 2–3**

Cross-curricular links
Literacy

Key vocabulary
Descriptive vocabulary: *il/elle a* (he/she has)... *les cheveux
courts/longs* (short/long hair), *les yeux bleus,* etc. (blue
eyes, etc.), *un chien* (a dog), *un frère/une sœur*
(brother/sister); *il/elle a sept ans* (he/she is seven years old)

Language structures and outcomes
Il/Elle a... (He/She's got...)

---

 1 Starter activity: **Tu es comment?** ⏲ 5–10 mins 📖 AT2.2 O4.1 O4.4

Materials
Unit 3 Flashcards 1–13 (Parts of the body; Eyes and hair),
puppets

Description
Pupils use previously covered structures and words to describe
themselves as fully as possible.

Delivery
● Quickly recap the key words and phrases from the flashcards.
● Write two questions on the board: *Tu es comment?* and *Quel
âge as-tu?* Point to one question, read it out, and make one of
the puppets answer the question. Do the same with the second
question.
● Ask the class to work in pairs, asking their partner the
questions from the board.
● Move around the room to monitor the activity.
● If time allows, ask a few pupils questions at random, which
they answer in front of the class.

 **Language Learning Strategies**

Recycling language
● This first lesson revisits language from Units 2 and 3,
rephrasing it in the third person using *il* and *elle* instead
of *j'ai.*
● Following the starter activity above, focus pupils on
all the *avoir* phrases they have learnt by writing *j'ai...* at
the top of the board, asking pupils to think of as many
phrases as they can.
● These can be either descriptions or other phrases: *j'ai
un stylo* (etc.), *j'ai huit ans, j'ai les yeux bleus, j'ai les
cheveux longs, j'ai un chien.* They could also be
encouraged to use language presented in other contexts
here, e.g. *j'ai un ordinateur, j'ai un frère.*

---

 2 Animated story: **La visite (1)** ⏲ 5–10 mins 📖 AT1.2–3 AT3.2–3 O4.2 L4.1 L4.2

Materials
CD-ROM

Description
● Watch and listen to this interactive animated story, based in
the château, presenting the language for Lessons 1 and 2
(introducing more ways of describing people, and the third
person of the verb *avoir* ['to have']).
● You can pause and rewind the story at any point.

Delivery
● This animated story can be used for both starter and plenary
activities – the whole animation can be played at the end of
the unit so that pupils can gauge their improved
understanding.
● At this point pupils watch the first half of the story only; the
second half is in Lesson 3.
Scene 1 (Polly and Didier in a room at the castle)
● Freeze the screen on the opening scene and ask *Comment
s'appellent-ils?* (What are their names?) to elicit and refresh
Il/Elle s'appelle...
● Ask pupils to tell you what they can see in the room, using
previously studied structures and words (e.g. *Il y a un
ordinateur*).
● Before playing the scene, pause and ask what pupils think
will happen. Play the scene, and compare their predictions
with the actual story.

---

 3 Presentation: **Qu'est-ce qu'il a?** ⏲ 5–10 mins 📖 AT1.2 AT2.2 AT3.2 O4.2 O4.3 L4.1 L4.3

Materials
CD-ROM

Description
Click on an indicated object in each room to hear the target
structure (*Il/Elle a* ['He/She has'] + noun). Use the additional
features to practise sound/spelling links.

Delivery
● Invite pupils to click on the indicated objects or physical
attributes, one by one. The Virtual Teacher will say the target
structure (*Il/Elle a* + noun).
● Pupils repeat the sentence each time. Repeat each item a
couple of times to reinforce the structure and words.

Sounds
To further reinforce accurate pronunciation, and to introduce
some basic reading skills:
● Point to each word on the text bar and ask the class to say
the word.
● Focus on the text on screen, click on the *Sound* icon, and
click on the different highlighted sounds to hear the Virtual
Teacher saying them.
● Repeat all together.

4 Oracy activity: **C'est qui?** ⏱ c. 10 mins 📖 AT1.2 / O4.2 / O4.3

Materials
CD-ROM

Description
Click on *Allez*. You will hear a description of someone in the third person. Click on the correct corresponding character, who will become animated.

Delivery
● Click on *Allez* to start (or invite a pupil to start) the activity. You will hear a description of someone in the third person form (e.g. *Elle a douze ans*). Click on the *Encore* button to listen again, if necessary. Encourage pupils to repeat the description they hear.

● Pupils must identify the character being described by clicking on them.

● If their selection is correct, the character will become animated and the Virtual Teacher will congratulate them.

● If their selection is wrong, the Virtual Teacher will invite pupils to have another try.

● Repeat a couple of times to reinforce the language.

Extension
● Make two teams. Each team takes it in turn to answer a question and scores a point for each correct answer.

Support
● Quickly revise numbers 6–12 before beginning the activity, paying particular attention to numbers 9 and 12, so that pupils will know what to listen out for for two of the characters' descriptions.

5 Plenary activity: **Il/Elle a…** ⏱ c. 5–10 mins 📖 AT1.2 / O4.2

Materials
Puppets, Unit 3 Flashcards 1–13 (Parts of the body and Eyes and hair) and other noun flashcards

Description
Pupils identify a person or character described in the third person.

Delivery
● Describe a character or a pupil in the class using one or two simple sentences with *Il/Elle a* + description or noun.

● Pupils must say the name of the person/character being described.

● If pupils are confident enough, the pupil who correctly identifies the person being described could also describe someone for the others to guess.

Extension
● Divide the class into two teams.

● Describe someone as above to each team in turn and award a point for each correct answer.

Support
● If pupils find this difficult initially, use a puppet, e.g. Polly, and ask simple, deliberately wrong questions, e.g. *Elle a les cheveux courts?* to elicit *Non, longs* and eventually *Non, elle a les cheveux longs!*

● Repeat with the Jake puppet as necessary.

Lesson summary

Context
Revision of ways to describe people

National criteria
KS2 Framework: **O4.1, O4.2, O4.3, O4.4, L4.1, L4.2, L4.3**
Attainment levels: **AT1.2–3, AT2.2, AT3.2–3**
Language ladder levels:
  Listening: **Grade 2–3;** Speaking: **Grade 2;**
  Reading: **Grade 2–3**

Cross-curricular links
Literacy

Key vocabulary
Descriptive vocabulary: *il/elle a* (he/she has)... *les cheveux courts/longs* (short/long hair), *les yeux bleus,* etc. (blue eyes, etc.), *un chien* (a dog), *un frère/une sœur* (brother/sister); *il/elle a sept ans* (he/she is seven years old)

Language structures and outcomes
Il/Elle a... (He/She's got...)

---

1   Starter activity: ⏱ 5–10 mins 📖 AT2.2
     Il/Elle est comment?   O4.1

Materials
n/a

Description
Pupils use previously covered structures and words to describe others in their class.

Delivery
● Invite one or two volunteers to come to the front. Chorally describe the pupils in one or two simple sentences (similar to the plenary activity from Lesson 1) to refresh memories!
● Divide the class into groups of three. Each pupil takes it in turn to describe one other pupil in their group, using *Il/Elle a...*
● Move around the groups to monitor the activity and help where needed.

2   Animated story: ⏱ 5–10 mins 📖 AT1.2–3
     La visite (1)   AT3.2–3
                                 O4.2
                                 L4.1 L4.2

Materials
CD-ROM

Description
● To refresh pupils' memories of the story from Lesson 1, watch and listen again to this interactive animated story, based in the chateau, presenting the language for Lessons 1 and 2, i.e. introducing more ways of describing people, and the third person of the verb *avoir* ('to have').
● You can pause and rewind the story at any point.

Delivery
● This animated story can be used for both starter and plenary activities – the whole animation can be played at the end of the unit so that pupils can gauge their improved understanding.
● At this point pupils watch the first half of the story only; the second half is in Lesson 3.
● Before playing the scene, pause and ask pupils what they remember happening. Play the scene, and compare their recollections with the actual story.

Scene 1 (Polly and Didier in a room at the castle)
● Ask pupils to listen out for how to say a bird (*un oiseau*) and how to say a girl (*une fille*).
● Ask pupils what instrument Marine brings with her (*une guitare*) and how to say she has a guitar (*Elle a une guitare*).
● Ask pupils what Marine's hair is like (*Elle a les cheveux longs*).

---

3   Oracy activity: ⏱ c. 10 mins 📖 AT1.2
     Il a... Elle a...   AT2.2
                                O4.3 O4.4

Materials
CD-ROM

Description
Click on *Allez* and correctly describe the character highlighted in the portrait. Click on *Allez* to go on to the next character.

Delivery
● Click (or invite a pupil to click) on *Allez* to start the activity. You will see a picture of a character, and an arrow pointing to the relevant piece of information about them (e.g. their hair or eyes, or an object they have).
● Pupils must correctly describe the character using *il/elle a*, referring to the indicated feature, e.g. *Elle a les cheveux longs* ('She's got long hair').
● If necessary, you can use the audio check button in the speech bubble to hear the correct answer. If pupils answered correctly, click on the tick and there will be a reward animation. If their answer was incorrect, click on the cross and the Virtual Teacher will invite pupils to try again.
● Click on *Allez* to see another character and feature highlighted, and to continue the activity.
● Go through each character twice if necessary.

Extension
● Make two teams. Each team takes it in turn to answer a question and scores a point for each correct answer.

Support
● Model the first couple of questions by giving pupils the main part of the phrase, e.g. *Il a les cheveux...*

🦉 **Knowledge About Language**

Plural agreements

● This is a good opportunity to introduce the concept of plural adjective agreements.
● Write the phrases *Il a un stylo bleu* and *Il a une trousse bleue* on the board. Remind pupils what these phrases mean, and ask them if they can remember why there is an extra 'e' on *bleue* (because *trousse* is a different kind of word from *stylo*, i.e. it is feminine).
● Now write up the phrase *Il a un stylo bleu* on the board, then write the phrase *Il a les yeux bleus* underneath it. Ask pupils if they can tell you what both phrases mean.
● Ask pupils to spot the difference between the two words for 'blue' (one has an 's'). See if they can suggest why this is – ask them to think how many eyes and pens are involved in each sentence (the adjective adds an 's' in the plural).
● If pupils have grasped this, reinforce the concept by writing out a list of singular and plural nouns and adjectives, leaving a blank letter space at the end of each adjective (e.g. *le stylo bleu_, les stylos bleu_*). Ask pupils what letter should go in each blank, if any.

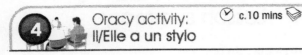

4 Oracy activity: Il/Elle a un stylo
c.10 mins — AT2.2 04.1

Materials
Units 1–6 Flashcards (nouns), puppets

Description
Pupils use puppets and flashcards to practise building more sentences using *Il/Elle a* + nouns covered so far.

Delivery
● Choose a puppet and hold a noun flashcard in its hand/paw.
● Chorally, make a sentence using the target structure.
● Repeat with another puppet and flashcard.
● Invite pupils to come to the front, choose a puppet and flashcard, and make a sentence.

Extension
● Display a selection of the flashcards on the board, and place the puppets on the front desk.
● Divide the class into small groups. Ask each group to make as many sentences as possible, using the displayed props, in five minutes.
● Go round each group asking how many sentences they managed, and ask for a few examples.

Support
● If you find pupils have difficulty in remembering nouns covered, go through some of the flashcards quickly before the activity to refresh their memories, asking *Qu'est-ce que c'est?* for each.

5 Literacy activity: Il a une guitare
c. 10 mins — AT1.2 AT3.2 04.2 L4.1 L4.3

Materials
CD-ROM

Description
Play bingo in teams, either using completed cards, or filling your own cards in on screen, or using a printed grid. Then mark off the sentences on your card if you see the sentence appear on-screen. The first player or team with all their sentences marked off wins.

Delivery
There are three ways of playing the bingo game:

● *Ready to go*: the computer automatically completes two grids for each team. Team members mark off sentences on their grid as pictures appear on-screen.

● *Make your own*: as above, but teams complete their grids with their choice of sentences on-screen.

● *Print your own*: as 'Ready to go', but print off blank lotto grids from the CD-ROM, which pupils fill with their choice of sentences from those listed on-screen.

● When you are ready to start the game, call up a member of each team to click on the card.

● Click on *Allez* to make each item appear. When pupils hear a sentence from their grid, they must either click on the relevant square, or mark the square off on their printed grid.

● When the first on-screen grid is complete, there will be a celebratory animation.

● If playing with printed grids, then the first player to fill their grid calls out *Gagné!*

Support
● You can play with or without sound using the *Audio on/Audio off* button on the taskbar at the bottom. With sound on, pupils will hear each sentence spoken as it appears.

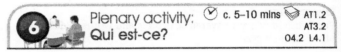

6 Plenary activity: Qui est-ce?
c. 5–10 mins — AT1.2 AT3.2 04.2 L4.1

Materials
Units 1–6 Flashcards (nouns)

Description
Pupils say the name of the person being referred to, using the target structure.

Delivery
● Hand out noun flashcards around the class.
● Make sentences using the target structure about the objects being held by pupils, e.g. *Il a un tambour*.
● Pupils must say the name of the person who is being referred to, i.e. the name of the pupil with the drum flashcard.

Extension
● In order to focus the listening more closely on *il* or *elle*, give out two cards for each object: one to a boy, one to a girl, so that pupils pay attention to whether they hear *Il a un tambour* or *Elle a un tambour*.
● Write the sentences on the board so pupils have to read the structure instead of listen for it.

Support
● If you find pupils have difficulty in remembering nouns covered, before starting the activity go quickly through some of the flashcards to refresh their memories, asking *Qu'est-ce que c'est?* for each.

Unit 7  Lesson 3

Context
Nationalities

National criteria
KS2 Framework: **O4.2, O4.3, O4.4, L4.1, L4.2, L4.3, L4.4, IU4.4**
Attainment levels: **AT1.1–3, AT2.2, AT3.1–3, AT4.1–2**
Language ladder levels:
   Listening: **Grade 1–3**; Speaking: **Grade 2**;
   Reading: **Grade 1–3**; Writing: **Grade 1–2**

Cross-curricular links
Geography, literacy

Key vocabulary
Nationalities: *français*(e) (French), *canadien*(ne) (Canadian), *britannique* (British)

Language structures and outcomes
Il/Elle est... (He/She is) + nationality

---

1 Starter activity: **Où est le Canada?** ⏱ 5 mins 📖 AT1.1 AT3.1 IU4.4

Materials
Wall map or whiteboard map of the world

Description
Pupils locate France, Canada and Great Britain on a world map.

Delivery
● Ask for volunteers to come and locate the above countries on the map, giving help where required.
● Introduce the French names for the countries (*la France, le Canada, la Grande-Bretagne*).
● Ask pupils if they have visited France or Canada. Ask if they know what languages are spoken in each country.

2 Animated story: **La visite (2)** ⏱ 5–10 mins 📖 AT1.2–3 AT3.2–3 O4.2 L4.1 L4.2

Materials
CD-ROM

Description
Watch and listen to this interactive animated story presenting the language for Lessons 3–4 (introducing nationalities and more ways of describing people). You can pause and rewind the story at any point.

Delivery
● This animated story can be used for both starter and plenary activities – the whole animation can be played at the end of the unit so that pupils can gauge their improved understanding.
● At this point pupils watch the second half of the story only; the first half is in Lesson 1.
Scene 2 (Polly, Didier, Marine and Bernard in a room at the castle)
● Pause the screen on the opening scene, point to Polly and Didier in turn and ask *Il/Elle est comment?* ('What is he/she like?') to elicit and refresh descriptions covered so far.
● Before playing the scene, ask what pupils think will happen next. Play the scene, and compare their predictions with the actual story.
● Ask pupils if they can tell you the names of Didier's cousin (Marine) and the bird (Bernard).

3 Presentation: **De quelle nationalité?** ⏱ 5–10 mins 📖 AT1.2 AT2.2 AT3.2 O4.2 O4.3 L4.1 L4.3

Materials
CD-ROM

Description
Click on a character to hear a presentation of their nationality. Use the additional features to practise sound/spelling links, word classes and spelling.

Delivery
● Invite pupils to click on the characters, one by one. The Virtual Teacher will say the nationality (*Il/Elle est* + nationality).
● Pupils repeat the sentence each time. Repeat each item a couple of times to reinforce learning.

Spelling
● For groups who have already done the alphabet: Point to a character and ask pupils to say/spell the nationality word. Check answer by clicking on the word then on the *Spell* icon.
● To simply introduce the concept of spelling in French, click on a character, then on the *Spell* icon, and point to the letters as the Virtual Teacher says them. Repeat, this time asking the whole class to join in. Continue in the same way with all the words.

Sounds
To further reinforce accurate pronunciation, and to introduce some basic reading skills:
● Point to each word on the text bar and ask the class to say the word.
● Focus on the text on screen, click on the *Sound* icon, and click on the different highlighted sounds to hear the Virtual Teacher saying them.
● Repeat all together.

Word class
● Focus on a word and ask the group what type of word it is (an adjective).
● Click on the *Word* icon to hear the Virtual Teacher say the word class.
● Repeat all together, copying the Virtual Teacher's gestures as you say the word class.

Oracy activity: Les nationalités

c. 10 mins — AT1.2 O4.2 O4.3

Materials
CD-ROM

Description
Click on *Allez*. You will hear an audio clip giving someone's nationality. Click on the correct character.

Delivery
● Click on *Allez* to start the activity. Pupils will hear a description of someone's nationality, e.g. *Il est britannique.* ('He is British.'). Click on the *Encore* button to listen again, if necessary.

● Encourage pupils to repeat the description they hear.

● Pupils must identify the character being described by clicking on them (the flags on their T-shirts indicate their nationality).

● If their selection is correct, the character will become animated and the Virtual Teacher will congratulate them.

● If their selection is wrong, the Virtual Teacher will invite pupils to have another try.

● Repeat a couple of times to reinforce the language.

● Click on *Allez* to hear the next character description.

Extension
● Make two teams. Each team takes it in turn to answer a question and scores a point for each correct answer.

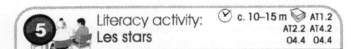

Literacy activity: Les stars

c. 10–15 m — AT1.2 AT2.2 AT4.2 O4.4 O4.4

Materials
Pictures of famous French, Canadian, and British people; Unit 7 Flashcards 12–14 (Flags)

Description
Pupils produce a photo collage of famous people with captions.

Delivery
● Go through the pictures of famous people and ask *Comment s'appelle-t-il/elle?* ('What is he/she called?'). Then ask *Il/Elle est de quelle nationalité?* ('What nationality is he/she?').

● Divide the class into groups. Each group has a large sheet of paper, on which they will stick the pictures and write captions.

● Divide each group into pairs, and give each pair a picture. They work together on writing the caption, then stick the text and picture on to the collage.

Support
● If pupils don't know the celebrities' nationalities, help them out by holding up the appropriately corresponding flag flashcard next to the picture.

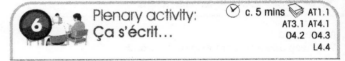

Plenary activity: Ça s'écrit…

c. 5 mins — AT1.1 AT3.1 AT4.1 O4.2 O4.3 L4.4

Materials
Pencils and paper

Description
Pupils identify a celebrity or classmate from the spelling of their name.

Delivery
● Write down a short list of celebrities' or pupils' names for yourself.

● Divide the class into two teams.

● Begin spelling a name; pupils can write down the letters as you spell them out. The first team to guess correctly the full name being spelled wins a point.

● Teams lose a point for each incorrect guess.

Unit 7  Lesson 4

Context
Describing people using various adjectives

National criteria
KS2 Framework: O4.1, O4.2, O4.3, O4.4, L4.1, L4.2, L4.3, L4.4
Attainment levels: AT1.2, AT2.1–2, AT3.1–2, AT4.2
Language ladder levels:
  Listening: **Grade 2**; Speaking: **Grade 1–2**;
  Reading: **Grade 1–2**; Writing: **Grade 2**

Cross-curricular links
Geography

Key vocabulary
Adjectives: *intelligent(e)* (clever), *sportif/sportive* (sporty), *sévère* (strict), *timide* (shy), *français(e)* (French), *canadien(ne)* (Canadian), *britannique* (British)

Language structures and outcomes
Il/Elle est... (He/She is ...)

---

 1 Starter activity: ⏱ 5 mins 📄 AT1.2 AT2.2 O4.2 O4.4
Il est de quelle nationalité?

Materials
Unit 7 Flashcards 1–3 (Nationalities)

Description
Pupils describe characters' nationalities using the flashcards as prompts.

Delivery
● Hold up the flashcards and point to the characters individually. For each character ask *Il/Elle est de quelle nationalité?* ('What nationality is he/she?')

● Elicit answers using *Il/Elle est* + nationality, giving help where needed.

 2 Presentation: ⏱ 5–10 mins 📄 AT1.2 AT2.2 AT3.2 O4.2 O4.3 L4.1 L4.3
Il est comment?
Elle est comment?

Materials
CD-ROM

Description
Click on a character to hear them described (*il/elle est* + adjective). Use the additional features to practise sound/spelling links, word classes and spelling.

Delivery
● Invite pupils to click on the characters, one by one. The Virtual Teacher will describe each one using the target structure (*il/elle est* + adjective).

● Pupils repeat the sentence each time. Repeat each item a couple of times to reinforce learning.

Spelling
● You can practise spelling using the language in this presentation. See the Introduction for notes on how to use this feature of the Language Presentation.

Sounds
● This is a good opportunity to practise sound/spelling links. See the Introduction for notes on how to use this feature of the Language Presentation.

Word class
● This is a good opportunity to practise word classes. See the Introduction for notes on how to use this feature of the Language Presentation.

 Knowledge About Language

Adjective agreements
● This is a good opportunity to revise and extend pupils' understanding of adjective agreements.

● Write the phrases *il est intelligent* and *elle est intelligente* on the board, and *il est français* and *elle est française*. Ask pupils what the difference is between the ways *intelligent* and *français* are spelt, and why this is (when you describe girls or women you have to add an 'e' to the end of the adjective).

● Now write the phrases *un stylo bleu* and *une trousse bleue* on the board. You can remind them that there are two types of noun in French, those that take *un* (masculine) and those that take *une* (feminine). In the same way as adjectives describing girls or women, adjectives describing *une* words also add an 'e'.

● Now write up the phrase *le stylo bleu* on the board, then write the phrase *les stylos bleus* underneath it. Ask pupils if they can tell you what both phrases mean ('the blue pen' and 'the blue pens').

● Ask pupils to spot the difference between the two words for 'blue' (one has an 's'). See if they can suggest why this is – ask them to think how many pens there are in each phrase. Comparing with English may help here.

● If pupils have grasped this, reinforce the concept by writing out pairs of singular and plural nouns and adjectives, leaving a blank letter space at the end of each adjective (e.g. *le stylo bleu_/les stylos bleu_, le stylo bleu_/la trousse bleu_*). Ask pupils what letter should go in each blank, if any.

● You can also point out the fact that not all adjectives follow this pattern – pupils have already met several which fall outside this model. See if they can work out which (*britannique, sévère, timide, jaune, rouge, rose, marron, orange, sympa, drôle*).

---

 3 Oracy activity: ⏱ c. 10 mins 📄 AT2.2 O4.3 O4.4
Il est intelligent

Materials
CD-ROM

Description
Click on *Allez*. You will see various characters highlighted. Correctly describe them using *il/elle est* + characteristics.

Delivery
● Click on *Allez* to start the activity. A character becomes illuminated and pupils must describe that character.

● If needed, you can click on the audio check button in the speech bubble to double-check their answer. Click on the tick or the cross to indicate whether the answer was correct or not.

• Click on *Allez* to move on to the next character.

• Repeat each character a couple of times to reinforce the language.

Extension
• Make two teams. Each team takes it in turn to answer a question and scores a point for each correct answer.

4 Oracy activity: c. 5–10 mins   AT2.2
Ils sont comment?   AT4.2
                   04.1 04.4
                   L4.4

Materials
Unit 7 Flashcards 4–11 (Characteristics), puppets, flashcards of *Rigolo* characters and pictures of characters from stories and films

Description
Pupils use puppets or flashcards and pictures of people or pupils in class to practise building more sentences using *il est/elle est* + characteristics adjectives covered so far.

Delivery
• Point to a puppet or flashcard, or a picture, or a pupil in class and, chorally, make a sentence using the target structure, e.g. *Il est intelligent*; *Elle est sportive*.

• Repeat, until you have covered as many of the adjectives as possible.

Extension
• Display a selection of the pictures and flashcards on the board, and place the puppets on the front desk.

• Divide the class into small groups. Ask each group to write as many sentences as possible, using the displayed props, in five minutes.

• Go round each group and ask how many sentences they managed to write. Ask also for a few examples.

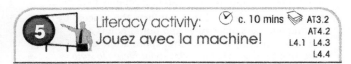

5 Literacy activity: c. 10 mins   AT3.2
Jouez avec la machine!   AT4.2
                   L4.1 L4.3
                   L4.4

Materials
CD-ROM

Description
Drag and drop words from a selection on screen to create descriptive sentences.

Delivery
• Ask pupils to come to the board and drag a word into Monsieur Chanson's machine. Continue until a sentence has been formed, e.g. *Elle est canadienne*.

• If the sentence is grammatically correct, a character matching the description will appear behind the shutter. Otherwise, the machine will 'malfunction', and pupils will be invited to try again.

Extension
• Divide the class into two teams. Each team takes it in turn to build a sentence and scores a point for each correct answer.

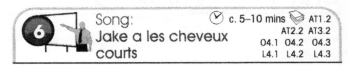

6 Song: c. 5–10 mins   AT1.2
Jake a les cheveux   AT2.2 AT3.2
courts   04.1 04.2 04.3
                   L4.1 L4.2 L4.3

Materials
• CD-ROM or Audio CD, track 13

• Unit 7 Flashcards 1–3 (Nationalities); 4, 5, 8, 9 (Characteristics)

• Prepare cards depicting numbers 8, 9, 10, 11 (enough for one from each category for each pupil)

Description
Watch and listen to the interactive song practising character descriptions. Choose either *Practice* or *Sing* mode: the former to go through the song line by line, the latter to sing it all the way through. Switch the music and words on or off as you prefer.

Delivery
• Hand out one nationality, number and characteristic flashcard to each pupil.

• Freeze the opening screen and ask, for each character, *Il/Elle est de quelle nationalité?* to elicit the lyrics for the chorus. Play the chorus through, asking pupils to join in and wave 'their' nationality flashcard each time they hear 'their' nationality.

• Freeze the screen and focus on the characters' appearances. Ask *Il/Elle est comment?* ('What's he/she like?'), or *Comment sont les cheveux/yeux de... ?* ('What is/are...'s hair/eyes like?') to elicit the next lyrics.

• Follow the same approach for each of the following verses, asking *Quel âge a-t-il/elle?* ('How old is he/she?') or *Il/Elle est comment?* ('What's he/she like?') to elicit the lyrics and get pupils to hold up the corresponding characteristic flashcard.

• Play the song again, this time asking pupils to wave the appropriate nationality, number and characteristic flashcard in the air when their word is sung!

• Go through song again as a whole-class activity, with or without the words or music.

Extension
• **Divide the class into groups of 6–8 pupils.**
• **Each group performs its own version of the song.**
• **The other groups can award points to see which version was the best.**

See the Introduction for more notes on the Song features.

7 Plenary activity: c. 5 mins   AT2.1
Les charades   AT3.1

Materials
Unit 7 Flashcards 4–14 (Characteristics)

Description
Pupils take it in turn to mime an adjective for their classmates to guess.

Delivery
• Divide the class into two teams. In turn, invite one pupil from each team to come and select a card. Alternatively, indicate an adjective from your list.

• The pupil must mime that adjective to their team mates. Teams score two points for a correct answer within 30 seconds; one point for under a minute.

Extension
• If the word has not been correctly guessed after a minute has passed, offer a bonus point to the other team if they have guessed correctly.

Unit 7  Extra!

Worksheet 1A

⏱ 10–15 mins 📖 AT2.2 AT3.3
AT4.2 O4.4
L4.1 L4.3 L4.4

Description
Worksheet to give further practice in reading, writing and saying what characters are like.

Notes
1 & 2 Go through each picture orally as a whole-class activity, before giving pupils a few minutes to write out the sentences.

3 Move around the class as pupils complete Activity 3, to monitor progress and provide help where needed.

Answers
1 a Elle a   c Il a   e Il a   g Elle a
   b Il a   d Elle a   f Elle a   h Il a
2 **Nathalie:** Elle a les cheveux noirs. Elle a un chat.
   Jake: Il a huit ans. Il a un dragon.
   Polly: Elle a les cheveux longs. Elle a un ordinateur.
   Bernard: Il a les yeux jaunes. Il a deux ans.

Worksheet 1B

⏱ 10–15 mins 📖 AT2.2 AT3.2
AT4.2 O4.4
L4.1 L4.3 L4.4

Description
Worksheet to give further practice in reading, writing, and saying what characters are like.

Notes
1 & 2 If necessary, go through each picture orally as a whole-class activity, before giving pupils a few minutes to write out the sentences.

3 Move around the class as pupils complete Activity 3, to monitor progress and provide help where needed.

Answers
1 a Elle a   c Elle a   e Elle a   g Il a
   b Elle a   d Il a   f Il a   h Il a
2 **Nathalie:** Elle a les cheveux noirs. Elle a un chat.
   Madame Moulin: Elle a une machine. Elle a un sandwich.
   Bernard: Il a les yeux jaunes. Il a un sac.
   Didier: Il a sept ans. Il a un gâteau.

Worksheet 2A

⏱ 10–15 mins 📖 AT2.1 AT3.1
AT4.1 O4.2
O4.3 L4.3 L4.4

Description
Worksheet to give further practice in nouns introduced so far.

Notes
1 If necessary, quickly go through each picture orally as a whole-class activity. Alternatively, pupils could work in pairs.

2 Move around the class as pupils complete Activity 2, to monitor progress and provide help where needed.

Answers
1 B – bras, bouche, banane
   C – chien, cahier, chaise
   D – deux, dragon, DVD
   G – garçon, guitare, gomme
   T – tortue, trompette, tambour

 ⚑ **Language Learning Strategies**

Sorting words into categories
● As pupils should now have accumulated a reasonable amount of French vocabulary, activities that help them to see patterns in spelling and sounds are a good way for them to work with language in different contexts.

● You can do further activities like this, getting pupils to count syllables in French words, or sort vocabulary into masculine and feminine groups.

Worksheet 2B

⏱ 10–15 mins 📖 AT2.1 AT3.1
AT4.1 O4.2
O4.3 L4.3 L4.4

Description
Worksheet to give further practice in nouns introduced so far.

Notes
1 If necessary, quickly go through each picture orally as a whole-class activity. Alternatively, pupils could work in pairs.

2 Move around the class as pupils complete Activity 2, to monitor progress and provide help where needed.

Answers
1 B – bras, bouche, banane
   C – chien, cahier, chaise
   D – deux, dragon, DVD
   G – garçon, guitare, gomme
   J – jus d'orange, jambe, jeu vidéo
   L – livre, lapin, lundi
   P – piano, pizza, pomme
   T – tortue, trompette, tambour

Worksheet 3A

⏱ 10–15 mins 📖 AT2.1 AT3.2
AT4.2 L4.1
L4.3 L4.4

Description
Worksheet to give further practice in reading, writing, and describing characters.

Notes
1 Move around the class as pupils complete Activity 1, to monitor progress and provide help where needed.

2 Go through each picture orally as a whole-class activity, by asking pupils to describe each character. Give the class a few minutes to complete the activity.

Answers
2 a Il est canadien.
    Il a les cheveux courts.
    Il a neuf ans.
   b Elle est drôle.
    Elle a les cheveux jaunes.
    Elle est française.
   c Elle est timide.
    Elle a les cheveux longs.
    Elle a le nez long.
   d Il est français.
    Il a les cheveux noirs.
    Il est bavard.

Worksheet 3B

⏱ 10–15 mins 📚 AT2.2 AT3.2
AT4.2 L4.1
L4.3 L4.4

Description
Worksheet to give further practice in reading, writing, and describing characters.

Notes
1. Go through each picture orally as a whole-class activity, by asking pupils to describe each character. Give the class a few minutes to complete the activity.
2. Move around the class as pupils complete Activity 2, to monitor progress and provide help where needed.
3. Pictures and captions from this activity could be used to make a wall display.

Answers
1. **a** Luc   **c** Mme Pomme
   b Sophie   **d** M. Legrand

Worksheet 4A

⏱ 10–15 mins 📚 AT2.1 AT3.1
O4.3 L4.3

Description
Worksheet to give practice in reading words and identifying rhyming patterns.

Notes
1. Go through Activity 1 orally before asking pupils to match the rhyming pairs.
2. Move around the group to monitor Activity 2.

Answers
1. **rhyming pairs:** lundi/samedi, pizza/sympa, Didier/janvier, marron/crayon, décembre/septembre, stylo/rigolo, grand/ans, tambour/bonjour, frère/mère, chien/bien
2. **a** Il a huit **ans**.   **c** Il est **marron**.
   b Il va très **bien**.   **d** Oh, c'est **beau**.

Worksheet 4B

⏱ 10–15 mins 📚 AT2.1 AT3.1
O4.3 L4.3

Description
Worksheet to give practice in reading words and identifying rhyming patterns.

Notes
1. Go through this orally before asking pupils to match the rhyming pairs.
2. Move around the group to monitor Activity 2.

Answers
1. **rhyming pairs:** souris/petit, chat/sympa, guitare/bavard, marron/crayon, tortue/salut, stylo/gâteau, grand/dans, tambour/court, lapin/vingt, chien/combien
2. **a** Il est **bavard**.   **c** Il a un **gâteau**.
   b Il a les yeux **marron**.   **d** Où est mon **chat**?

Project work: Describing someone

⏱ 30–60 mins 📚 AT2.2
AT3.2 AT4.2 O4.1
L4.1 L4.4

Description
Pupils choose someone to describe, and then prepare and deliver a presentation about them.

Materials
Flashcards of *Rigolo* characters, pictures of celebrities, internet access, map of the world

Delivery
● Ask the class if they have a favourite *Rigolo* character. Using the appropriate flashcard, get the class to think about ways of describing someone. Ask deliberately wrong questions so that pupils have to correct you, e.g. for Jake ask, *Il a les cheveux longs?* to elicit *Non – courts!* and eventually *Non! Il a les cheveux courts* or *Il a un chien?* to elicit *Non! Il a un dragon*, and so on.

● Explain that pupils are going to pick somebody to describe to the class. This can be a *Rigolo* character or a celebrity.

● Divide the class into groups. Provide a list of suggested *Rigolo* characters and French, British and Canadian celebrities for the groups to choose from, or, if confident, they can think of one for themselves.

● Provide access to information via magazines and/or the internet, and ask each group to find some information on their chosen person.

● Pupils should then do some research and write up a short report on what they have discovered. Encourage them to add captions to any pictures in French where possible.

● Invite each group to come to the front of the class to deliver their presentation and display any visual aids. These could then be displayed around the classroom.

Support
● You can provide some prompts for the type of information they should look for. These can either be one-word prompts in French or English, or more detailed prompts such as:

● Name: *Il/Elle s'appelle…*

● Age: *Il/Elle a (9) ans*

● Nationality: *Il/Elle est français(e)/canadien(ne)/britannique* (pinpoint on the map which country the person is from)

● Appearance: *Il/Elle a les cheveux (longs/courts)*
Il/Elle a les yeux (bleus/verts/marron) Il/Elle est petit(e)/grand(e)

● Personality: *Il/Elle est intelligent(e)/sportif (sportive)/sévère/ timide/drôle/sympa*

● Other background information: *Il/Elle a (un frère/une sœur).*
Il/Elle s'appelle… Il/Elle a (10) ans
Il/Elle a (un chien/un chat). Il/Elle s'appelle…

Rigolo 1

Unit 8: Quelle heure est-il?

National criteria

KS2 Framework objectives

O4.1	Memorise and present a short spoken text
O4.2	Listen for specific words and phrases
O4.3	Listen for sounds, rhyme and rhythm
O4.4	Ask and answer questions on several topics
L4.1	Read and understand a range of familiar written phrases
L4.2	Follow a short familiar text, listening and reading at the same time
L4.3	Read some familiar words and phrases aloud and pronounce them accurately
L4.4	Write simple words and phrases using a model and some words from memory
IU4.2	Know about some aspects of everyday life and compare them to their own

QCA Scheme of Work

Unit 1	Je parle français
Unit 5	Mon anniversaire
Unit 9	Les sports

Language ladder levels

Listening:	Breakthrough, Grade 1–3
Reading:	Breakthrough, Grade 1–3
Speaking:	Breakthrough, Grade 1–2
Writing:	Breakthrough, Grade 1–2

5–14 guideline strands   Levels A–C

Listening		Reading	
Listening for information and instructions	A, C	Reading for information and instructions	A, C
Listening and reacting to others	A–C	Reading aloud	A, C

Speaking		Writing	
Speaking to convey information	A, C	Writing to exchange information and ideas	A, C
Speaking and interacting with others	B, C	Writing to establish and maintain personal contact	A, C
Speaking about experiences, feelings and opinions	A, B	Writing imaginatively/to entertain	n/a

Unit objectives

- talk about free-time activities
- learn to tell the time
- say what activities you do at certain times

Key language

- activities: *je regarde* (I am watching)… *la télé* (TV), *un DVD* (a DVD); *j'écoute* (I am listening to)… *mes CD* (my CDs), *la radio* (the radio); *je joue* (I'm playing)… *au football* (football), *au tennis* (tennis)
- telling the time: *il est… heure(s)*
- activities at certain times: *Je regarde la télé à cinq heures*, etc.

Grammar and skills

- use several present tense verbs to describe activities
- produce short phrases orally and in writing
- express the time separately or in phrases with other verbs

Unit outcomes

Most children will be able to:

- recognise and repeat various activities
- learn to tell the time in a simple phrase (*Il est cinq heures*, etc.)

Some children will also be able to:

- produce phrases about various activities
- tell the time separately, or in combination with above phrases to create full sentences, e.g. *Je joue au football à cinq heures.*

Unit 8  Lesson 1

Context
Talking about activities

National criteria
KS2 Framework: O4.2, O4.3, L4.1, L4.2, L4.3
Attainment levels: AT1.2–3, AT2.2, AT3.1–3
Language ladder levels:
 Listening: **Grade 2–3**; Speaking: **Grade 1–2**;
 Reading: **Grade 1–3**

Cross-curricular links
PE

Key vocabulary
je regarde (I am watching)… *la télé* (TV), *un DVD* (a DVD);
j'écoute (I am listening to)… *mes CD* (my CDs), *la radio*
(the radio); *je joue* (I'm playing)… *au football* football),
au tennis (tennis)

Language structures and outcomes
As above

---

 1 Starter activity: ⏱ 5–10 mins 📖 AT3.1
Bof dit… O4.2

Materials
Bof puppet

Description
Game based on 'Simon says' to practise classroom instructions.

Delivery
● Revise the target instructions by saying them and doing the actions all together.

● Hold up the Bof puppet and remind pupils of the rules, which are the same as 'Simon says', but each correct instruction will be preceded by *Bof dit* – the usual French game being *Jacques a dit…*

● Begin giving instructions. Pupils must only respond if the instruction is preceded by *Bof dit*, otherwise they are out of the game. The last pupil remaining in the game is the winner.

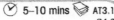 **2** Animated story: ⏱ 5–10 mins 📖 AT1.2–3
Le football (1) AT3.2–3
O4.2
L4.1 L4.2

Materials
CD-ROM

Description
Watch and listen to this interactive animated story presenting the language for Lessons 1 and 2 (leisure activities). You can pause and rewind the story at any point.

Delivery
● This animated story can be used for both starter and plenary activities – the whole animation can be played at the end of the unit so that pupils can gauge their improved understanding.

● At this point pupils watch the first half of the story only; the second half is in Lesson 3.

Scene 1: Polly, Marine, Jake, Didier and Bof

● Tell the class they are going to hear the characters talking about leisure activities. Ask them to predict which ones will feature in this scene.

● Write their suggestions on the board, in French and English if possible. Play the scene through and ask which predictions were correct.

● Leave just the correct suggestions on the board, in random order. Play the scene again, this time asking pupils to note down the order in which the activities appear in the animated story.

● Check the answers at the end of the viewing. Depending on how well the pupils coped with this activity, you may wish to replay the scene for them one more time.

 3 Presentation: ⏱ 5–10 mins 📖 AT1.2
Mes activités AT2.2 AT3.2
O4.2 O4.3
L4.1 L4.3

Materials
CD-ROM

Description
Click on a portrait to hear model sentences describing what activity the character in the portrait is performing. Use the additional features to practise sound/spelling links and word classes.

Delivery
● If possible, ask pupils to stand up to view this presentation, so they can mime the actions as they repeat them.

● Invite pupils to click on the portraits, one by one. The character in the portrait becomes animated and says what they are doing. Pupils repeat the sentence and mime the activity as they do so. Click *Continuez* to return to the "gallery" and click on another portrait, or click *Encore* to listen again.

● Repeat each item a couple of times to reinforce learning.

Word class
● Focus on a phrase, and ask the group what class of word is at the start (a verb).

● Click on the *Word* icon to hear the Virtual Teacher say the word class.

● Repeat all together, copying the Virtual Teacher's gestures as you say the word class.

Sounds
To further reinforce accurate pronunciation, and to introduce some basic reading skills:

● Point to each word on the text bar and ask the class to say the word.

● Focus on the text on screen, click on the *Sound* icon, and click on the different highlighted sounds to hear the Virtual Teacher saying them.

● Repeat all together.

Knowledge About Language

Word classes
● *Rigolo* provides ample opportunity to focus on individual word classes in Units 1–6. As pupils are now encountering longer phrases with several word classes, you can focus on them several at a time.

● In this lesson, take one of the activity phrases above and focus firstly on the verb at the start (*je regarde, j'écoute* or *je joue*). Then focus on the nouns that form the end of each phrase (*la téle, un DVD, mes CD, la radio, football, tennis*).

● Encourage pupils to identify as many word classes as they can in phrases they meet.

4 Oracy activity: Je joue
⏱ c. 10 mins 📓 AT1.2 O4.2

Materials
CD-ROM

Description
Click on *Allez*. You will hear someone describing an activity in the first person. Click on the correct character according to the description.

Delivery
● Click on *Allez* to start (or invite a pupil to start) the activity. You will hear a voice describing an activity one of the characters is doing in the first person, and see three activities. Click on the *Encore* button to listen again, if necessary. Encourage pupils to repeat the description they hear.

● Pupils must identify the character being described by clicking on them.

● If their selection is correct, the character will become animated and the Virtual Teacher will congratulate them. If their selection is wrong, the Virtual Teacher will invite pupils to have another try.

● Click on *Allez* to proceed to the next question.

● Repeat a couple of times to reinforce the language.

Extension
● Make two teams. Each team takes it in turn to answer a question and scores a point for each correct answer.

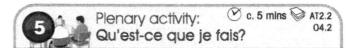

5 Plenary activity: Qu'est-ce que je fais?
⏱ c. 5 mins 📓 AT2.2 O4.2

Materials
Unit 8 Flashcards 1–6 (Leisure activities)

Description
Pupils mime an activity for others to guess, in order to consolidate vocabulary from this lesson.

Delivery
● Ask a pupil to come to the front of the class. Show them a flashcard and ask them to mime the activity for the rest of the class to guess.

● The pupil who guesses correctly then comes to the front to mime another activity.

● Continue as long as time allows.

Extension
● Divide the class into two teams. Pupils mime to their team-mates and score two points for correct answers given within 30 seconds; one point for answers within one minute.

● Offer a bonus point to the other team if the correct answer isn't given after one minute.

Unit 8  Lesson 2

Context
Further practice in talking about activities

National criteria
KS2 Framework: O4.1, O4.2, O4.4, L4.1, L4.2, L4.3, L4.4

Attainment levels: AT1.2–3, AT2.2, AT3.2–3, AT4.2

Language ladder levels:
  Listening: **Grade 2–3**; Speaking: **Grade 2**;
  Reading: **Grade 2–3**; Writing: **Grade 2**

Cross-curricular links
PE

Key vocabulary
Activities: *je regarde* (I am watching)… *la télé* (TV), *un DVD* (a DVD); *j'écoute* (I am listening to)… *mes CD* (my CDs), *la radio* (the radio); *je joue* (I'm playing)… *au football* (football), *au tennis* (tennis)

Language structures and outcomes
As above

---

 1 Starter activity: ⏱ 5 mins 📖 AT2.2 AT4.2 O4.1 O4.4 L4.4
Les passe-temps

Materials
Unit 8 Flashcards 1–6 (Leisure activities)

Description
Pupils use flashcards as prompts for making sentences about leisure activities.

Delivery
● Divide the class into teams.

● Stick the flashcards on the board.

● Point to the cards, one by one, and ask each team to make a sentence, either orally or in writing, using structures and vocabulary already covered. The teams can confer, and score two points for a correct answer within 30 seconds.

● Offer a bonus point to the other team if time runs out.

---

 2 Animated story: ⏱ 5–10 mins 📖 AT1.2–3 AT3.2–3 O4.2 L4.1 L4.2
Le football (1)

Materials
CD-ROM

Description
● To refresh pupils' memories of the story from Lesson 1, watch and listen again to this interactive animated story, presenting the language for Lessons 1 and 2 (sports and activities).

● You can pause and rewind the story at any point.

Delivery
● This animated story can be used for both starter and plenary activities – the whole animation can be played at the end of the unit so that pupils can gauge their improved understanding.

● At this point pupils watch the first half of the story only; the second half is in Lesson 3.

● Before playing the scene, pause and ask pupils what they remember happening. Play the scene, and compare their recollections with the actual story.

---

 3 Oracy activity: ⏱ c. 10 mins 📖 AT1.2 AT2.2 O4.2 O4.4
J'écoute la radio

Materials
CD-ROM

Description
Click on *Allez*. You must correctly describe the activity taking place in each portrait.

Delivery
● Click (or invite a pupil to click) on *Allez* to start the activity. You will see a picture of Bof doing an activity.

● Pupils must make a sentence describing the activity in the first person (e.g. *Je regarde la télé*).

● If necessary, you can use the audio check button in the speech bubble to hear Bof's correct answer. If the pupils answered correctly, click on the tick. If their answer was incorrect, click on the cross, and the Virtual Teacher will invite pupils to try again.

● Click on the *Allez* button to see another picture and to continue the activity.

● Go through each picture twice if necessary, to reinforce learning.

Extension
● Make two teams. Each team takes it in turn to answer a question and scores a point for each correct answer.

---

 4 Literacy activity: ⏱ c. 10 mins 📖 AT3.2 L4.1 L4.3
Je joue au tennis

Materials
CD-ROM

Description
Look at what activity the character is doing and drag the correct speech bubble to the person.

Delivery
● Ask pupils to come to the board and drag the appropriate speech bubble to the character.

● If their answer is correct, the character becomes animated and says what they are doing. In the case of an incorrect answer, the speech bubble will return to its base, and pupils will be invited to try again.

● Click on *Allez* to continue the activity, or *Encore* to hear the phrase again.

● Repeat a couple of times to reinforce the language, if necessary.

Extension
● Divide the class into two teams. Each team takes it in turn to match a picture and a sentence, and scores a point for each correct answer.

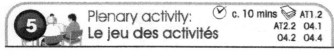

5 Plenary activity: ⏱ c. 10 mins   📚 AT1.2
Le jeu des activités   AT2.2   O4.1
                                            O4.2   O4.4

Materials
Unit 8 Flashcards 1–6 (Leisure activities)

Description
Pupils set up a 'live' multiple-choice game to consolidate vocabulary from this lesson.

Delivery
● Divide the class into groups of four pupils.

● Each group chooses an activity and prepares the game as follows: one pupil will mime the activity (e.g. watching TV), and the other three will each say a sentence describing the activity. Only one of the sentences will correctly describe the activity being mimed, e.g. *Je joue au football, Je regarde la télé, Je joue au tennis.*

● When they have completed their preparation, the groups come to the front one by one. Pupil 1 performs the mime, then the class listens to the three sentences before selecting the correct answer.

Support
● If you find pupils have difficulty in remembering language covered, go through some of the flashcards quickly before the activity to refresh their memories, asking *Qu'est-ce que tu fais?* for each.

Lesson summary

Context
Telling the time

National criteria
KS2 Framework: **O4.1, 4.2, O4.3, O4.4, L4.1, L4.2, L4.3, L4.4**

Attainment levels: **AT1.2–3, AT2.1–2, AT3.2–3, AT4.2**

Language ladder levels:
Listening: **Grade 1–3**; Speaking: **Grade 2;**
Reading: **Grade 1–3**; Writing: **Grade 2**

Cross-curricular links
Numeracy, Literacy, PE

Key vocabulary
Numbers 1–12
Telling time: *il est... heure(s)*

Language structures and outcomes
Quelle heure est-il? (What time is it?)
Il est... [cinq] heures. (It's... [five] o'clock.)

1 Starter activity: ⏱ 5 mins 📖 AT2.1 O4.2
Un, deux, trois...

Materials
Rigolo puppets, soft toys or small beanbags

Description
Pupils practise numbers up to 12 with a fun physical activity.

Delivery
● Quickly revise numbers 1–12 orally as a class.

● Divide the class into two large groups of 10–15 pupils, and give each group a soft toy/beanbag.

● Each group must simply say the numbers 1–12, in order, as fast as possible. A pupil must be in possession of the soft toy to say the number; they must therefore throw the toy to each other as quickly as possible.

● Needless to say, it is vital to lay down some ground rules about throwing the toy gently, or pupils will be eliminated from the game!

2 Animated story: ⏱ 5–10 mins 📖 AT1.2–3
Le football (2) AT3.2–3 O4.2
L4.1 L4.2

Materials
CD-ROM

Description
Watch and listen to this interactive animated story presenting the language for Lessons 3–4 (saying what time you do certain activities). You can pause and rewind the story at any point.

Delivery
● This animated story can be used for both starter and plenary activities – the whole animation can be played at the end of the unit so that pupils can gauge their improved understanding.

● At this point pupils watch the second half of the story only; the first half is in Lesson 1.

Scene 2: Polly and Marine with the clock

● Ask pupils to listen out for what activities Polly and Marine do at four o'clock

● Ask pupils to tell you what the time really is (two o'clock, as Madame Moulin says at the end of the scene).

Extension
● Write numbers 1–5 in a column on the board.

● Ask pupils to jot down the numbers and to place a tick next to each number each time they hear it in the animated story.

● Play the scene through, go through the answers (1 appears twice, 2 appears three times, 3 and 4 appear five times each, and 5 appears four times), then play a second time for pupils to confirm the correct answers.

Support
● If pupils have difficulty in listening out for all numbers 1–5, arrange the class in pairs groups and assign each pair/group one number to listen out for. Then tally their results on the board and watch the story again.

3 Presentation: ⏱ 5–10 mins 📖 AT1.2
Quelle heure est-il? AT2.2 AT3.2
O4.2 O4.3
L4.1 L4.3

Materials
CD-ROM

Description
Click on the numbers on the clock face to see and listen to an animated presentation of the time, from one to 12 o'clock. Use the additional features to practise sound/spelling links.

Delivery
● Pupils click on numbers on the clock face to see and listen to an animated presentation of the time, from one to 12 o'clock.

● This presentation can be done in any order, although you may wish to do it in chronological order first.

● Pupils should repeat each time as they hear it.

● Repeat each item a couple of times to reinforce learning.

Sounds
● This is a good opportunity to practise sound/spelling links. See page ix of the Introduction for notes on how to use this feature of the Language Presentation.

 Knowledge About Language

Question forms
● Point out to pupils that *Quelle heure est-il?* is another question.

● It's a good idea to revise questions that pupils have met so far so they can be aware of the stock of questions (and answers) they now know: *Comment t'appelles-tu?, Ça va?, Qu'est-ce que c'est?, Qu'est-ce que tu as?, C'est de quelle couleur?, Quel âge as-tu?, Tu est comment?, Tu as un animal?, C'est qui?, Qu'est-ce que tu veux?, Il/Elle est comment?, Qu'est-ce que tu fais?* and now *Quelle heure est-il?*

4 Oracy activity: L'heure   c. 10 mins   AT1.2 04.2–3

Materials
CD-ROM

Description
Click on *Allez*. You will hear an audio prompt and must click on the correct number on the clock according to what time you hear.

Delivery
● Click on *Allez* to start the activity. Pupils will hear Madame Moulin say the time.

● Pupils must click on the number on the clock face that corresponds to the time they hear.

● If their selection is correct, the clock sets itself to the correct time, there is an animation and the Virtual Teacher will congratulate them.

● If their selection is wrong, the Virtual Teacher will invite pupils to have another try.

● Click on *Allez* to move on to the next item, or *Encore* as necessary to hear the item again.

● Repeat a couple of times to reinforce the language.

Extension
Make two teams. Each team takes it in turn to answer a question and scores a point for each correct answer.

 5 Literacy activity: Les horloges   c. 10 mins   AT1.2 AT2.2 AT3.2 AT4.2 04.2 L4.1 L4.3 L4.4

Materials
One sheet of blank clock faces for each pupil; 'teaching' clock. Optionally, add sentences under each clock of *Il est _____ heure(s)*.

Description
Dictate times for pupils to complete their clock faces.

Delivery
● Hand out the activity sheets.

● Call out six to eight different times using *Il est... [huit] heures*. (It's [eight] o'clock). Keep a note of the times you call.

● Pupils must draw the hands in the correct positions on their sheets, and write the number into the gap if you have added these underneath.

● Go through the answers by repeating the time you called and asking different pupils to come to the front. Pupils at the front should indicate the time they heard on the teaching clock. Ask the rest of the class if they agree, and confirm (or correct) the answer.

 6 Song: Tic Tac   10–15 mins   AT1.2 AT2.2 04.1 04.2 04.3 L4.1 L4.2 L4.3

Materials
CD-ROM or Audio CD, track 14; Unit 8 Flashcards 8, 11, 13 and 15 (Telling the time)

Description
Watch and listen to the interactive song practising telling the time. Choose either *Practice* or *Sing* mode: the former to go through the song line by line, the latter to sing it all the way through. Switch the music and words on or off as you prefer.

Delivery
● Ask pupils to write the numbers 1–12 on their piece of paper. Ask them to circle each number they hear as they listen to the song.

● Play the song through once in *Sing* mode, and quickly check the answers (2, 5, 7, 9). You can explain that *faire dodo* is French children's slang for 'going to sleep'.

● Go through each verse in *Practice* mode, pausing to check comprehension. Chorally repeat each line, copying the characters' gestures where appropriate.

● Hand out one flashcard to each pupil, ensuring an even distribution of the different times in the class, and also that pupils can remember how to say the time on their card. Play the song again in *Sing* mode; this time pupils must stand up for the verse containing 'their' time and sing along to that verse. You could make it into a competition to see which group sings the best.

● Sing the complete song all together.

Extension
● Divide the class into groups of 6–8 pupils.

● **Each group performs its own version of the song.**

● **The other groups can award points to see which version was the best.**

See the Introduction for more notes on the Song features.

 7 Plenary activity: Quelle heure est-il, Monsieur le Loup?   c. 10 mins   AT1.2 AT2.2 04.2 04.4

Materials
n/a

Description
Game based on 'What's the time, Mr Wolf?'

Delivery
● This game is best played in a large area such as a hall (or playground).

● One player is the 'wolf' (*Le Loup*) and will stand about 5 metres from the others with their back turned.

● The others call out *Quelle heure est-il, Monsieur le Loup?* ('What's the time Mr. Wolf?'). The wolf turns to face the others and shouts out a time, e.g. *Il est [cinq] heures*. ('It's [five] o'clock.'). The others then take five (or however many) steps toward the wolf. If there are space restrictions, pupils can advance one step at a time as is traditional.

● Each time the wolf says a time, the pupils take the corresponding number of steps.

● The wolf turns away from the group again, whilst the others ask the time, turning to face them only as he says the time.

● When the group gets close to the wolf, the wolf will reply *Il est douze heures!* (It's 12 o'clock, i.e. dinnertime!) and will turn to the others. Pupils must try to return to their 'base' before the wolf catches one of them.

● If time allows, the pupil who is caught by the wolf becomes the wolf in the next game.

Extension
● If you think pupils can manage it, introduce the French phrase *Allez! On mange!* alongside *Il est douze heures*. The phrase *on mange* will come up in Unit 11.

Support
You may choose to be the wolf for the first game, or ask a pupil, in which case you need to explain the rules and be on hand with suggestions of times to call out.

Unit 8  Lesson 4

Context
Talking about what time you do activities

National criteria
KS2 Framework: **O4.2, O4.3, O4.4, L4.1, L4.3, L4.4**
Attainment levels: **AT1.2, AT2.2, AT3.2, AT4.2**
Language ladder levels:
Listening: **Grade 2;** Speaking: **Grade 2;**
Reading: **Grade 2;** Writing: **Grade 2**

Cross-curricular links
Numeracy

Key vocabulary
Activities: *je regarde* (I am watching)… *la télé* (TV), *un DVD* (a DVD); *j'écoute* (I am listening to)… *mes CD* (my CDs), *la radio* (the radio); *je joue* (I'm playing)… *au football* (football), *au tennis* (tennis)
Times: …*à [trois] heures*

Language structures and outcomes
As above

---

 1 Starter activity: **Il est une heure**   ⏱ 5 mins 📖 AT2.2 O4.2

Materials
Rigolo puppets, soft toys or small beanbags

Description
Pupils practise telling the time with a fun physical activity.

Delivery
● Quickly revise times (*Il est une heure.* to *Il est douze heures.*) orally as a class.

● Divide the class into two groups of e.g. 10–15 pupils, and give each group a soft toy/beanbag.

● Each group must simply say the time from one to 12 o'clock in order, as fast as possible. A pupil must be in possession of the soft toy to say the time; they must therefore throw the toy to each other as quickly as possible.

● Needless to say, it is vital to lay down some ground rules about throwing the toy gently, or pupils will be eliminated from the game!

---

 2 Oracy activity: **Je joue au tennis à trois heures**   c. 10 mins 📖 AT1.2 AT2.2 O4.2 O4.3 O4.4

Materials
CD-ROM

Description
Look at the images of three different activities happening at different times, listen to the question and say the correct answer out loud.

Delivery
● Click on *Allez* to start the activity. There are three images of a character doing different activities at a specific time, indicated by a different clock for each image.

● Pupils will hear a question asking what the character is doing at a certain time, e.g. *Qu'est-ce que tu fais à quatre heures?* ('What are you doing at four o'clock?').

● Pupils must identify the corresponding image for the question, read the clock time and give the correct answer orally, e.g. *Je joue au football à quatre heures.* ('I'm playing football at four o'clock').

● You can check the answer is correct, if necessary, by clicking on the audio check button in the speech bubble. Click on the tick or the cross to register the pupils' answers. Click on *Encore* to hear the question again.

● If their answer is wrong, the Virtual Teacher will invite pupils to have another try. Correct answers lead to animation of the character doing the activity.

● Click on *Allez* to go on to the next screen.

● Repeat a couple of times to reinforce the language.

Extension
● Make two teams. Each team takes it in turn to answer a question and scores a point for each correct answer.

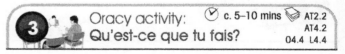 **3** Oracy activity: **Qu'est-ce que tu fais?**   ⏱ c. 5–10 mins 📖 AT2.2 AT4.2 O4.4 L4.4

Materials
Unit 8 Flashcards 1–18 (Leisure activities and Telling the time)

Description
Pupils use flashcard prompts to practise building dialogues about scheduled activities, using language covered so far.

Delivery

● Stick all the flashcards face down on the board, with the time flashcards on the right side and the activity flashcards on the left.

● Model the activity at the front of the class with two pupils. Pupil 1 chooses a flashcard depicting an activity (e.g. watching TV) and asks *Qu'est-ce que tu fais?* and *Tu [regardes la télé] à quelle heure?* ('What are you doing? At what time do you [watch TV]?').

● Pupil 2 selects a time flashcard from the board and makes a reply based on the time on the card (e.g. *Je regarde la télé à [sept heures]*).

● Repeat with another two pupils, using flashcard prompts to make a dialogue based on the same structures.

● Repeat until you have covered as many of the flashcards as possible.

Extension

● Make multiple copies of the flashcards and arrange the class in small groups.

● Each group places the cards face down on their table, and plays the game as above.

● Move around the groups to monitor the activity and offer help where required.

● Encourage those who are able to write down their sentences as well. You can provide a model on the board for the phrases if this will help.

Support

● Help pupils structure their answers by getting them to answer the first half before giving the time, e.g. they say *Je regarde la télé* and then add *à sept heures*.

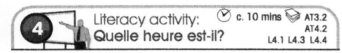

Materials
CD-ROM

Description
Drag word tiles to build sentences describing the time.

Delivery

● Pupils must drag three word tiles, in the correct order, into the designated spaces under the clock face to make a sentence that indicates the time.

● If their answer is correct, the clock becomes animated and sets itself to the time indicated. In case of an incorrect answer, the clock malfunctions and pupils are invited to try again.

● Repeat a couple of times to reinforce the language, if necessary.

Extension

● Divide the class into two teams. Each team takes it in turn to make a sentence, and scores a point for each correct answer.

● Encourage pupils to write down all the sentences that have been created.

Materials
Unit 8 Flashcards 1–18 (Leisure activities and Telling the time)

Description
Pupils match flashcards with sentences on the board.

Delivery

● Choose and copy a set of activity and time flashcards, and make four or five sentences matching the cards, e.g. *J'écoute mes CD à cinq heures*. Write these on the board, with a space next to each phrase where pupils can stick the cards.

● Mix up all the flashcards and stick them in a group at the bottom of the board. Then ask pupils to choose the right cards to match each sentence, and stick these next to the phrase.

● Encourage pupils to read out the sentence before matching the cards.

Extension

● Divide the class into groups, with copies of the same cards for each group. Then ask pupils to repeat the activity as above using large sheets of paper, on which they stick the cards.

Unit 8  Extra!

Worksheet 1A
⏱ 10–15 mins 📖 AT2.2 AT3.2
AT4.1 L4.1
L4.3 L4.4

Description
Worksheet to give further practice of regular verbs in the first person singular.

Notes
1 Go through each picture orally as a whole-class activity, before giving pupils a couple of minutes to write in the missing verbs.
2 Repeat as above.
3 Move around the class as pupils complete Activity 3, to monitor progress and provide help where needed.

Answers
1 a Je **joue** au football.   c Je **regarde** la télé.
  b J'**écoute** mes CD.   d Je **regarde** un DVD.

2 a Je **joue** au tennis.   c J'écoute la **radio**.
  b Je joue au **tennis**.   d Je regarde la **télé**.

Worksheet 1B
⏱ 10–15 mins 📖 AT2.2 AT3.2
AT4.1 04.2
L4.1 L4.3 L4.4

Description
Worksheet to give further practice of regular verbs in the first person singular.

Notes
1 Go through each verb, discussing all the possible options, before giving pupils a few minutes to complete the activity.
2 Look at each gapped sentence and discuss all possible options as a whole-class activity before pupils complete the activity.
3 Move around the class as pupils complete Activity 3, to monitor progress and provide help where needed.

Answers
2 a Je **joue** au tennis.   c J'écoute la **radio**.
  b Je joue au **tennis**.   d Je regarde la **télé**.
  Le mot mystère: Je joue au **football**.

Worksheet 2A
⏱ 10–15 mins 📖 AT2.2 AT3.1–2
AT4.1–2
L4.1 L4.3 L4.4

Description
Worksheet to give further practice in describing leisure activities.

Notes
1 Go through each picture orally as a whole-class activity, before giving pupils a couple of minutes to write in the missing letters.
2 Look at each verb and discuss all possible options as a whole-class activity before pupils complete Activity 2.
3 & 4 Move around the class as pupils complete these two activities, to monitor progress and provide help where needed.

Answers
1 a mes CD   c la télé   e au tennis
  b un DVD   d au football   f la radio

2 j'écoute... mes CD, la radio
  je regarde... la télé, un DVD
  je joue... au football, au tennis

Worksheet 2B
⏱ 10–15 mins 📖 AT2.2 AT3.2
AT4.2
L4.1 L4.3 L4.4

Description
Worksheet to give further practice in describing leisure activities.

Notes
1 Go through verbs and options orally as a whole-class activity, before giving pupils a couple of minutes to write in the words.
2 & 3 Move around the class as pupils complete these activities, to monitor progress and provide help where needed.

Answers
1 j'écoute... mes CD, la radio
  je regarde... la télé, un DVD
  je joue... au football, au tennis

Worksheet 3A
⏱ 10–15 mins 📖 AT2.2 AT3.1
04.2
L4.1 L4.3

Description
Worksheet to give further practice in telling the time.

Notes
1 Give pupils a few minutes to complete Activity 1, then go through the answers.
2 Move around the class as pupils complete Activity 2, to monitor progress and provide help where needed.

Answers
1 a neuf heures   c cinq heures
  b une heure   d onze heures

Worksheet 3B
⏱ 10–15 mins 📖 AT2.2 AT3.2
AT4.1 04.2
L4.1 L4.3 L4.4

Description
Worksheet to give further practice in telling the time.

Notes
1 Give pupils a few minutes to complete Activity 1, then go through the answers.
2 Move around the class as pupils complete Activity 2, to monitor progress and provide help where needed.

Answers
1 a Il est une heure.   c Il est cinq heures.
  b Il est neuf heures.   d Il est onze heures.

Worksheet 4A & 4B
⏱ 10–15 mins 📖 AT2.2 AT3.2
AT4.2
L4.1 L4.3 L4.4

Description
Worksheet to give further practice in writing about scheduled activities.

Notes
1 Give pupils a few minutes to complete Activity 1, then go through the answers.
2 Move around the class as pupils complete Activity 2, to monitor progress and provide help where needed.

Answers

1 a J'écoute la radio à sept heures.
   b Je joue au tennis à dix heures.
   c Je regarde mes DVD à onze heures.
   d Je joue au football à une heure.
   e J'écoute un CD à quatre heures.
   f Je regarde la télé à six heures.

Project work: ⏲ 30–60 mins 📓 IU4.2
Finding out about famous French people

Description
Pupils research famous French-speaking people such as footballers or actors.

Materials
Internet access

Delivery
NB. You may wish to cut out magazine articles and preview some websites via standard search engines before starting this activity. This will save classroom preparation time, and guide pupils to appropriate content on the web.

● Find out if pupils know of any contemporary famous people from France. Are there any sporting personalities, actors or pop stars they know? Pupils' knowledge will probably depend on current media exposure, e.g. a film with a leading French actor, a French tennis player doing well at Wimbledon, or a French racing driver in the news.

● Explain to pupils that in this activity, they will be researching one famous French person. Pupils may work individually or in pairs.

● Provide access to information via magazines and/or the internet, and ask each group to find some basic biographical information on their chosen person. This information can include:
– Personal facts such as how old they are, whether they are married, etc.
– Where they are from (pinpoint which country on the map).
– What they are famous for.
– A photo or picture.
– What they like best about this person.
– Other appropriate information, e.g. for footballers, what team they play for, or for actors, what films they have been in.

● Pupils should then do some research and write up a short report in English (and French where possible) on what they have discovered. Encourage them to add captions to any pictures, in French where possible.

● Once they have completed their research, invite each group to come to the front of the class to deliver their presentation to the class and display any visual aids. These could then be displayed around the classroom.

Support
Pupils may need help in choosing whom to research; if so, suggest some of the following French people:

● Actors: pupils may know Gérard Depardieu from *102 Dalmatians* or the *Astérix et Obélix* films, Jean Reno from various films including *Godzilla*, *The Pink Panther*, *Mission: Impossible* and *The Da Vinci Code*, and Audrey Tautou, also from *The Da Vinci Code*.

● Football players: Thierry Henry, Zinédine Zidane, Patrick Vieira, David Trézéguet, Éric Cantona

● Fictional French characters: Astérix and Obélix, Tintin, Inspector Jacques Clouseau, Jean-Luc Picard from *Star Trek*.

Sound/spelling activity
⏲ 15–20 mins 📓 AT1.1
AT2.1 AT3.1
O4.2 O4.3 L4.3

Description
Practise listening to and pronouncing the sounds *i* and *ch*, and compare your recording to the original. Then count how many times you hear the sounds.

Delivery
● This sound/spelling activity focuses specifically on the *i* and *ch* sounds.

● There are two parts to the activity: the first (*Practice*) allows pupils to familiarise themselves with the two sounds and to compare their pronunciation with Virtual Teacher model. The second part (*Activity*) is an exercise where pupils have to listen out for the sounds within a list of French words that they have encountered so far in *Rigolo*.

● Select *Practice* and click on *Next* to start this part. Then click on *Allez*. The Virtual Teacher will say the *i* sound first on its own, and then as part of three words that have already been used in the Units 7 and 8. For each of these, get the class to repeat the sound or word chorally several times, checking the model each time using the *Encore* button to see how close they are.

● Once you have finished this part, relaunch the activity and choose *Activity* from the selection menu to move on to test pupils' recognition of these sounds. Click on *Allez* to start the activity. Pupils will hear 12 words read out. For each word they must work out whether they can hear the *i* sound or the *ch* sound, then click on the correct button on screen: red if they hear an *i* sound, or green if they hear a *ch* sound. They'll have to listen carefully and click on the right button before the time runs out! Click on *Encore* if you need to hear the word again. You can ask the whole class to vote on what sound they hear, or ask individual pupils to step forward to press the correct button. Once they have completed each answer, you can use the *Encore* button to hear the word again, in order to review their understanding.

● Pupils score a point when they correctly identify the sound within the word. Encourage pupils to try to get all 12 words right to get the highest possible score!

● Repeat the activity again if you feel pupils need further practice.

Extension
● You can continue the practice activity using more words with *i* or *ch* if you feel that pupils have grasped this well, even words not yet covered in *Rigolo*. Can pupils tell you which French word they have met contains both *ch* and *i*? If necessary, give them a clue, e.g. that it's a type of animal. (Answer: *un chien*).

Assessment for Units 7–8

Écoutez!

Play the recording as many times as necessary. Pause the recording during each activity as required.

Total marks for listening: 20. If pupils are getting 8–14/20, they are working at level 1. If they achieve 15–20/20, they are working towards level 2.

Activity 1a   (AT1.1; O4.2, O4.3)
Mark out of 5

Answers
1M   2W   3W   4M   5M

Activity 1b (AT1.1; O4.2)
Mark out of 5

Answers
a1 **b**3 **c**2 **d**5 **e**4

> **1** Il est timide.   **4** Il est britannique.
> **2** Elle est intelligente. **5** Il est français.
> **3** Elle est sévère.

Activity 2 (AT1.1; O4.2)
Mark out of 5

Answers
(*example:* **1** Il est 2 heures.)
2 Il est 6 heures.   **5** Il est 5 heures.
3 Il est 10 heures.   **6** Il est 4 heures.
4 Il est 8 heures.

> **1** (*example*) Il est 2 heures.   **4** Il est 8 heures.
> **2** Il est 6 heures.   **5** Il est 5 heures.
> **3** Il est 10 heures.   **6** Il est 4 heures.

Activity 3a (AT1.2; O4.2)
Mark out of $2\frac{1}{2}$: $\frac{1}{2}$ for each correct answer

Answers
a3 **b**4 **c**1 **d**5 **e**2

> **1** J'écoute mes CD à trois heures. (× 2)
> **2** Je joue au tennis à dix heures. (× 2)
> **3** Je regarde la télé à huit heures. (× 2)
> **4** Je regarde un DVD à six heures. (× 2)
> **5** J'écoute la radio à sept heures. (× 2)

Activity 3b
Mark out of $2\frac{1}{2}$: $\frac{1}{2}$ for each correct answer

Answers
a 8:00   **c** 3:00   **e** 10:00
b 6:00   **d** 7:00

Parlez!

Pupils can work in pairs for the speaking tasks. If it is not possible to assess each pair, then assess a few pairs for each assessment block and mark the rest of the class based on the spoken work they do in class.

Total marks for speaking: 10. Pupils achieving 5/10 are working at level 1; pupils achieving more than 5/10 are working towards level 2.

Activity 1 (AT2.1; O4.4)
5 marks

Answers
example:
A Quelle heure est-il?
B Il est **cinq** heures. (etc.)

Activity 2 (AT2.2; O4.1, O4.4)
5 marks

Answers
Elle a les yeux bleus.
Elle a les cheveux longs.
Elle a un chat.
Elle a un ordinateur.
Elle a dix ans.
Il a les yeux marron.
Il a les cheveux courts.
Il a un chien.
Il a un CD.
Il a neuf ans.

Lisez!

Total marks for reading: 15. Pupils achieving 6–10/15 are working at level 1. Pupils achieving 10 or more out of 15 are working towards level 2.

Activity 1 (AT3.1–2; L4.1, L4.3)
Mark out of 5

Answers
(*example:* 1d) **2**e **3**b **4**a **5**c **6**f

Activity 2 (AT3.2; L4.1)
Mark out of 10

Answers
A Il a les yeux bleus.
Il a neuf ans.
Il a les cheveux longs.
Il a un frère.
Il a un chat.
Il a un DVD.
B Elle a les cheveux courts.
Elle a dix ans.
Elle a les yeux marron.
Elle a un chien.
Elle a un ordinateur.

Écrivez!

For the writing tasks, the copying of words can be approximate.
Total marks for writing: 15. Pupils achieving 6–10/15 are working at level 1. Pupils achieving 10 or more out of 15 are working towards level 2.

Activity 1 (AT4.1; L4.4)
Mark out of 10

Answers
1 quatre   **6** neuf
2 une   **7** trois
3 deux   **8** onze
4 sept   **9** six
5 huit   **10** dix

Activity 2 (AT4.2; L4.4)
Mark out of 5

Answers
a Elle est sportive.   **d** Elle est sévère.
b Il est intelligent.   **e** Il est sportif.
c Elle est timide.

National criteria

KS2 Framework objectives

O4.1	Memorise and present a short spoken text
O4.2	Listen for specific words and phrases
O4.3	Listen for sounds, rhyme and rhythm
O4.4	Ask and answer questions on several topics
L4.1	Read and understand a range of familiar written phrases
L4.2	Follow a short familiar text, listening and reading at the same time
L4.3	Read some familiar words and phrases aloud and pronounce them accurately
L4.4	Write simple words and phrases using a model and some words from memory
IU4.1	Learn about festivals and celebrations in different cultures

QCA Scheme of Work

Unit 1	Je parle français
Unit 2	Je me presente
Unit 3	En famille
Unit 4	Les animaux
Unit 5	Mon anniversaire
Unit 8	Qu'est-ce que tu veux?
Unit 9	Les sports

Language ladder levels

Listening:	Breakthrough, Grade 1–3
Speaking:	Breakthrough, Grade 1–2
Reading:	Breakthrough, Grade 1–3
Writing:	Breakthrough, Grade 1–2

5–14 guideline strands · Levels A–C

Listening

Listening for information and instructions	A, C
Listening and reacting to others	A–C

Speaking

Speaking to convey information	A, C
Speaking and interacting with others	B, C
Speaking about experiences, feelings and opinions	A, B

Reading

Reading for information and instructions	A, C
Reading aloud	A, C

Writing

Writing to exchange information and ideas	A, C
Writing to establish and maintain personal contact	A, C
Writing imaginatively/to entertain	n/a

Unit objectives

- say the names and dates of several French festivals
- identify and ask for certain presents at festivals
- recognise and use numbers 31–60
- give and understand more instructions

Key language

- festivals: *le Nouvel An* (New Year), *la Fête des Rois* (Feast of Kings/Epiphany), *la Saint-Valentin* (St Valentine's day), *Pâques* (Easter), *la Fête Nationale* (Bastille Day), *Noël* (Christmas)
- presents: *un vélo* (bike), *un jeu* (a game), *un livre* (a book), *un ballon* (a ball), *un Père Noël en chocolat* (chocolate Father Christmas), *un œuf de Pâques* (Easter egg)
- numbers 31–60
- instructions: *touchez le nez/les pieds!* (touch your nose/feet!), *comptez!* (count!), *sautez!* (jump!), *levez les bras!* (raise your arms!), *tournez!* (turn around!), *hochez la tête!* (nod your head!)

Grammar and skills

- give more dates for festivals through the year
- ask for various presents
- count up to 60
- understand and give imperative instructions
- recognise plural forms

Unit outcomes

Most children will be able to:

- recognise names of French festivals, and list their dates separately
- identify names of various presents suitable for festivals
- count up to 60
- understand more instructions

Some children will also be able to:

- produce fuller phrases giving dates of festivals, e.g. *Le nouvel an, c'est le premier janvier.*
- create sentences asking for gifts, using *je voudrais...*

Unit 9   Lesson 1

Context
Talking about festivals and dates

National criteria
KS2 Framework: **O4.2, O4.3, O4.4, L4.1, L4.2, L4.3, IU4.1**
Attainment levels: **AT1.1–3, AT2.1–2, AT3.1–3**
Language ladder levels:
Listening: **Grade 1–3**; Speaking: **Grade 1–2**;
Reading: **Grade 1–3**

Cross-curricular links
Numeracy, PE, Citizenship

Key vocabulary
Festivals: *le Nouvel An* (New Year), *la Fête des Rois* (The Feast of Kings/Epiphany), *la Saint-Valentin* (St Valentine's day), *Pâques* (Easter), *la Fête Nationale* (Bastille Day), *Noël* (Christmas)

Language structures and outcomes
Le [*nouvel an*], c'est le [*premier janvier.*] ([New Year] is on the [1st January.])

---

1 Starter activity: ⏱ 5 mins 📖 IU4.1
Les fêtes et les jours fériés

Materials
n/a

Description
Starter discussion to focus pupils' attention on the topic of festivals and significant dates.

Delivery
● Talk about pupils' own favourite national and cultural festivals.

● Ask pupils to tell you in which month (or, possibly, on which date) the festival takes place.

● Explain that French people also celebrate some of their own festivals, in addition to some others.

2 Oracy activity: ⏱ c. 5–10 mins 📖 AT1.2 AT2.2 O4.4
Les dates et les nombres

Materials
n/a

Description
Pupils answer questions in order to revise dates.

Delivery
● Quickly revise numbers up to 31 and the months, chorally.

● Ask *Quelle est la date aujourd'hui?*. If no-one answers, write the date on the board, repeat the question and say the answer, pointing to it at the same time.

● Now ask *C'est quand, ton anniversaire?* to see if pupils remember and can answer the question. Prompt if necessary.

● Ask both questions quickly and randomly to pupils across the classroom to continue the revision.

3 Animated story: ⏱ 5–10 mins 📖 AT1.2–3 AT3.1–3 O4.2 O4.3 L4.1 L4.2 IU4.1
La machine magique (1)

Materials
CD-ROM

Description
Watch and listen to this interactive animated story, based in the castle kitchen, presenting the language for Lessons 1 and 2 (dates and festivals). You can pause and rewind the story at any point.

Delivery
● This animated story can be used for both starter and plenary activities – the whole animation can be played at the end of the unit so that pupils can gauge their improved understanding.

● At this point pupils watch the first half of the story only; the second half is in Lesson 3.

Scene 1: Polly and Marine in the castle kitchen

● Freeze the screen on the characters standing in the kitchen. Ask pupils to introduce them, using as much as possible of the language covered so far.

● Continue playing the scene until the magic machine is revealed. Freeze the screen and ask pupils what they think the machine is for. Play the rest of the scene through and ask if their predictions were correct.

● Ask pupils which, if any, festivals they remember seeing on the screens.

● Summarise the scene together.

4 Presentation: ⏱ 5–10 mins 📖 AT1.2 AT2.2 AT3.2 O4.2 O4.3 L4.1 L4.3 IU4.1
Les fêtes

Materials
CD-ROM

Description
Click on an image to hear the festivals and their dates. Use the additional features to practise sound/spelling links.

Delivery
● Invite pupils to click on the images, one by one. The image becomes animated and the Virtual Teacher or audio says what the festival is, and what date it is. Click on *Continuez* to reset and move on to the next image.

● The audio can be repeated as many times as necessary by clicking on *Encore*, and pupils can repeat the language.

● Repeat each item a couple of times to reinforce learning.

Sounds
To further reinforce accurate pronunciation, and to introduce some basic reading skills:

● Point to each word on the text bar and ask the class to say the word.

● Focus on the text on screen, click on the *Sound* icon, and click on the different highlighted sounds to hear the Virtual Teacher saying them.

● Repeat all together.

NB. If the *Sound* icon is not illuminated, that means it is not applicable for that particular word.

Cultural information

French festivals

- Although several French festivals are featured on the CD-ROM in this lesson, due to language restrictions the best way to explain the origin of these festivals is to discuss them with your class in English. Below is some basic information about each festival.

- **le Nouvel An** (New Year): celebrated in a similar way to the UK, with a countdown to midnight. Most French people have a meal with friends or family. In Paris, everybody stops what they are doing at midnight, and drivers honk their car horns for several minutes. Parties will go on until 5 or 6am, and people eat onion soup for breakfast.

- **la Fête des Rois** (Feast of Kings/Epiphany): celebrated on 6th January. The tradition is to eat a flat round pastry cake called *une galette des rois*, filled with almond paste or fruit. There is a charm (*la fève*) hidden inside, and the person who discovers it in their portion is crowned the king or queen and wears a paper crown. You could compare this with Christmas pudding in the UK.

- **la Saint-Valentin** (St Valentine's Day): again, similar to the UK, although in France couples don't send each other cards, but offer gifts or go out for a meal instead.

- **Pâques** (Easter): as in the UK, children receive presents of eggs or chocolate rabbits. There is usually a treasure hunt round the garden or house where children search for eggs. The traditional family meal at Easter is lamb.

- **la Fête Nationale** (also called *La fête de la Bastille*: Bastille Day): on the 14th July, the whole of France celebrates the day when the Bastille prison was overthrown and burnt down at the start of the French Revolution in 1789. There is a big fireworks display in most cities, and everyone holds parties.

- **Noël** (Christmas): Christmas is similar between the two countries for those who celebrate it, with a few notable differences as well. The Christmas tree (*le sapin de Noël*) is decorated only a few days before the 25th, and parents – or *le Père Noël* – hang toys, sweets and fruit on the tree on Christmas Eve while children are asleep. Christian families also arrange a *crèche* (crib) display with wooden or plastic figures representing the birth of Jesus. They also go to a mass in church at midnight. There is a bigger traditional meal in France on Christmas Eve than in the UK, called *le réveillon*. The usual meal on Christmas Day involves oysters, turkey or goose.

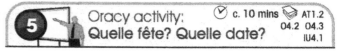

5 Oracy activity: **Quelle fête? Quelle date?** c. 10 mins AT1.2 04.2 04.3 IU4.1

Materials
CD-ROM

Description
Click on *Allez* to hear audio prompts about festivals and dates, decide if the statement is correct or not, and click on *Oui* or *Non*.

Delivery
- Click on *Allez* to start (or invite a pupil to start) the activity. You will hear the name of a festival and see an image. Click on the *Encore* button to listen again, if necessary. Encourage pupils to repeat the description they hear.

- Pupils must decide whether or not the information they hear is correct and/or matches the image, then click on *Oui* or *Non* as appropriate.

- If their selection is correct, the image will become animated and the Virtual Teacher will congratulate them.

- If their selection is wrong, the Virtual Teacher will invite pupils to have another try.

- Repeat a couple of times to reinforce the language.

- Click on *Allez* to go to the next image/audio.

Extension
Make two teams. Each team takes it in turn to answer a question and scores a point for each correct answer.

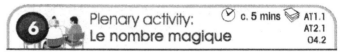

6 Plenary activity: **Le nombre magique** c. 5 mins AT1.1 AT2.1 04.2

Materials
Ball or soft toy

Description
Pupils throw the ball to each other as they say numbers from 1 to 31, in order.

Delivery
- Quickly revise numbers orally as a class.
Ask the class to choose a 'magic' number (*un nombre magique*). Anyone who says this number is eliminated from that round of the game, and must sit down until someone else has said the magic number.

- All pupils stand in a circle, and throw the ball/toy to each other. Pupils must say the numbers 1–31, in order, as fast as possible. A pupil must be in possession of the soft toy to say the number; they must therefore throw the toy to each other as quickly as possible. Pupils saying the *nombre magique* miss a turn, as described above.

- As always, it is vital to lay down some ground rules about throwing the toy gently, or pupils will be eliminated from the game!

Extension
- Divide the class into groups and give each group a magic number.

- Pupils can play the game in smaller groups as above.

Unit 9 — Lesson 2

Context
Talking about presents at festivals

National criteria
KS2 Framework: **O4.2, O4.3, O4.4, L4.1, L4.3, L4.4**
Attainment levels: **AT1.1–2, AT2.1–2, AT3.1–2**
Language ladder levels:
  Listening: **Grade 1–2;** Speaking: **Grade 1–2;**
  Reading: **Grade 1–2;** Writing: **Grade 2**

Cross-curricular links
Citizenship

Key vocabulary
Presents: *un vélo* (bike), *un jeu* (a game), *un livre* (a book), *un ballon* (a ball), *un Père Noël en chocolat* (chocolate Father Christmas), *un œuf de Pâques* (Easter egg)

Language structures and outcomes
Qu'est-ce que tu veux [comme cadeau]? (What [present] would you like?)
Je voudrais [+ *nom.*] (I'd like [+ noun.])

 1 Starter activity: Encore des fêtes — ⏱ 5 mins AT2.1

Materials
Unit 9 Flashcards 1–6 (Festivals)

Description
Starter game, using flashcards to revise French festivals and dates.

Delivery
● Divide the class into two teams.
● Hold up one flashcard to one of the teams and ask them to tell you which festival it is in French (*C'est quelle fête?*). Teams win one point if they name the festival correctly, and an extra point if they can tell you the date.
● Alternate questions between the two teams, and add up points at the end.

 2 Presentation: Les cadeaux — ⏱ 5–10 mins AT1.1–2 AT2.1–2 AT3.1–2 O4.2 O4.3 L4.1 L4.3

Materials
CD-ROM

Description
Click on a present to hear its name. Use the additional features to practise sound/spelling links, word classes and spelling.

Delivery
● Invite pupils to click on the presents, one by one. Pupils will hear the name of the object, then Bof will say that he would like that particular present, using the target structure (*je voudrais* + noun). The unwrapped present is shown in his thought bubble.
● Pupils repeat the object and target structure sentence.
● Repeat each item a couple of times to reinforce learning.
● Click on another object to continue.

Spelling
● For groups who have already done the alphabet: Point to an image and ask pupils to say/spell the word. Check answer by clicking on the word then on the *Spell* icon.
● To simply introduce the concept of spelling in French, click on an image, then on the *Spell* icon, and point to the letters as the Virtual Teacher says them. Repeat, this time asking the whole class to join in. Continue in the same way with all the words.

Word class
● Focus on a word and ask the group what type of word it is.

● Click on the *Word* icon to hear the Virtual Teacher say the word class.
● Repeat all together, copying the Virtual Teacher's gestures as you say the word class.

Sounds
To further reinforce accurate pronunciation, and to introduce some basic reading skills:
● Point to each word on the text bar and ask the class to say the word.
● Focus on the text on screen, click on the *Sound* icon, and click on the different highlighted sounds to hear the Virtual Teacher saying them.
● Repeat all together.

 3 Oracy activity: Qu'est-ce que tu veux comme cadeau? — ⏱ c. 10 mins AT2.2 O4.4

Materials
CD-ROM

Description
Click on *Allez*. Imagine you are Didier. Look at the present he is thinking of and say out loud what you would like.

Delivery
● Click on *Allez* to start (or invite a pupil to start) the activity. You will see a present appear in Didier's thought bubble. Pupils must identify the present, then answer on behalf of Didier by saying what he would like, using *Je voudrais*. You can click on the audio check button in the speech bubble to confirm the answer if necessary.
● If pupils' guess is correct, click on the tick button. The scene will be animated and the Virtual Teacher will congratulate them.
● If their selection is wrong, click on the cross, and the Virtual Teacher will invite pupils to have another try.
● Repeat a couple of times to reinforce the language.
● Click on *Allez* to go to the next present.

Extension
Make two teams. Each team takes it in turn to answer a question and scores a point for each correct answer.

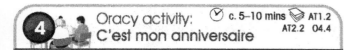

4 Oracy activity: c. 5–10 mins AT1.2 AT2.2 O4.4
C'est mon anniversaire

Materials
Units 1, 2, 4 and 5 Flashcards (nouns)

Description
Pupils use flashcard prompts to practise the target structure of *Je voudrais* + noun.

Delivery
- Quickly revise the nouns on the flashcards chorally.
- Stick the flashcards face down on the board.
- Invite a pupil to the front to take a flashcard off the board. Ask *Qu'est-ce que tu veux (comme cadeau)?*. They must reply using *Je voudrais* + the noun on the card.
- Repeat several times with different pupils and cards.

5 Literacy activity: c. 10 mins AT3.2 L4.1 L4.3
Je voudrais…

Materials
CD-ROM

Description
Drag and drop words to build two sentences describing what gifts you would like for different special occasions.

Delivery
- Ask pupils to come to the board and drag words into the gaps in the two sentences at the top of the machine.
- If their sentences are grammatically correct, the corresponding image will come out of the machine. In the case of a grammatically incorrect answer, the machine will malfunction and black smoke appears.

- If the sentence is grammatically correct but illogical (e.g. asking for an Easter egg for Christmas) there is appropriate animation to show that this is a strange, but grammatically acceptable, answer.
- Repeat a couple of times to reinforce the language if necessary.

Extension
Make two teams. Each team takes it in turn to make sentences, and scores a point for each correct answer.

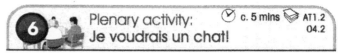

6 Plenary activity: c. 5 mins AT1.2 O4.2
Je voudrais un chat!

Materials
Units 1, 2, 4 and 5 Flashcards (nouns)

Description
Pupils run to the front of the class with their flashcard when they hear 'their' word called out.

Delivery
- Quickly hand out a few of the flashcards from the previous flashcard activity to pairs or small groups of pupils around the room.
- Make a sentence e.g. *Je voudrais [un chat]*. The pupil with the cat flashcard must come as quickly as they can to the front and stick their card on the board.
- Repeat as often as possible in the time allowed.

Support
If you find pupils have difficulty in remembering the nouns, go through some of the flashcards quickly to refresh their memories, asking *Qu'est-ce que c'est?* for each.

Unit 9 Lesson 3

Context
Numbers 31–60

National criteria
KS2 Framework: **O4.2, O4.3, O4.4, L4.1, L4.2, L4.3**
Attainment levels: **AT1.1–3, AT2.1, AT3.1–3**
Language ladder levels:
  Listening: **Grade 1–3**; Speaking: **Grade 1**;
  Reading: **Grade 1–3**

Cross-curricular links
Numeracy, PE

Key vocabulary
Numbers 31–60

Language structures and outcomes
As above

---

1 Starter activity:
Le jeu des nombres

⏱ 5 mins 📖 AT1.1
AT2.1 AT3.1
O4.2 L4.1

Materials
Pieces of paper with each of numbers 1 to 31 written on them,
either as a numeral or a word.

Description
Starter game to give further practice of numbers 1–31.

Delivery
● Distribute the pieces of paper to pupils, randomly. If you
have fewer than 31 pupils, give more than one piece of paper
to more confident pupils.

● Pupils must look at their number and memorise it, without
showing it to the others.

● Ask the pupil who has got number 1 to begin by shouting
out their number. The rest of the class follows, saying their
numbers in order. This can be in a military style if you wish.

● Once pupils are familiar with the game, repeat, this time as
fast as possible.

● Try varying the game by having words instead of numerals
on the pieces of paper.

2 Animated story:
La machine
magique (2)

⏱ 5–10 mins 📖 AT1.2–3
AT3.2–3
O4.2 O4.3
L4.1 L4.2

Materials
CD-ROM

Description
Watch and listen to this interactive animated story presenting
the language for Lessons 3–4 (numbers up to 60 and
imperatives). You can pause and rewind the story at any
point.

Delivery
● This animated story can be used for both starter and plenary
activities – the whole animation can be played at the end of the
unit so that pupils can gauge their improved understanding.

● At this point pupils watch the second half of the story only;
the first half is in Lesson 1.

Scene 2: Polly, Marine and Madame Moulin in the castle dungeon

● Before playing the scene, ask pupils to recap the first half of
the animated story. Ask them if they think Madame Moulin is
happy with the children.

● Freeze the screen on the opening scene so pupils can see
that the children have been taken down to the basement/
dungeon. Now ask the class what exercises they think
Madame Moulin will make the children do as punishment.

● Play the rest of the scene through and ask if their
predictions were correct.

● Summarise the scene together.

3 Presentation:
Les nombres 31–60

⏱ 5–10 mins 📖 AT1.1
AT2.1 AT3.1
O4.2 O4.3
L4.1 L4.3

Materials
CD-ROM

Description
Click on a number to hear and see it presented, or listen to a
group of numbers presented in sequence. Use the additional
features to practise sound/spelling links and spelling.

Delivery
● First of all select the group of numbers you would like to
present, using the *31-40*, *41-50* and *51-60* buttons on the right-
hand side. To listen to the whole group counted in sequence,
click on *Comptez*. There will be an audio presentation of those
numbers, with gaps to enable pupils to repeat. The numbers
will be highlighted as the Virtual Teacher says them.

● Once the Virtual Teacher has read out the sequence, the
numbers can be presented in isolation, by clicking on the
individual numbers along the bottom of the screen. The audio
can be repeated as many times as necessary.

● Use the buttons on the right-hand side to change to a
different group of numbers at any point.

● Repeat each group of numbers a couple of times to reinforce
learning.

Spelling
● For groups who have already done the alphabet: Point to a
number and ask pupils to say/spell the word. Check answer
by clicking on a number then on the *Spell* icon.

● To simply introduce the concept of spelling in French, click on
a number, then on the *Spell* icon, and point to the letters as the
Virtual Teacher says them. Repeat, this time asking the whole
class to join in. Continue in the same way with all the words.

Sounds
To further reinforce accurate pronunciation, and to introduce
some basic reading skills:

● Focus on the text on screen, click on the *Sound* icon, and
point to the highlighted sounds as they are being said by the
Virtual Teacher.

● Repeat all together.

Extension
● Divide the class into three groups. Each group must chant
the numbers 31–40, 41–50, or 51–60, as in the presentation.

4 Oracy activity: Qui gagne? ⏱ c. 10 mins 📖 AT1.1 AT2.1 O4.2 O4.4

Materials
CD-ROM

Description
Click on *Allez*. Predict which numbered dragon will win in a series of races, and practise numbers up to 60.

Delivery
● Click on *Allez* to start the activity. At the end of each dragon race pupils will hear *Qui gagne? C'est quel numéro?* ('Who wins? Which number is it?') and must say the number of the winning dragon.

● If necessary, you can verify the answer by clicking on the audio check button in the speech bubble.

● If the pupil's answer is correct, click on the tick to see the reward animation; otherwise, click on the cross and the Virtual Teacher will invite pupils to try again.

● Click on *Allez* to go to the next race.

Extension
● Make two teams. Each team takes it in turn to say which dragon wins, and scores a point for each correct answer.

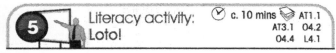

5 Literacy activity: Loto! ⏱ c. 10 mins 📖 AT1.1 AT3.1 O4.2 O4.4 L4.1

Materials
CD-ROM

Description
Play bingo in teams, either using completed cards, or filling in your own cards on-screen or using a printed grid. Then mark off the sentences on your card if you see the sentence appear on-screen. The first player or team with all their sentences marked off wins!

Delivery
There are three ways of playing the bingo game:

● *Ready to go*: the computer automatically completes two grids for each team. Team members mark off sentences on their grid as pictures appear on-screen.

● *Make your own*: as above, but teams complete their grids with their choice of sentences on-screen.

● *Print your own*: as *Ready to go*, but print off blank lotto grids from the CD-ROM, which pupils fill in with their choice of sentences from those listed on-screen.

● When you are ready to start the game, call up a member of each team to click on the card.

● Click on *Allez* to make each number appear. When pupils hear a number from their grid, they must either click on the relevant square, or mark the square off on their printed grid.

● When the first on-screen grid is complete, there will be a celebratory animation.

● If playing with printed grids, then the first player to complete filling in their grid calls out *Gagné!*

● Click on the *Jouez encore?* ✓ again to play another game, if time allows.

Support
● You can play with or without sound by clicking on the *Audio on/Audio off* button on the taskbar at the bottom. With sound on, pupils will hear each number spoken as it appears.

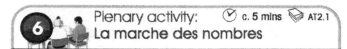

6 Plenary activity: La marche des nombres ⏱ c. 5 mins 📖 AT2.1

Materials
n/a

Description
Pupils march or chant numbers military-style, as in this lesson's Language Presentation.

Delivery
● Quickly revise the target numbers orally as a class.

● Divide the class into three groups. Each group must chant – as they march, if space allows – their number group (31–40, 41–50, or 51–60).

● Swap groups/number groups and repeat, if time allows.

NB. You will need a large area (hall or playground) if you opt for the marching version of this activity!

Unit 9 — Lesson 4

Lesson summary

Context
Giving and understanding instructions

National criteria
KS2 Framework: **O4.1, O4.2, O4.3, O4.4, L4.1, L4.2, L4.3, L4.4**
Attainment levels: **AT1.1–2, AT2.1–2, AT3.1–2, AT4.1**
Language ladder levels:
Listening: **Grade 1–2**; Speaking: **Grade 1–2**;
Reading: **Grade 1–2**; Writing: **Grade 1**

Cross-curricular links
Numeracy, Literacy, ICT

Key vocabulary
Instructions: *touchez le nez/les pieds!* (touch your nose/feet!), *comptez!* (count!), *sautez!* (jump!), *levez les bras!* (raise your arms!), *hochez la tête!* (nod your head!)

Language structures and outcomes
As above

---

1 Starter activity: **Levez-vous!** ⏱ 5 mins 📖 AT1.2 / AT2.1 / O4.2

Materials
Seven strips of paper with instructions written on

Description
Starter activity to revise instructions covered so far in the units.

Delivery
● Write down instructions pupils met in Unit 2 on seven separate strips of paper: *regardez* (look/watch), *levez-vous* (stand up), *asseyez-vous* (sit down), *écoutez* (listen), *écrivez* (write), *lisez* (read), *chantez* (sing)
● Choose a pupil to come to the front of the class and give them a strip of paper.
● The pupil must mime the action and other pupils have to guess quickly what the instruction is.
● The first pupil who correctly guesses the instruction comes to the front of the class and performs the next mime.
● Continue in the same way with all seven instructions, keeping the pace as brisk as possible.

2 Presentation: **Les ordres** ⏱ 5–10 mins 📖 AT1.1–2 / AT2.1–2 AT3.1–2 / O4.2 O4.3 / L4.1 L4.3

Materials
CD-ROM

Description
Click on an icon to hear and see a presentation of new commands. Use the additional features to practise sound/spelling links.

Delivery
● Invite pupils to click on an icon, one by one. Madame Moulin will shout the corresponding order at the children on screen, who will respond accordingly. The Virtual Teacher then repeats the order if she is switched on.
● Pupils should repeat the sentence each time they hear it, and copy the action.
● Repeat each item a couple of times to reinforce the language.

Sounds
● This is a good opportunity to practise sound/spelling links. See the Introduction for notes on how to use this feature of the Language Presentation.

 Knowledge About Language

Plurals
● Focus on plural forms of nouns at this point. Pupils have already encountered *les yeux* and *les cheveux* in Units 3 and 7, so you can draw upon several different nouns that will be familiar to them.
● Write the words *le pied* and *les pieds* on the board, and ask pupils what they mean ('the foot' and 'the feet').
● Ask pupils to point out the differences between the two phrases which show that *les pieds* is plural. (*Les* is the word for 'the' when there is more than one of a noun, and there is an 's' at the end of the word.)
● Compare between English and French by asking how you usually form plurals in English (also by adding an 's').
● Ask pupils who have easily grasped this point if they can think of any exceptions to this rule in English. An immediate one is listed above ('foot/feet'). Explain that in French there are exceptions as well: *le bras/les bras* (already ends in an 's'), *le cheveu/les cheveux* (uses an 'x' instead) or the most extreme case, *l'œil/les yeux* (different words altogether!). They will learn more of these exceptions as they progress in French.

3 Oracy activity: **Quel ordre?** ⏱ c. 10 mins 📖 AT1.2 / O4.2 O4.4

Materials
CD-ROM

Description
Click on *Allez*. Listen to the commands and identify which character is performing the right action.

Delivery
● Click on *Allez* to start the activity. You will hear Madame Moulin giving an instruction and see three characters demonstrating three different actions.
● Pupils click on the character performing the action that corresponds to the command they hear.
● Click on *Encore* to listen again, if necessary. Encourage pupils to repeat the instruction they hear.
● If their selection is correct, the character will become animated and the Virtual Teacher will congratulate them.
● If their selection is wrong, pupils lose one of three lives, and the Virtual Teacher will invite pupils to have another try. If all three lives are lost, the activity is ended and pupils are invited to try again.
● Repeat a couple of times to reinforce the language.

Extension
● Make two teams. Each team takes it in turn to answer a question and scores a point for each correct answer.

4 Oracy activity: Jeu de rôle   ⏱ c. 5 mins   AT1.2 AT2.2 O4.2

Materials
n/a

Description
Pupils re-enact extracts from the Language Presentation activity to revise commands.

Delivery
● Ask pupils to tell you which commands Madame Moulin gives the children in the Language Presentation. Go through them, making sure the pupils understand which actions are required: *touchez le nez/les pieds!* (touch your nose/feet!), *comptez!* (count!), *sautez!* (jump!), *levez les bras!* (raise your arms!), *hochez la tête!* (nod your head!)

● Write the commands in French on the board as pupils remember them.

● Divide the class into small groups. Each group will act out Madame Moulin giving the children orders.

● One pupil takes on the role of Madame Moulin and the others must obey her orders.

● Encourage a brisk pace so that pupils have time to practise all the commands in the time allocated.

Support
● Be on hand to prompt the pupils if they have difficulty in remembering what the commands mean.

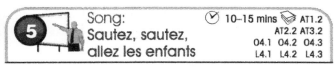

5 Song: Sautez, sautez, allez les enfants   ⏱ 10–15 mins   AT1.2 AT2.2 AT3.2 O4.1 O4.2 O4.3 L4.1 L4.2 L4.3

Materials
CD-ROM or Audio CD, track 15

Description
Watch and listen to the interactive song practising numbers and orders. Choose either *Practice* or *Sing* mode: the former to go through the song line by line, the latter to sing it all the way through. Switch the music and words on or off as you prefer.

Delivery
● Play the first verse through, and ask pupils to join in with the actions.

● Pause the song and ask pupils to tell you and show you the actions from that verse.

● Play the remaining verses, asking pupils to join in with the actions and commands.

● Divide the class into three groups: each group is responsible for singing the numbers in a given verse. Quickly go through their numbers chorally. Go through the song all the way through: everyone joins in with the actions in each verse, and the individual groups sing their group of numbers.

Extension
● Divide the class into groups of 6–8 pupils.

● **Each group performs its own version of the song.**

● **The other groups can award points to see which version was the best.**

See the Introduction for more notes on the Song features.

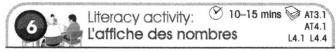

6 Literacy activity: L'affiche des nombres   ⏱ 10–15 mins   AT3.1 AT4.1 L4.1 L4.4

Materials
Paper, pencils and colour crayons; possibly computer Clip Art; Units 1, 2, 4 and 5 Flashcards – Nouns

Description
Pupils combine French numbers and nouns learned so far to make a number wall chart for the classroom.

Delivery
● Either prepare a list of numbers with nouns (e.g. *trente chats*), or ask pupils to choose their own combination (using the flashcards as prompts if you wish). If Clip Art isn't available, it may not be feasible to produce multiple pictures for the higher numbers, so you may want pupils simply to add the number in numerical and word form.

● Pupils then draw/write out their number + noun(s) on a piece of A4 card or paper.

● When everyone has finished, the papers can be taped together to make a wall display.

NB. If preferred, the chart could be produced on computer, with pupils using Clip Art for visuals.

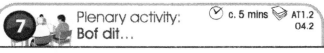

7 Plenary activity: Bof dit...   ⏱ c. 5 mins   AT1.2 O4.2

Materials
Bof puppet

Description
Game based on 'Simon says', to practise giving and understanding instructions.

Delivery
● Go through the target instructions by saying them and performing the actions all together.

● Hold up the Bof puppet and explain the rules of the game: as 'Simon says', but each correct instruction will be preceded by *Bof dit* – the usual French game being *Jacques a dit...*

● Begin giving instructions. Pupils must only respond if the instruction is preceded by *Bof dit*, otherwise they are out of the game. The last pupil remaining in the game is the winner.

Extension
● In order to practise giving more polite instructions, leave out *Bof dit*, and pupils respond only if the instruction is followed by *s'il vous plaît*.

● Ask pupils who are out of the game to come to the front and help you give the instructions.

Unit 9  Extra!

 Worksheet 1A
10–15 mins 📖 AT2.1 AT3.1 AT4.1 L4.1 L4.3 L4.4

Description
Worksheet to give further practice in reading, writing, and saying names of festivals.

Notes
1 Go through each picture orally as a whole-class activity, before giving pupils a couple of minutes to write in the names of the festivals.

2 Move around the class as pupils complete Activity 2, to monitor progress and provide help where needed.

Answers
1 a le Nouvel An
  b la Fête des Rois
  c la Saint-Valentin
  d Pâques
  e la Fête Nationale
  f Noël

 Worksheet 1B
10–15 mins 📖 AT2.1 AT3.1 AT4.1 L4.1 L4.3 L4.4

Description
Worksheet to give further practice in reading, writing and saying names of festivals.

Notes
1 Go through each picture orally as a whole-class activity, before giving pupils a couple of minutes to write in the names of the festivals.

2 If necessary, you can also do this question first as a class activity

3 Move around the class as pupils complete Activity 3, to monitor progress and provide help where needed.

Answers
1 & 2 a le Nouvel An/le premier janvier
     b la Fête des Rois/le six janvier
     c la Saint-Valentin/le quatorze février
     d Pâques/c'est en mars ou en avril
     e la Fête Nationale/le quatorze juillet
     f Noël/le vingt-cinq décembre

 Worksheet 2A
10–15 mins 📖 AT3.1 AT4.1 L4.1 L4.4

Description
Worksheet to give further practice in reading, writing and saying names of presents.

Notes
1 Go through each picture orally as a whole-class activity, before giving pupils a couple of minutes to write in the names of the presents.

2 Monitor progress in Activity 2 as required.

3 Move around the class as pupils complete Activity 3, to monitor progress and provide help where needed.

Answers
1 a un jeu vidéo
  b un ballon
  c un vélo
  d un père Noël en chocolat
  e un œuf de Pâques
  f un livre
  g un chat
  h un CD

 Worksheet 2B
10–15 mins 📖 AT2.2 AT3.1 AT4.1–2 O4.4 L4.1 L4.3 L4.4

Description
Worksheet to give further practice in reading, writing, and saying names of presents.

Notes
1 Go through each picture orally as a whole class-activity, before giving pupils a couple of minutes to write in the names of the presents.

2 Monitor progress in Activity 2 as required.

3 Move around the class as pupils complete Activity 3, to monitor progress and provide help where needed.

Answers
1 a un jeu vidéo
  b un ballon
  c un vélo
  d un père Noël en chocolat
  e un œuf de Pâques
  f un livre
  g un chat
  h un CD

Worksheet 3A
10–15 mins 📖 AT2.1 AT3.1 AT4.1 L4.1 L4.3 L4.4

Description
Worksheet to give further practice in reading, writing and saying numbers.

Notes
1 & 2 Go through each number orally as a whole-class activity, before giving pupils a couple of minutes to write in the numbers.

3 Move around the class as pupils complete Activity 3, to monitor progress and provide help where needed.

Answers
1 41 quarante et un
  42 quarante-deux
  43 quarante-trois
  44 quarante-quatre
  45 quarante-cinq
  46 quarante-six
  47 quarante-sept
  48 quarante-huit
  49 quarante-neuf
  50 cinquante

2 51 cinquante et un
  52 cinquante-deux
  53 cinquante-**trois**
  54 cinquante-**quatre**
  55 cinqu**ante-cinq**
  56 cinqu**ante**-six
  57 cinqu**ante**-sept
  58 cinquante-**huit**
  59 cinquante-**neuf**
  60 soix**ante**

 Worksheet 3B
10–15 mins 📖 AT2.1 AT3.1 AT4.1 L4.1 L4.3 L4.4

Description
Worksheet to give further practice in reading, writing and saying numbers.

Notes
1 & 2 If necessary, go through each number orally as a whole-class activity before giving pupils a few minutes to write in the numbers.

Answers

1 41 quarante et un
42 quarante-deux
43 quarante-trois
44 quarante-quatre
45 quarante-cinq
46 quarante-six
47 quarante-sept
48 quarante-huit
49 quarante-neuf
50 cinquante

2 **a** trente et un, trente-deux, trente-trois, **trente-quatre**
b quarante-deux, quarante-quatre, quarante-six, **quarante-huit**
c cinquante et un, cinquante-trois, cinquante-cinq, **cinquante-sept**
d trente-six, trente-huit, **quarante**, quarante-deux
e vingt et un, trente et un, **quarante et un**, cinquante et un

Worksheet 4A

⏱ 10–15 mins 📖 AT1.2 AT2.2
AT3.2 AT4.2 O4.2
L4.1 L4.3 L4.4

Description
Worksheet to give further practice in reading, writing and saying commands.

Notes
1 & 2 Go through each picture orally as a whole-class activity before giving pupils a few minutes to do the activities. Pupils can simply draw 'stick' people if they're not confident of their artistic ability!

3 Move around the class as pupils complete Activity 3, to monitor progress and provide help where needed.

Answers
1 **a** Comptez!   **c** Sautez!
b Touchez la tête!   **d** Levez les bras!

Worksheet 4B

⏱ 10–15 mins 📖 AT1.2 AT2.2
AT3.2 AT4.2 O4.2
L4.1 L4.3 L4.4

Description
Worksheet to give further practice in reading, writing and saying commands.

Notes

1 & 2 Go through each picture orally as a whole-class activity before giving pupils a few minutes to do the activities. Pupils simply just draw 'stick' people if they're not confident of their artistic ability!

3 Move around the class as pupils complete Activity 3, to monitor progress and provide help where needed.

Answers
1 **a** Comptez!
b Touchez la tête!
c Sautez!
d Tournez!
e Touchez le nez!
f Levez les bras!

Project work: Festivals

⏱ c. 30–60 mins 📖 IU4.1

Description
Pupils conduct research to find out about festivals celebrated in one of their twin towns.

Materials
Research tools such as the internet, library access, photographs, etc.

Delivery
● Ask pupils if they know which town(s) their hometown is twinned with. Tell them if necessary!

● Ask them how they could find out about festivals that people in this town celebrate (e.g. library, internet, talking to people).

● If pupils are from a different cultural background, they may wish to talk about a festival particular to their culture/religion.

● Pupils are then given the opportunity to do some research and write up a short report on what they have discovered. Encourage them to add captions to any pictures, in French where possible.

Extension
● Pupils could prepare a short presentation, individually or in pairs/small groups, about their project. Their work could then be displayed around the classroom.

Rigolo 1 — Unit 10: Où vas-tu?

National criteria

KS2 Framework objectives

O4.1 Memorise and present a short spoken text
O4.2 Listen for specific words and phrases
O4.3 Listen for sounds, rhyme and rhythm
O4.4 Ask and answer questions on several topics
L4.1 Read and understand a range of familiar written phrases
L4.2 Follow a short familiar text, listening and reading at the same time
L4.3 Read some familiar words and phrases aloud and pronounce them accurately
L4.4 Write simple words and phrases using a model and some words from memory
IU4.2 Know about some aspects of everyday life and compare them to their own
IU4.4 Learn about ways of travelling to the country/countries

QCA Scheme of Work

Unit 2 Je me présente
Unit 6 Le monde
Unit 11 J'habite

Language ladder levels

Listening: Breakthrough, Grade 1–3
Speaking: Breakthrough, Grade 1–2
Reading: Breakthrough, Grade 1–3
Writing: Breakthrough, Grade 1–2

5–14 guideline strands   Levels A–C

Listening		Reading	
Listening for information and instructions	A, C	Reading for information and instructions	A, C
Listening and reacting to others	A–C	Reading aloud	A, C

Speaking		Writing	
Speaking to convey information	A, C	Writing to exchange information and ideas	A, C
Speaking and interacting with others	B, C	Writing to establish and maintain personal contact	A, C
Speaking about experiences, feelings and opinions	A, B	Writing imaginatively/to entertain	n/a

Unit objectives

- name and recognise various French cities
- give and understand basic directions
- talk about the weather
- talk about the weather in a particular city

Key language

- saying where you are going: *Je vais à* (I'm going to)... *Paris/Bordeaux/Strasbourg/Nice/Grenoble.*
- directions: *tournez à droite* (right), *tournez à gauche* (left), *allez tout droit* (straight on), *arrêtez* (stop)
- weather: *Quel temps fait-il?* (What's the weather like?), *Il fait beau.* (It's sunny), *Il fait froid.* (It's cold), *Il fait chaud.* (It's hot), *Il pleut.* (It's raining), *Il neige.* (It's snowing)
- weather in a particular town: *À Paris/Bordeaux/ Strasbourg/Nice/Grenoble, il fait beau/il fait froid/il fait chaud/il pleut/il neige.* (In Paris [etc.], it's sunny/cold/hot/raining/snowing.)

Grammar and skills

- recognise various French cities
- ask and answer where you are going, using *je vais à...*
- understand and give imperative instructions for directions
- form weather expressions using impersonal *il...* expressions
- describe the weather in a certain location in a short sentence

Unit outcomes

Most children will be able to:

- recognise names of various French cities
- use *je vais à...* to say which city they are going to
- understand and use weather expressions
- understand and use direction expressions
- understand descriptions of weather in certain locations

Some children will also be able to:

- produce phrases describing weather in certain locations

Unit 10  Lesson 1

Context
Going to French cities

National criteria
KS2 Framework: **O4.2, O4.3, O4.4, L4.1, L4.2, L4.3**
Attainment levels: **AT1.1–3, AT2.2, AT3.1–3**
Language ladder levels:
  Listening: **Grade 1–3**; Speaking: **Grade 2**;
  Reading: **Grade 1–3**

Cross-curricular links
Geography

Key vocabulary
Je vais à (I'm going to)...
Paris/Bordeaux/Strasbourg/Nice/Grenoble

Language structures and outcomes
Où vas-tu? (Where are you going?), *Je vais à...*
(I'm going to)...

---

 1 Starter activity: ⏲ c. 5–10 mins 📖 IU4.4
Les villes de France

Materials
Large map of France; if possible, pictures or photos of key
monuments/places

Description
Pupils talk about French towns and cities they know of, or
have visited.

Delivery
● Display the map of France. Ask pupils if they have been to
any French towns, or if they know of any.

● Invite pupils to come up and locate key places on the map,
providing help where required.

● If you have pictures of key places, stick them near the
relevant towns or cities.

Extension
● If some pupils have been to France, ask them if they
remember where they went and to tell you what they saw
(monuments or tourist attractions, for example).

● If none of your pupils have been to France, show photos of
key monuments and places, and talk briefly about them.

 2 Animated story: ⏲ 5–10 mins 📖 AT1.2–3
Je vais à Nice (1) AT3.2–3
O4.2 O4.3
L4.1 L4.2 IU4.4

Materials
CD-ROM, map of France

Description
● Watch and listen to this interactive animated story
presenting the language for Lessons 1 and 2 (directions and
cities in France).

● You can pause and rewind the story at any point.

Delivery
● This animated story can be used for both starter and plenary
activities – the whole animation can be played at the end of
the unit so that pupils can gauge their improved
understanding.

● At this point pupils watch the first half of the story only; the
second half is in Lesson 3.

Scene 1: Bof and Jake at the château

● Write the city name *Nice* on the board. Ask if anyone knows
where Nice is, and locate it on the map if possible.

● Explain that Bof and Jake want to go to Nice, and ask pupils
to note down how many times the word is said in the first
scene (4).

● Play the scene all the way through.

Scene 2: Bof and Jake flying

● Freeze the opening screen.

● Write the following cities on the board and ask pupils to
copy them down: Grenoble, Nice, Bordeaux, Strasbourg, Paris.

● Ask pupils to number the cities in the order they hear them.

● Play the scene all the way through.

● Check pupils' answers and play again if necessary to reconfirm
the order: 1 Paris 2 Nice 3 Strasbourg 4 Bordeaux 5 Grenoble

● Summarise the scene together.

 3 Presentation: ⏲ c. 5 mins 📖 AT1.2
Où vas-tu? AT2.2 AT3.2
O4.2 O4.3 O4.4
L4.1 L4.3 IU4.4

Materials
CD-ROM

Description
Click on a city to hear how to say you are going there. Use the
additional features to practise sound/spelling links.

Delivery
● Invite pupils to click on the cities on the map of France, one
by one. We see Bof fly to the city in question, and hear the
target question and appropriate answer.

● The Virtual Teacher (if activated) repeats what Bof says.
The audio can be replayed as many times as necessary for
pupils to repeat the language accurately.

● Repeat each item a couple of times to reinforce learning.

Sounds
To further reinforce accurate pronunciation, and to introduce
some basic reading skills:

● Point to each phrase on the text bar and ask the class to say
the phrase.

● Focus on the text on screen, click on the *Sound* icon, and
click on the different highlighted sounds to hear the Virtual
Teacher saying them.

● Repeat all together.

4 Oracy activity:
Où vas-tu, Bof?

c. 5–10 mins AT1.2
04.2 04.3 04.4
IU4.4

Materials
CD-ROM

Description
Watch where Bof is going, and predict what he will say.

Delivery
● Click on *Allez* to start the activity. Bof flies directly towards a city, and we hear Polly ask *Où vas-tu, Bof?* ('Where are you going, Bof?').

● Pupils must answer the question as if they were Bof using *Je vais à* ('I'm going to')…

● You may check the answer before proceeding, if necessary, by clicking on the audio check button in the speech bubble.

● If pupils produce the correct language, click on the tick. The image will become animated and the Virtual Teacher will congratulate them. If not, click on the cross and the Virtual Teacher will invite pupils to have another try.

● Click on *Allez* to see Bof go to the next destination.

● Repeat a couple of times to reinforce the language.

Extension
● Make two teams. Each team takes it in turn to answer a question and scores a point for each correct answer.

 Knowledge About Language

Question forms
● Point out to pupils that *Où vas-tu?* is another question they have learnt in French. Quickly revise the ones encountered up to this point (see Unit 8, Lesson 3 for a list of these).

5 Plenary activity:
Quelle ville?

c. 5 mins AT1.1
AT3.1 04.2
L4.1 IU4.4

Materials
Two sets of cards with the names of five French towns; music cassette/CD (French, if possible)

Description
Pupils move around to music before trying to predict which town or city will host the winning team.

Delivery
● Quickly go through the five towns/cities on the cards to make sure pupils can pronounce and understand them comfortably (Grenoble, Nice, Bordeaux, Strasbourg and Paris).

● Place one set of cards in a cloth bag or an envelope. Place the other cards randomly around the room. Play the music and ask pupils to move around. When the music stops, they must quickly move to a town of their choice.

● Without looking, pick a card out of the bag/envelope and read it out. Pupils in that town go through to the next round. All the others are out. Put the card to one side.

● Repeat the activity until there is just one winning pupil, or only one town left!

Unit 10  Lesson 2

Context
Giving and understanding basic directions

National criteria
KS2 Framework: **O4.2, O4.3, L4.1, L4.3, IU4.4**
Attainment levels: **AT1.1–2, AT2.2, AT3.2**
Language ladder levels:
  Listening: **Grade 1–2**; Speaking: **Grade 2**;
  Reading: **Grade 2**

Cross-curricular links
Geography, PE

Key vocabulary
Directions: *tournez à droite* (right), *tournez à gauche* (left), *allez tout droit* (straight on), *arrêtez* (stop)

Language structures and outcomes
As above

---

 1 Starter activity: ⏱ 5 mins 📖 AT1.1 IU4.4
Encore une visite en France!

Materials
Large map of France

Description
Starter revision game to further familiarise pupils with places in France.

Delivery
● Say the name of a town or city in France that you covered last lesson (Grenoble, Paris, Nice, Bordeaux, Strasbourg) and ask for a volunteer to come up and locate it on the map.
● Ask the others if they think the answer is correct or not, before confirming the answer.
● Repeat for all towns/cities.

 **2** Presentation: ⏱ 5–10 mins 📖 AT1.2
Arrêtez! AT2.2 AT3.2
O4.2 O4.3
L4.1 L4.3

Materials
CD-ROM

Description
Click on a direction icon to hear the instruction and see Bof carry it out. Use the additional features to practise sound/spelling links and word classes.

Delivery
● Invite pupils to click on the direction icons, one by one. We hear Polly give the instruction and see Bof fly or stop as instructed.
● The Virtual Teacher (if activated) repeats Polly's instruction; this can be replayed as many times as necessary for pupils to repeat the language accurately.
● Repeat each item a couple of times to reinforce the language.
● Click on another direction icon to move on to the next instruction.

Word class
● Focus on a word and ask the group what type of word it is.
● Click on the *Word* icon to hear the Virtual Teacher say the word class.
● Repeat all together, copying the Virtual Teacher's gestures as you say the word class.

Sounds
To further reinforce accurate pronunciation, and to introduce some basic reading skills:
● Point to each word on the text bar and ask the class to say the word.

● Focus on the text on screen, click on the *Sound* icon, and click on the different highlighted sounds to hear the Virtual Teacher saying them.
● Repeat all together.

 3 Oracy activity: ⏱ c. 5–10 mins 📖 AT1.2
Allez tout droit! O4.2

Materials
CD-ROM

Description
Click on *Allez*. Listen to the audio directions and click on the correct direction icon to help Jake and Bof to find the hidden ghosts.

Delivery
● Click on *Allez* to start the activity. You will hear Polly giving a direction. Pupils must click on the corresponding icon to make Jake and Bof move in that direction. There are five commands for each sequence.
● When they reach their destination, the ghost becomes visible and is caught by Jake and Bof.
● Click on *Allez* to go to the next set of directions.

Extension
Make two teams. Each team takes it in turn to follow directions and scores a point for each one caught by Jake and Bof.

 4 Oracy activity: ⏱ 5–10 mins 📖 AT1.2
Bof dit… O4.2

Materials
Bof puppet, Unit 10 Flashcards 6–9 (Directions)

Description
Pupils play a game based on 'Simon says' to practise directions.

Delivery
● Work through the target directions by saying them and performing the actions all together (these can be done on the spot if there is limited space). You may wish to use the flashcards as prompts to elicit the target language.
● Hold up the Bof puppet and explain the rules of the game, i.e. the same as 'Simon says', but each correct instruction will be preceded by *Bof dit* – the usual French game being *Jacques a dit…*
● Begin giving directions. Pupils must respond only if the instruction is preceded by *Bof dit*, otherwise they are out of the game. The last pupil remaining in the game is the winner.

5 Literacy activity: ⏱ c. 5–10 mins 📚 AT3.2
Je vais à… L4.1

Materials
CD-ROM

Description
Click on *Allez*. Read where Bof says he is going, then click on the correct direction.

Delivery
● Click on *Allez* to start the activity.

● Pupils read Bof's speech bubble to see which city he will visit. They must then click on one of the three blue direction buttons on screen to indicate the way he needs to go.

● If their answer is correct, Bof goes to the city in question. Otherwise, pupils are invited to try again.

● Click on *Allez* to see where Bof wants to go next.

Extension
● Divide the class into two teams. Each team takes it in turn to get Bof to his destination, and scores a point for each correct answer.

6 Plenary activity: ⏱ c. 5–10 mins 📚 AT1.2
Une course d'obstacles! AT2.2 AT3.2
O4.2 L4.3

Materials
Classroom furniture or brightly coloured paper to create obstacle course, puppets or soft toys, two scarves or similar to use as blindfolds; Unit 10 Flashcards 6–9 (Directions).

Description
Pupils create an obstacle course in the classroom, with your guidance, and give instructions to two blindfolded pupils to help them reach their destination.

Delivery
● Divide the class into groups. Assign one puppet or soft toy to each group, but hold onto them for now. Ask two pupils in each group to leave the room.

● The other pupils help you rearrange the tables and chairs in the room to create an obstacle course. If this is not feasible, you can create obstacles by placing brightly coloured pieces of paper on the floor – pupils will have to be careful not to step on them.

● Place the puppets/soft toys around the room.

● Call the other pupils back into the room. Blindfold the first two pupils. Their team-mates must give directions to lead them to the correct puppet/toy in under two minutes.

● The team scores 10 points if they are successful.

● Repeat for all teams.

Extension
● If time allows, repeat with different pupils doing the obstacle course.

Support
● Remind pupils of the instructions for giving directions by writing them on the board, or going through them orally using the flashcards as prompts at any time during the activity.

Unit 10  Lesson 3

Context
Talking about the weather

National criteria
KS2 Framework: **O4.2, O4.3, O4.4, L4.1, L4.2, L4.3, IU4.4**
Attainment levels: **AT1.2–3, AT2.2, AT3.1–3**
Language ladder levels:
  Listening: **Grade 2–3**; Speaking: **Grade 2**;
  Reading: **Grade 1–3**

Cross-curricular links
Geography, Science, ICT

Key vocabulary
Weather: *Quel temps fait-il?* (What's the weather like?), *Il fait beau.* (It's sunny), *Il fait froid.* (It's cold), *Il fait chaud.* (It's hot), *Il pleut.* (It's raining), *Il neige.* (It's snowing)

Language structures and outcomes
As above

---

1 Starter activity: **Où vas-tu?** ⏱ 5–10 mins 📖 AT1.2 AT2.2 AT3.1 O4.2 O4.4 IU4.4

Materials
Puppets, large map of France

Description
Starter revision game with puppets to further familiarise pupils with places in France.

Delivery
● Divide the class into two teams. Invite two pupils, one from each team, to the front and give each a puppet.
● Invite another two pupils – again, one from each team – to the front of the class, or to stand in front of the large wall map.
● The first pair of pupils must recreate a dialogue using the puppets, along the lines of: *Où vas-tu?* ('Where are you going?')/*Je vais à [Paris.]* ('I'm going to [Paris.]')
● The second pair of pupils then race to be the first to touch the city mentioned on the wall map.
● Give one point to the fastest team each time.

Extension
● Invite new pairs up to the front, to enable as many as possible to participate.

Support
● If pupils have difficulty in remembering the cities covered in the previous lesson, write them on the board for reference (Paris, Strasbourg, Grenoble, Nice, Bordeaux).

2 Animated story: **Je vais à Nice (2)** ⏱ 5–10 mins 📖 AT1.2–3 AT3.2–3 O4.2 O4.3 L4.1 L4.2

Materials
CD-ROM, Unit 10 Flashcards 1–5 (Weather), map of France

Description
Watch and listen to this interactive animated story presenting the language for Lessons 3–4 (weather expressions). You can pause and rewind the story at any point.

Delivery
● This animated story can be used for both starter and plenary activities – the whole animation can be played at the end of the unit so that pupils can gauge their improved understanding.
● At this point pupils watch the second half of the story only; the first half is in Lesson 1.

Scene 3: Jake, Bof, Marine and Bernard on a beach in Nice
● Write Grenoble, Nice, Bordeaux and Paris on the board, in a vertical list, and ask pupils to copy them down.
● On the other side of the board, stick flashcards of different weather conditions.
● Play the first part of the scene where the children discuss Grenoble. Freeze the screen and ask which town was mentioned, and what the weather was like. Stick the appropriate cards (*Il fait froid.* – 'it's cold', and *Il neige.* – 'it's snowing') next to 'Grenoble' on the board.
● Repeat for the other towns.
● Play through once more, this time without stopping.
● Summarise the scene together.

Extension
● If you have time, once pupils have assigned the correct weather flashcards to the towns, ask them if they can point to where the town is on the map, and stick the weather flashcards by the towns.

3 Presentation: **Quel temps fait-il?** ⏱ c. 5 mins 📖 AT1.2 AT2.2 AT3.2 O4.2 O4.3 L4.1 L4.3

Materials
CD-ROM

Description
Click on a weather icon to hear a presentation of the weather. Use the additional features to practise sound/spelling links, word classes.

Delivery
● Invite pupils to click on the weather icons, one by one.
● The scene changes to the selected weather and the Virtual Teacher says what the weather is like.
● The audio can be repeated as many times as necessary (by clicking on the appropriate icon) for pupils to repeat the language accurately.

Word class
● Focus on a word and ask the group what type of word it is.
● Click on the *Word* icon to hear the Virtual Teacher say the word class.
● Repeat all together, copying the Virtual Teacher's gestures as you say the word class.

Sounds

To further reinforce accurate pronunciation, and to introduce some basic reading skills:

● Point to each phrase on the text bar and ask the class to say it.

● Focus on a phrase on screen, click on the *Sound* icon, and click on the different highlighted sounds to hear the Virtual Teacher saying them.

● Repeat all together.

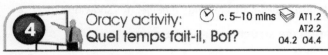

4 Oracy activity: ⏱ c. 5–10 mins 📚 AT1.2 AT2.2
Quel temps fait-il, Bof? O4.2 O4.4

Materials
CD-ROM

Description
Click on *Allez*. Look at the different kinds of weather, and say in French what the weather is like.

Delivery

● Click on *Allez* to start the activity. The window shutters open to reveal Bof outside in different weather conditions.

● Each time, pupils must correctly say what the weather is like. You may check the answer before proceeding, if necessary, by clicking on the audio check button in the speech bubble.

● If pupils produce the correct language, click on the tick. If not, click on the cross. You can replay the audio if required.

● If the pupils' answer is correct, Bof will become animated and the Virtual Teacher, if activated, will congratulate them. If their selection is wrong, the Virtual Teacher will invite pupils to have another try.

● Click on *Allez* to go to the next question.

● Repeat a couple of times to reinforce the language.

Extension
● Make two teams. Each team takes it in turn to answer a question and scores a point for each correct answer.

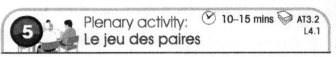

5 Plenary activity: ⏱ 10–15 mins 📚 AT3.2 L4.1
Le jeu des paires

Materials
Multiple sets of Unit 10 Flashcards 1–5 (Weather), using separate copies of words and images, or one such set to play on the board at the front of class.

Description
Pupils match picture and word Weather flashcards.

Delivery

● Mini-group memory pairs game: give one set of word and picture cards to each table; the cards are placed face down in the centre of the table. Pupils take it in turn to turn over two cards and to say/read the weather expression shown. If the two cards match, the pupil keeps those cards as points for the rest of the game. Continue until all pairs have been found.

● Large-group memory pairs game: arrange the class in two teams and place all the flashcards face down on the board. Invite two pupils from team A to turn over two cards and to say/read the weather expression shown. If the two cards match, the pupil keeps those cards as points for the rest of the game.

● Invite two pupils from team B to play in the same way. Continue until all pairs have been found and count the points!

Extension
● Pupils could create their own weather pair games on the computer.

Unit 10  Lesson 4

Context
Weather and places in France

National criteria
KS2 Framework: O4.1, O4.2, O4.3, O4.4, L4.1, L4.2, L4.3, IU4.4

Attainment levels: AT1.2, AT2.2, AT3.2, AT4.2

Language ladder levels:

Listening: **Grade 2**; Speaking: **Grade 2**;
Reading: **Grade 2**; Writing: **Grade 2**

Cross-curricular links
Geography

Key vocabulary
Weather: *Quel temps fait-il?* (What's the weather like?) *À Paris/Bordeaux/Strasbourg/Nice/Grenoble, il fait beau/il fait froid/il fait chaud/il pleut/il neige.* (In Paris [etc.], it's sunny/cold/hot/raining/snowing.)

Language structures and outcomes
À [Paris] [il pleut.] (It's [raining] in [Paris.])

---

1 Starter activity: **Le temps**   ⏲ 5 mins   AT2.2   O4.4

Materials
Unit 10 Flashcards 1–5 (Weather – pictures only)

Description
Starter revision team game, with flashcards, to revise weather expressions.

Delivery
- Divide the class into two teams.
- Hold up a weather flashcard and ask Team A to say what weather is shown, using *Quel temps fait-il?* If they answer correctly within 30 seconds they score two points. Otherwise, after that time, offer a bonus point to the other team if they can answer correctly.
- Hold up another card, and ask Team B to answer.
- Repeat until you have gone through all the cards.

2 Presentation: **À Paris, il fait beau**   ⏲ c. 5 mins   AT1.2 AT2.2 AT3.2 O4.2 O4.3 L4.1 L4.3 IU4.4

Materials
CD-ROM

Description
Click on a weather icon to hear a presentation of what the weather is like in a particular town. Use the additional features to practise sound/spelling links.

Delivery
- Invite pupils to click on the weather icons, one by one. You will hear and see the Virtual Teacher saying and demonstrating what the weather is like in relation to a particular town.
- Encourage pupils to copy both words and gestures.
- Repeat each item a few times to reinforce the language.

Sounds
To further reinforce accurate pronunciation, and to introduce some basic reading skills:
- Point to each phrase on the text bar and ask the class to say it.
- Focus on the text on screen, click on the *Sound* icon, and click on the different highlighted sounds to hear the Virtual Teacher saying them.
- Repeat all together.

3 Oracy activity: **À Bordeaux, il fait beau!**   ⏲ c. 5–10 mins   AT1.2 O4.2 IU4.4

Materials
CD-ROM

Description
Click on *Allez*. Listen to the audio about the weather and drag the correct weather symbol to the correct town.

Delivery
- Click on *Allez* to start the activity. You will hear a description of the weather in one of the places on the map, e.g. *À Paris il pleut.* ('It's raining in Paris.'). Click on the *Encore* button to listen again if necessary.
- Pupils must drag the appropriate weather icon to the correct place.
- If their answer is correct, the image will become animated and the Virtual Teacher, if activated, will congratulate them.
- If their selection is wrong, the Virtual Teacher will invite pupils to have another try.
- Click on *Allez* to hear the next sentence.
- Repeat a couple of times to reinforce the language.

Extension
- Make two teams. Each team takes it in turn to answer a question and scores a point for each correct answer.

4 Song: **C'est la fête à la grenouille!**   ⏲ 10–15 mins   AT1.2 AT2.2 AT3.2 O4.1 O4.2 O4.3 L4.1 L4.2 L4.3 IU4.4

Materials
CD-ROM or Audio CD, track 16; Unit 10 Flashcards 1–5 (Weather – large size for the board, and as many individual cards as necessary for pupils have one each)

Description
Watch and listen to the interactive song practising weather expressions in relation to places in France. Choose either *Practice* or *Sing* mode: the former to go through the song line by line, the latter to sing it all the way through. Switch the music and words on or off as you prefer.

Delivery

● Write the weather expressions that feature in the song on the board in random order (*Il neige./Il fait chaud./Il pleut./Il fait froid./Il fait beau.*), or stick up the corresponding weather flashcards. Ask pupils to copy down the words or pictures.

● Play the song through, and ask pupils to number the weather expressions in the order they appear in the song (*Il pleut./Il fait beau./Il neige./Il fait chaud./Il fait froid.*)

● Check through answers and replay the song. Encourage all pupils to join in with the chorus at this stage.

● Hand out a weather card to each pupil. Play the song again. This time, pupils must stand up and sing along to the verse with 'their' weather expression.

Extension

● Divide the class into groups of 6–8 pupils.

● **Each group performs its own version of the song.**

● **The other groups can award points to see which version was the best.**

See the Introduction for more notes on the Song features.

Knowledge About Language

Learning through rhyme

● The song in this lesson contains clear rhymes in each verse, to help pupils to remember the weather expressions.

● Most of the sounds that are used in the verses (*eu, oi, eau*) are covered explicitly in the Sound/Spelling activities in the *Extra!* sections on the CD-ROM. You can follow the song with a whole-class activity, collecting together all the words pupils have met using these sounds. These are listed in the relevant Sound/Spelling activities.

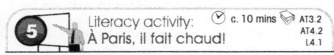

5 | Literacy activity: ⏱ c. 10 mins   📖 AT3.2
À Paris, il fait chaud!   AT4.2
                                               L4.1

Materials
CD-ROM

Description
Drag words into the newspaper headline to form sentences about the weather.

Delivery
● Ask pupils to come to the board and drag word tiles into the gaps in the sentence to make a newspaper headline about the weather.

● When satisfied with the sentence built, click on *Fini*. If the sentence is grammatically correct, the weather in the cover image of the newspaper will change to match the sentence. Otherwise, pupils are invited to try again.

● Repeat a couple of times to reinforce the language, if necessary.

Extension
● Divide the class into two teams. Each team takes it in turn to make sentences, and scores a point for each correct answer.

6 | Plenary activity: ⏱ c. 10 mins 📖 AT1.2
Quel temps!   AT2.2 AT3.2
                                      O4.2   L4.3

Materials
Unit 10 Flashcards 1–5 (Weather); weather 'props' (e.g. umbrella, sunglasses, fan, woolly scarf, etc.)

Description
Game based on 'Chinese Whispers', to practise saying and recognising weather expressions.

Delivery
● Divide the class into two teams. Each team must line up facing the front, as far away from the other team as possible.

● Place the box of props at the front of the class, equidistant from both teams.

● Invite the pupils at the back of each line to come forward to you. (Ensure you are far enough away from the other pupils not to be overheard).

● Show them both the same weather card, and whisper the corresponding expression to them both at the same time.

● On your count of three, the pupils must run to their place at the back of the line and whisper the weather expression to the pupil immediately in front of them. Pupil 2, in turn, whispers the expression to the pupil in front of them, and so on until the front of the line is reached.

● The pupil at the front must race to the props box, grab an item relating to the target weather expression, put it on and shout out the expression.

● The first (correct!) team scores five points.

● Choose two more pupils to come out and listen to your whisper, and repeat as long as time allows, or until all expressions have been covered.

Extension
● Don't whisper the expression to the pupils who see the card – they have to remember it themselves.

● Alternatively, use the word flashcard only, to encourage pupils to read it correctly.

Unit 10  Extra!

Worksheet 1A
⏱ 10–15 mins 📚 AT1.2 AT2.2
AT3.2 AT4.1 O4.2 O4.4
L4.1 L4.3 L4.4

Description
Worksheet to give further practice in reading, writing and saying French towns, and revising days of the week.

Notes
1 Go through each destination orally as a whole-class activity, before giving pupils a couple of minutes to write in the names of the places.
2 Move around the class as they complete Activity 2, to monitor progress and provide help as required. Encourage pupils to ask *Quel temps fait-il?* to elicit the information.

Answers
1 a Lundi, je vais à Strasbourg.
  b Mardi, je vais à Paris.
  c Mercredi, je vais à Grenoble.
  d Jeudi, je vais à Nice.
  e Vendredi, je vais à Bordeaux.

Worksheet 1B
⏱ 10–15 mins 📚 AT1.2 AT2.2
AT3.2 AT4.1 O4.2
O4.4 L4.1 L4.3 L4.4

Description
Worksheet to give further practice in reading, writing, and saying French towns and revising days of the week.

Notes
1 Give pupils a few minutes to prepare their itinerary, and move around the class to monitor progress and help where necessary. Give another few minutes for them to complete the sentences.
2 Again, move around the class as pupils complete Activity 2, to monitor progress and provide help where needed.

Answers
1 a Lundi, je vais à Strasbourg.
  b Mardi, je vais à Paris.
  c Mercredi, je vais à Grenoble.
  d Jeudi, je vais à Nice.
  e Vendredi, je vais à Bordeaux.

Worksheets 2A & 2B
⏱ 10–15 mins 📚 AT1.2 AT2.2
AT3.2 AT4.2 O4.2
L4.1 L4.3 L4.4

Description
Worksheet to give further practice in reading, writing and saying directions.

Notes
1 Go through each icon orally as a whole-class activity, before giving pupils a couple of minutes to write in the correct direction for each one.
2 Move around the class as pupils complete Activity 2, to monitor progress and provide help where needed.

Answers
1 a tournez à droite
  b tournez à gauche
  c arrêtez
  d allez tout droit

Worksheet 3A
⏱ 10–15 mins 📚 AT1.1 AT2.1
AT3.1 AT4.1
O4.2 L4.1 L4.4

Description
Worksheet to give further practice in reading, writing and saying weather expressions.

Notes
1 Quickly revise key weather expressions, if necessary. Give pupils a few minutes to do the activity on their own before checking through answers.
2 Move around the class as pupils complete Activity 2, to monitor progress and provide help where needed.

Answers
1 a Il pleut.   d Il fait froid.
  b Il fait beau.   e Il neige.
  c Il fait chaud.

Worksheet 3B
⏱ 10–15 mins 📚 AT1.1 AT2.1
AT3.1 AT4.1
O4.2 L4.1 L4.4

Description
Worksheet to give further practice in reading, writing and saying weather expressions, directions, and months.

Notes
1 Quickly revise key weather expressions, if necessary. Give pupils a few minutes to do the activity on their own before checking through answers.
2 Move around the class as pupils complete Activity 2, to monitor progress and provide help where needed.

Answers
1
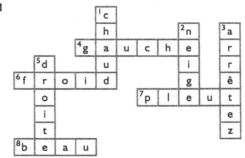

Worksheet 4A
⏱ 10–15 mins 📚 AT1.2 AT2.2
AT3.2 AT4.2 O4.2
L4.1 L4.3 L4.4

Description
Worksheet to give further practice in reading, writing and saying weather expressions and French towns.

Notes
1 Quickly revise key weather expressions, if necessary. Give pupils a few minutes to do the activity on their own, and move around the class to monitor progress and help as required
2 Move around the class as pupils complete Activity 2 in pairs, to monitor progress and provide help where needed. Encourage them to elicit the information using the question *Quel temps fait-il?*

Worksheet 4B

⏱ 10–15 mins 📖 AT1.2 AT2.2
AT3.2 AT4.2 O4.2
L4.1 L4.3 L4.4

Description
Worksheet to give further practice in reading, writing and saying weather expressions and French towns.

Notes
1 Quickly revise key weather expressions, if necessary. Give pupils a few minutes to do the activity on their own, and move around the class to monitor progress and help as required

2 Move around the class as pupils complete Activity 2 in pairs, to monitor progress and provide help as required. Encourage pupils to elicit the information using the question *Quel temps fait-il?*

Project work:
Une ville française

⏱ c. 60 mins 📖 IU4.2
IU4.4

Description
Pupils choose a French town or city, prepare and deliver a presentation about it.

Materials
Books and pictures about France, holiday brochures, internet access, maps

Delivery
● Arrange the class in groups.

● Each group selects a French town or city (allow them to look through holiday brochures for ideas if necessary). You may wish to suggest the towns that have come up so far in Unit 10, i.e. Paris, Grenoble, Strasbourg, Nice, Bordeaux, or choose somewhere different.

● Provide access to information via brochures or books and/or internet access, and ask each group to find some information on their chosen place.

● Pupils should then do some research and write up a short report on what they have discovered. Encourage them to add captions to any pictures in French where possible.

● Invite each group to come to the front of the class to deliver their presentation and display any visual aids. These could then be displayed around the classroom.

Support
● It may be a good idea to give some headings, e.g. population, location, leisure facilities, industry, etc. for pupils to work on. Pairs in each group could then focus on one aspect, and collate the information at the end.

Sound/spelling Activity

⏱ 15–20 mins 📖 AT1.1
AT2.1 AT3.1
O4.2 O4.3 L4.3

Description
Practise listening out for and pronouncing the *j* and *oi* sounds, and compare your recording to the original. Then count how many times you hear the sounds.

Delivery
● This sound/spelling activity focuses specifically on the *j* and *oi* sounds.

● There are two parts to the activity: the first (*Practice*) allows pupils to familiarise themselves with the two sounds and to compare their pronunciation with Virtual Teacher model. The second part (*Activity*) is an exercise where pupils have to listen out for the sounds within a list of French words that they have encountered so far in *Rigolo*.

● Select *Practice* and click on *Next* to start this part. Then click on *Allez*. The Virtual Teacher will say the *j* sound first on its own, and then as part of three words that have already been used in the Units 9 and 10. For each of these, get the class to repeat the sound or word chorally several times, checking the model each time using the *Encore* button to see how close they are.

● Once you have finished this part, relaunch the activity and choose *Activity* from the selection menu to move on to test pupils' recognition of these sounds. Click on *Allez* to start the activity. Pupils will hear 12 words read out, most of which they have already encountered in *Rigolo*. You may wish to pre-teach *roi* (king). For each word they must work out whether they can hear the *j* sound or the *oi* sound, then click on the correct button on screen: red if they hear a *j* sound, or green if they hear a *oi* sound. They'll have to listen carefully and click on the right button before the time runs out! Click on *Encore* if you need to hear the word again. You can ask the whole class to vote on what sound they hear, or ask individual pupils to step forward to press the correct button. Once they have completed each answer, you can use the *Encore* button to hear the word again, in order to review their understanding.

● Pupils score a point when they correctly identify the sound within the word. Encourage pupils to try to get all 12 words right to get the highest possible score!

● Repeat the activity again if you feel pupils need further practice.

Extension
● You can continue the practice activity using more words with these sounds if you feel that pupils have grasped this well, even words not yet covered in *Rigolo*. Pupils can then hold up cards marked with the sounds to show when they hear the appropriate one.

Assessment for Units 9–10

Écoutez!

Play the recordings 2–3 times, or more if necessary. Pause the recording during each activity as required.

Total marks for listening: 20. If pupils are getting 8–14/20, they are working at level 1. If they achieve 15–20/20, they are working towards level 2.

Activity 1   (AT1.1; O4.2)
Mark out of 10. Pupils should join up the numbers in this order, making a picture of a cat: 31, 34, 38, 40, 43, 46, 49, 50, 51, 55, 58, 60.

Numbers spoken as follows:
31, 34, 38, 40, 43, 46, 49, 50, 51, 55, 58, 60
(*all* × 2)

Activity 2a   (AT1.2; O4.2)
Mark out of 5

Answers
a4 (*example:* b1) c5 d6 e2 f3

(*example:* 1 Le nouvel an, c'est le premier janvier.)
2 Noël, c'est le vingt-cinq décembre.
3 La Saint-Valentin, c'est le quatorze février.
4 Pâques, c'est en mars ou en avril.
5 La fête nationale, c'est le quatorze juillet.
6 La fête des rois, c'est le six janvier.

Activity 2b (AT1.2; O4.2; L4.2)
Mark out of 5

Answers
a en mars ou avril
b (*example:* le 1 janvier)
c le 14 juillet
d le 6 janvier
e le 25 décembre
f le 14 février

Parlez!

Pupils can work in pairs for the speaking tasks. If it is not possible to assess each pair, then assess a few pairs for each assessment block and mark the rest of the class based on the spoken work they do in class.

Total marks for speaking: 10. Pupils achieving 5/10 are working at level 1; pupils achieving more than 5/10 are working towards level 2.

Activity 1 (AT2.1–2; O4.4)
5 marks

Answers
(in any order)
(*example:* Je voudrais un Père Noël en chocolat.)
Je voudrais un vélo.
Je voudrais un ballon.
Je voudrais un livre.
Je voudrais un œuf de Pâques.
Je voudrais un jeu vidéo.

Activity 2 (AT2.2; O4.4)
5 marks. First, practise pronunciation of the question with pupils. Less able pupils could just say the town for the question and the weather for the answer.

Answers
example:
A Quel temps fait-il à Strasbourg?
B À Strasbourg il fait beau.
A Quel temps fait-il à Paris?
B À Paris il pleut.
A Quel temps fait-il à Bordeaux?
B À Bordeaux il fait froid.
A Quel temps fait-il à Nice?
B À Nice il fait chaud.
A Quel temps fait-il à Grenoble?
B À Grenoble il neige.

Lisez!

Total marks for reading 20. Pupils achieving 8–14/20 are working at level 1. Pupils achieving 15 or more out of 20 are working towards 2.

Activity 1 (AT3.1–2 L4.1)
Mark out of 10

Answers
a Sautez!
b Tournez à droite!
c Touchez le nez!
d Tournez!
e Allez tout droit!
f Levez les pieds!
g Touchez les pieds!
h Tournez à gauche!
i Allez tout droit!
j Comptez!

Activity 2a (AT3.1–2; L4.1)
Mark out of 5

Answers
Pupils draw symbols for the following:
a fine weather; b hot; c rain; d snow; e cold

Activity 2b (AT3.2; L4.1, L4.2)
Mark out of 5

Answers
a À Blois – il fait froid
b À Bayeux – il pleut
c À Pau – il fait beau/chaud
d À Liège – il neige
e À Bordeaux – il fait beau/chaud

Écrivez!

For the writing tasks, the copying of words can be approximate.

Total marks for writing: 20. Pupils achieving 8–14/20 are working at level 1. Pupils achieving 15 or more out of 20 are working towards level 2.

Activity 1 (AT4.1; L4.4)
Mark out of 10

Answers

towns:	presents:
Paris	un vélo
Strasbourg	un livre
Grenoble	un Père Noël en chocolat
Bordeaux	un ballon
Nice	un œuf de Pâques

Activity 2 (AT4.2; L4.4)
Mark out of 10 (6 for sentences, 4 for general accuracy)

Answers
(*example:* Tournez à droite. Allez tout droit.)
a Tournez à gauche. Allez tout droit.
b Allez tout droit. Tournez à gauche.
c Tournez à gauche. Arrêtez.

Unit 11: On mange!

National criteria

KS2 Framework objectives

O4.1	Memorise and present a short spoken text
O4.2	Listen for specific words and phrases
O4.3	Listen for sounds, rhyme and rhythm
O4.4	Ask and answer questions on several topics
L4.1	Read and understand a range of familiar written phrases
L4.2	Follow a short familiar text, listening and reading at the same time
L4.3	Read some familiar words and phrases aloud and pronounce them accurately
L4.4	Write simple words and phrases using a model and some words from memory
IU4.2	Know about some aspects of everyday life and compare them to their own

QCA Scheme of Work

Unit 1	Je parle français!
Unit 2	Je me presente
Unit 3	En famille
Unit 4	Les animaux
Unit 5	Mon anniversaire
Unit 8	Qu'est-ce que tu veux?

Language ladder levels

Listening:	Breakthrough, Grade 1–3
Speaking:	Breakthrough, Grade 1–2
Reading:	Breakthrough, Grade 1–3
Writing:	Breakthrough, Grade 1–2

5–14 guideline strands · Levels A–C

Listening

Listening for information and instructions	A, C
Listening and reacting to others	A–C

Speaking

Speaking to convey information	A, C
Speaking and interacting with others	B, C
Speaking about experiences, feelings and opinions	A–C

Reading

Reading for information and instructions	A, C
Reading aloud	A, C

Writing

Writing to exchange information and ideas	A, C
Writing to establish and maintain personal contact	A, C
Writing imaginatively/to entertain	n/a

Unit objectives

- ask for food in a shop
- ask for and understand how much something costs
- talk about activities at a party
- give opinions about activities and food

Key language

- asking and answering what you want: *Qu'est-ce que tu veux?* (What do you want?); *Je voudrais* (I'd like)…
- food items: *du pain* (bread), *du fromage* (cheese), *de la limonade* (lemonade), *de la crème* (cream), *des fraises* (strawberries), *des tomates* (tomatoes)
- using money: *C'est combien?* (How much is it?); *C'est [cinq] euros.* (It's [five] euros.)
- party activities: *On boit.* (We are drinking.), *On mange.* (We are eating.), *On danse.* (We are dancing.), *On chante.* (We are singing.), *On s'amuse.* (We are having fun.)
- opinions: *c'est chouette* (it's great), *c'est nul* (it's rubbish), *c'est bizarre* (it's weird)

Grammar and skills

- ask what someone wants
- say what you want
- talk about food using the partitive article
- use *on* to talk about first-person plural activities
- give basic opinions about activities and food

Unit outcomes

Most children will be able to:
- identify various food items
- describe various party activities, using *on* expressions
- give various opinions in isolation

Some children will also be able to:
- ask and answer what others/they want
- give opinions in a sentence: *Le football, c'est chouette*, etc.

Unit 11  Lesson 1

Context
Shopping for food

National criteria
KS2 Framework: **O4.2, O4.3, O4.4, L4.1, L4.2, L4.3, L4.4**
Attainment levels: **AT1.2–3, AT2.1–2, AT3.2–3, AT4.2**
Language ladder levels:
  Listening: **Grade 2–3;** Speaking: **Grade 1–2;**
  Reading: **Grade 2–3**

Cross-curricular links
Numeracy

Key vocabulary
Food items: *du pain* (bread), *du fromage* (cheese), *de la limonade* (lemonade), *de la crème* (cream), *des fraises* (strawberries), *des tomates* (tomatoes)

Language structures and outcomes
Qu'est-ce que tu veux? (What do you want?)
Je voudrais [du pain.] (I'd like [some bread.])

---

 1 Starter activity: ⏱ 5–10 mins 📗 AT2.1
Une révision des nombres

Materials
Unit 6 Flashcards 1–6 (Food and drink – pictures only)

Description
Starter revision game to give further practice in numbers and food vocabulary.

Delivery
● If required, quickly go through the numbers and food items (using Unit 6 Flashcards 1–6) to revise/check the vocabulary.

● Stick the flashcards face down on the board, in a 9-square grid (3 × 3 squares, as in *Morpion* or 'Noughts and Crosses').

● Number the back of each square/card with random numbers (anything up to 30).

● Divide the class into two teams. In turn, each team must say a number, flip the card over and correctly identify the card in that square to 'take control of' the square. The winning team is the team that has 'won' three squares in a row, horizontally, vertically or diagonally.

 2 Animated story: ⏱ 5–10 mins 📗 AT1.2–3
La fête (1)
AT3.2–3
O4.2 O4.3
L4.1 L4.2 IU4.2

Materials
CD-ROM, Unit 6 Flashcards 1–6 (Food and drink), Unit 11 Flashcards 1–6 (More food and drink)

Description
● Watch and listen to this interactive animated story presenting the language for Lessons 1 and 2 (shopping and paying for food).

● You can pause and rewind the story at any point.

Delivery
● This animated story can be used for both starter and plenary activities – the whole animation can be played at the end of the unit so that pupils can gauge their improved understanding.

● At this point pupils watch the first half of the story only; the second half is in Lesson 3.

Scene 1: Polly and Olivier in a grocery shop

● Stick the food flashcards on the board. Ask pupils to watch the scene all the way through and note which foods are mentioned, and in which order, in the dialogue.

● Play the scene through and check their answers: *du pain* (bread), *de la limonade* (lemonade), *du fromage* (cheese), *des fraises* (strawberries), *des tomates* (tomatoes), *des pommes vertes* (green apples).

● Ask pupils for a summary of the scene to ensure they have understood the general gist.

● Play the scene again if required.

 3 Presentation: ⏱ 5–10 mins 📗 AT1.2
Je voudrais…
AT2.2 AT3.2
O4.2 O4.3
L4.1 L4.3

Materials
CD-ROM

Description
Click on any food item in the shop to hear it presented, and Polly then asking for that item. Use the additional features to practise sound/spelling links and word types.

Delivery
● Invite pupils to click on the food/drink items, one by one. You will hear the word presented, e.g. *du pain*.

● You will then hear Polly request the same item using *Je voudrais [du pain], s'il vous plaît.* ('I'd like [some bread], please.').

● The food item will then float into Polly's basket.

● Repeat each item a couple of times to reinforce learning.

Word class
● Focus on a word and ask the group what type of word it is.

● Click on the *Word* icon to hear the Virtual Teacher say the word class.

● Repeat all together, copying the Virtual Teacher's gestures as you say the word class.

Sounds
To further reinforce accurate pronunciation, and to introduce some basic reading skills:

● Point to each word on the text bar and ask the class to say the word.

● Focus on the text on-screen, click on the *Sound* icon, and click on the different highlighted sounds to hear the Virtual Teacher saying them.

● Repeat all together.

NB. If the *Sound* icon is not illuminated, that means it is not applicable for that particular word.

Knowledge About Language

Question forms

Qu'est-ce que tu veux?/Je voudrais... is another pair of questions and answers that pupils will have encountered in *Rigolo 1*. Draw their attention to the question, and remind them of the other questions they know: these are listed in Unit 8, Lesson 3.

Oracy activity:
Au magasin

c. 5–10 mins · AT1.2 O4.2 O4.3

Materials
CD-ROM

Description
Click on *Allez*. Listen to the food or drink item Olivier asks for, and click on the appropriate items in the shop display.

Delivery
● Click on *Allez* to start the activity. You will hear Olivier tell the shopkeeper what food or drink item he wants, and pupils must click on the corresponding item(s) he requests. They can replay the audio as required.

● If their answer is correct, the item(s) will fly into Olivier's bag and the Virtual Teacher will congratulate them.

● If their selection is wrong, the Virtual Teacher will invite pupils to have another try.

● Click on *Allez* to move on to the next exchange.

Extension
● Make two teams. Each team takes it in turn to answer a question and scores a point for each correct answer.

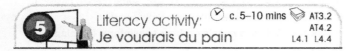

Literacy activity:
Je voudrais du pain

c. 5–10 mins · AT3.2 AT4.2 L4.1 L4.4

Materials
CD-ROM

Description
Drag tiles into the appropriate spaces, to create sentences asking for food items in the shop, then click on *Fini* to see the correct sentences animated.

Delivery
● Pupils drag words, or word groups, into the spaces on the notepad to create a sentence which correctly asks for one or two food items, e.g. *Je voudrais du pain.* or *Je voudrais du pain et du fromage.* (Both are correct.)

● Click on *Fini*. If the sentence is grammatically correct, the requested items fly into the shopping bag. Otherwise pupils are invited to try again.

● Repeat as above to create more sentences.

Extension
● Divide the class into two teams. Each team takes it in turn to compose a sentence and scores a point for each correct answer.

Plenary activity:
Jeu de rôle: au magasin

c. 10 mins · AT1.2 AT2.2 O4.2 O4.4

Materials
Unit 6 Flashcards 1–6 (Food and drink), Unit 11 Flashcards 1–6 (More food and drink); possible real food items: an apple, a banana, a sandwich, cake, bread, cheese, pizza, a carton of orange juice, lemonade, some tomatoes, some strawberries, cream; puppets

Description
Pupils set up role-plays using puppets to practise requesting food items in a small shop situation.

Delivery
● Model a dialogue using two puppets and the food flashcards (or real food props) along the lines of the animated story:
– *Bonjour./Bonjour.*
– *Qu'est-ce que tu veux?/Je voudrais...*
– *Voilà./Merci.*
– *Au revoir./Au revoir.*

● Invite two pupils at a time up to the front to do a similar role-play using the puppets.

● Repeat with as many pupils as time allows.

Unit 11  Lesson 2

Context
Asking how much something costs

National criteria
KS2 Framework: O4.1, O4.2, O4.3, O4.4, L4.1, L4.3, L4.4, IU4.2
Attainment levels: AT1.1–2, AT2.1–2, AT3.2, AT4.2
Language ladder levels:
  Listening: **Grade 1–2**; Speaking: **Grade 1–2**;
  Reading: **Grade 2**; Writing: **Grade 2**

Cross-curricular links
Numeracy, Literacy, ICT

Key vocabulary
Using money: *C'est combien?* (How much is it?); *C'est [cinq] euros.* (It's [five] euros.)

Language structures and outcomes
As above

---

1 Starter activity: Trouvez le bon nombre!
⏱ 5–10 mins 📖 AT1.1 O4.2

Materials
Individual cards with numbers up to 40

Description
Starter revision game, to give further practice in saying and recognising numbers up to 40.

Delivery
● If required, quickly go through the numbers using the cards.
● Place a random selection of number cards on the board, face up.
● Divide the class into two teams. Invite a pupil from each team to come up to the board.
● Call out a number from the board. The first pupil to grab the correct flashcard wins a point for their team.
● Repeat with two more pupils, and so on. When the time is up, add up the points!

2 Presentation: C'est cinq euros!
⏱ c. 5 mins 📖 AT1.2 AT2.2 AT3.2 O4.2 O4.3 L4.1 L4.3 IU4.2

Materials
CD-ROM

Description
Click on a food or drink item to hear Polly asking the price and the shopkeeper responding. Use the additional features to practise sound/spelling links.

Delivery
● Invite pupils to click on the food and drink items, one by one.
● We hear Polly ask how much each one is (*C'est combien?*), and the shopkeeper replies (e.g. *C'est cinq euros*).
● The Virtual Teacher, if activated, then repeats the exchange.
● Repeat each item chorally a couple of times to reinforce the language.

Sounds
To further reinforce accurate pronunciation, and to introduce some basic reading skills:
● Point to each word on the text bar and ask the class to say the word.
● Focus on the text on screen, click on the *Sound* icon, and click on the different highlighted sounds to hear the Virtual Teacher saying them.
● Repeat all together.

 Cultural information

French money
● It's a good idea to reinforce the *Rigolo* presentation above by showing pupils some real (French) euros of various denominations. If you want to use the money for role-plays, then it's best for now to use only whole euro coins or notes.

3 Oracy activity: C'est combien?
⏱ c. 5–10 mins 📖 AT1.2 AT2.1 O4.2 O4.4

Materials
CD-ROM

Description
Click on *Allez*. Listen to Bof asking for different types of food or drink, then say in French how much you think it will cost.

Delivery
● Click on *Allez* to start the activity. You will hear Bof asking for various items in the grocery store, and asking for the total price. Click on *Encore* to hear the prompt again, as necessary.
● Pupils must look at the prices displayed on the appropriate item(s), and say the total price e.g. *C'est dix euros*.
● You can click on the speech bubble for confirmation after pupils have given their answer, as required.
● If their answer is correct, click on the tick, otherwise click on the cross.
● Click on *Allez* to hear Bof asking for more items.

Extension
Make two teams. Each team takes it in turn to answer a question, and scores a point for each correct answer.

4 Oracy activity: Le juste prix!
⏱ c.10 mins 📖 AT1.2 AT2.2 O4.2 O4.4

Materials
Unit 6 Flashcards 1–6 (Food and drink), Unit 11 Flashcards 1–6 (More food and drink); sticky labels, pens

Description
Game using flashcards, in which pupils must guess the price of food and drink items.

Delivery

● Stick price labels, in euros and as realistic-looking as possible, on the back of the Unit 11 flashcards.

● Hold up the flashcards to the class, being careful not to let them see the prices on the back.

● Ask pupils to guess the price of each item, e.g. *C'est combien?* /*C'est deux euros.* You could play this individually or in teams.

● The pupil who guesses correctly, or who guesses the price closest to the correct answer, takes the card. The pupil or team with the most cards at the end of the game is the winner.

Extension

● Divide the class into small groups and give a different food flashcard, e.g. from Unit 6, to each group.

● Each group must set a price for the food item on its flashcard, write the price (in euros) on a sticky label, and stick it to the back of the card.

● Ask each group, in turn, to hold up their food item. The other groups must guess a price for each item apart from their own.

● The group which guesses correctly, or which guesses the price closest to the answer, takes the card. The team with the most cards at the end of the game is the winner.

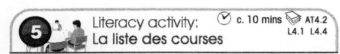

Literacy activity: La liste des courses

⏱ c. 10 mins   📖 AT4.2   L4.1 L4.4

Materials

Unit 6 Flashcards 1–6 (Food and drink), Unit 11 Flashcards 1–6 (More food and drink); paper and pencils

Description

Pupils write out shopping lists and food inventories, in preparation for the role-play in the plenary activity *Jeu de rôle: C'est combien?* (below).

Delivery

● Divide the class into pairs. Using the flashcards, with pictures and/or words as you prefer, as prompts, one partner in each pair writes a shopping list for themselves, the other writes an inventory of items and prices in 'their' shop.

● If time is limited, you may wish to restrict pupils to a maximum of, say, five items per pair.

Extension

● The shopping lists and inventories could be created on the computer.

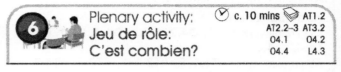

Plenary activity: Jeu de rôle: C'est combien?

⏱ c. 10 mins   📖 AT1.2   AT2.2–3 AT3.2   O4.1 O4.2   O4.4 L4.3

Materials

Unit 6 Flashcards 1–6 (Food and drink), Unit 11 Flashcards 1–6 (More food and drink); mock euro coins/notes, if possible; real food items, if possible: an apple, a banana, a sandwich, cake, bread, cheese, pizza, a carton of orange juice, lemonade, some tomatoes, some strawberries, cream

Description

Pupils set up role-plays using the shopping lists or shop inventories they prepared in the literacy activity *La liste des courses* (above).

Delivery

● Match up pairs of shopkeepers with pairs of shoppers to form a group of four pupils.

● Model a role-play using language covered in this lesson, e.g.

  – *Bonjour, [Monsieur/Mademoiselle]./Bonjour, [Monsieur/Mademoiselle].*
  – *Qu'est-ce que tu veux?/Je voudrais [des tomates]… et [du pain], s'il vous plaît.*
  – *C'est [douze] euros./Voilà.*
  – *Merci./Merci.*
  – *Au revoir [Monsieur/Mademoiselle]./Au revoir [Monsieur/Mademoiselle].*

● Each group then sets up role-plays using their lists.

Support

● Move around the groups to provide help where needed and ensure that everyone has a turn!

Extension

● Ask pupils to memorise their dialogue and present it to the rest of the class.

Unit 11 — Lesson 3

Context
Talking about activities at a party

National criteria
KS2 Framework: **O4.1, O4.2, O4.3, O4.4, L4.1, L4.2, L4.3, L4.4**
Attainment levels: **AT1.1–3, AT2.1–2, AT3.1–3, AT4.1**
Language ladder levels:
  Listening: **Grade 1–3;** Speaking: **Grade 1–2;**
  Reading: **Grade 1–3;** Writing: **Grade 1**

Cross-curricular links
Literacy

Key vocabulary
Party activities: *On boit.* (We are drinking.), *On mange.* (We are eating.), *On danse.* (We are dancing.), *On chante.* (We are singing.), *On s'amuse.* (We are having fun.)

Language structures and outcomes
Qu'est-ce qu'on fait pour la fête? (What are we doing for the party?)
On [danse.] (We are [dancing.])

---

1 Starter activity: Un quiz
⏱ 5–10 mins 📖 AT2.1

Materials
Unit 6 Flashcards 1–6 (Food and drink), Unit 11 Flashcards 1–6 (More food and drink)

Description
Starter revision game to give further practice in food and drink vocabulary.

Delivery
● Divide the class into teams.

● Hold up a flashcard and ask Team 1 to name the food or drink item. They score two points if they produce a correct answer within 10 seconds. Otherwise, offer a bonus point to the other teams: the first team to give the correct response wins the point.

● Hold up the next card and ask Team 2 to name the item. Proceed as above until all cards have been exhausted.

2 Animated story: La fête (2)
⏱ 5–10 mins 📖 AT1.2–3
AT3.2–3
O4.2 O4.3
L4.1 L4.2

Materials
CD-ROM

Description
Watch and listen to this interactive animated story presenting the language for Lessons 3–4 (talking about activities at a party). You can pause and rewind the story at any point.

Delivery
● This animated story can be used for both starter and plenary activities – the whole animation can be played at the end of the unit so that pupils can gauge their improved understanding.

● At this point pupils watch the second half of the story only; the first half is in Lesson 1.

Scene 2: Grand Hall of the château

● Freeze the screen and ask pupils what they think will happen in this scene (if pupils need prompting, ask them what Polly and Olivier were shopping for in the first part of the animated story, and whose birthday it is).

● Ask them to tell you what we might talk about doing at parties. Introduce some key vocabulary to accompany their suggestions, such as *on danse* ('we're dancing'), *on mange* ('we're eating'), *on s'amuse* ('we're having fun').

● Play the scene through and ask pupils if their suggestions were correct.

● Ask pupils for a summary of the scene to ensure they have understood the general gist.

● Play the scene again if required.

3 Presentation: On s'amuse!
⏱ c. 5 mins 📖 AT1.2
AT2.2 AT3.2
O4.2 O4.3
L4.1 L4.3

Materials
CD-ROM

Description
Click on the characters to hear them describing activities at a party. Use the additional features to practise sound/spelling links, word classes.

Delivery
● Invite pupils to click on the images of the characters at a party.

● The characters become animated and the Virtual Teacher says the relevant action, e.g. *on danse* ('we dance/we're dancing').

● Repeat each item a couple of times to reinforce the language. If you want pupils to echo the language, ask them to repeat the phrases in groups of twos or threes, to emphasise that *on* means 'we'.

Word class
● This is a good opportunity to practise word classes. See the Introduction for notes on how to use this feature of the Language Presentation.

Sounds
This is a good opportunity to practise sound/spelling links. See the Introduction for notes on how to use this feature of the Language Presentation.

Knowledge About Language

Different persons

● This is a good opportunity to focus on the different persons that pupils have met with verbs in *Rigolo 1*, i.e. *je, tu, il, elle* and *on*.

● Write the following phrases on the board: *je voudrais du pain, tu as un animal?, il est intelligent, elle est britannique* and *on mange*, underlining *je, tu, il, elle* and *on*. Ask pupils what these phrases mean and, in particular, to tell you what the five underlined words mean.

● Then write three forms of the same verb on the board: *je mange, tu manges, il mange, elle mange* and *on mange*, underlining *je, tu, il, elle* and *on*. Again, get pupils to tell you what the three phrases mean, and the five pronouns as well.

● Tell pupils that they will meet many more verbs in French, and that they should look out for the different pronouns as a way of working out what they mean.

Oracy activity: Qu'est-ce qu'on fait pour la fête?
c. 10 mins — AT1.1–2 · 04.2 04.4

Materials
CD-ROM

Description
Click on *Allez*. Listen to the audio prompt and click on the picture that illustrates the activity described.

Delivery
● Click on *Allez* to start the activity. You will hear a description of an activity and see three images of three different activities. Encourage pupils to repeat the description they hear. Click on *Encore* to hear the audio prompt again, if needed.

● Pupils must click on the picture that corresponds to the audio that they hear.

● If their selection is correct, the characters will become animated and the Virtual Teacher, if activated, will congratulate them. If their selection is wrong, the Virtual Teacher will invite pupils to have another try.

● Click on *Allez* to proceed to the next item.

● Repeat a couple of times to reinforce the language.

Extension
● Make two teams. Each team takes it in turn to answer a question and scores a point for each correct answer.

Support
● Play each scenario twice using the *Encore* button before asking pupils to respond.

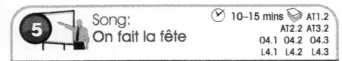

Song: On fait la fête
10–15 mins — AT1.2 AT2.2 AT3.2 · 04.1 04.2 04.3 · L4.1 L4.2 L4.3

Materials
CD-ROM or Audio CD, track 17; Unit 11 Flashcards 7–11 (Party activities)

Description
Watch and listen to the interactive song practising party activities. Choose either *Practice* or *Sing* mode: the former to go through the song line by line, the latter to sing it all the way through. Switch the music and words on or off as you prefer.

Delivery
● Play the song through, pausing after each verse to check comprehension.

● Divide the class into two groups.

● Play the song again. This time, each group must sing along, karaoke-style, in turn – this will mean repeating each verse twice.

● Encourage each group to do as many actions as possible as they sing or to hold up flashcards when they hear the corresponding action being sung.

● Set up a competition: each group must perform the whole song (again, karaoke-style). You will judge the best performance and reward the best group!

Extension
● Divide the class into groups of 6–8 pupils.

● **Each group performs its own version of the song.**

● **The other groups can award points to see which version was the best.**

See the Introduction for more notes on the Song features.

Literacy activity: On s'amuse!
c. 10 mins — AT2.1 AT3.1 AT4.1 · 04.2 L4.1 L4.4

Materials
Unit 11 Flashcards 7–11 (Party activities) or blank cards and pencils

Description
Literacy activity, in which pupils read cards and mime the action they have read.

Delivery
● If you have time, pupils could write out the flashcards themselves. Go through the verbs covered in the lesson and write them up on the board: *On mange./On boit./On danse./On chante./On s'amuse.*

● Give a card to each pupil and ask them to select one of the verbs to write on their card. Monitor this to ensure a reasonably even distribution of verbs.

● Collect all the cards, or have your set of cards ready.

● Divide the class into two teams. Ask two pupils from Team A to come to the front and select a card, presented face down. Pupils must read the card and do the corresponding mime for their team.

● Allow two points for a relevant mime, i.e. which shows they correctly read the card, and two points if the team correctly guesses the verb within 30 seconds. Offer a bonus point to the other team if Team A doesn't guess correctly.

● When their team has guessed the answer – or likewise if they haven't! – encourage the two pupils at the front to repeat the phrase together: e.g. *Oui, on mange!* or *Non, on chante!* This will further emphasise the meaning of *on*.

● Do the same for Team B.

● Continue until all verbs have been covered.

Extension
● Add other verbs which have already been introduced, this time using the *on* + [verb] format, e.g. *on saute, on tourne, on parle, on écoute*, etc.

● Pupils could create the cards on a computer.

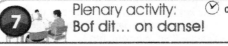

Plenary activity: Bof dit... on danse!
c. 5 mins — AT2.1 04.2

Materials
Bof puppet; Unit 11 Flashcards 7–11 (Party activities)

Description
Game based on 'Simon says' to practise verbs with *on*.

Delivery

● Run through the target verbs by saying them and performing the actions all together: *On danse*. ('We are dancing.'), *On mange*. ('We are eating.'), *On boit*. ('We are drinking.'), *On chante*. ('We are singing.'), *On s'amuse*. ('We are having fun.'). Alternatively you may wish to use the flashcards as prompts to elicit the target language.

● Hold up the Bof puppet and explain the rules of the game, i.e. the same as 'Simon says', but each correct instruction will be preceded by *Bof dit* – the usual French game being *Jacques a dit...*

● Begin giving instructions using the form *Bof dit + on +* [verb] e.g. *Bof dit on danse*, *Bof dit on chante*, etc.

● Pupils must only do the action if it is preceded by *Bof dit*, otherwise they are out of the game. The last pupil remaining in the game is the winner.

Extension

● Add other verbs which have already been introduced, this time using the *on +* [verb] format, e.g. *on saute, on tourne, on parle, on écoute*, etc.

Unit 11  Lesson 4

Context
Giving opinions about food and various activities

National criteria
KS2 Framework: **O4.2, O4.3, O4.4; L4.1, L4.3, L4.4**
Attainment levels: **AT1.2, AT2.1–2, AT3.1–2, AT4.2**
Language ladder levels:
  Listening: **Grade 2;** Speaking: **Grade 1–2;**
  Reading: **Grade 1–2;** Writing: **Grade 2**

Cross-curricular links
n/a

Key vocabulary
Opinions: *c'est chouette* (it's great), *c'est nul* (it's rubbish),
c'est bizarre (it's weird)

Language structures and outcomes
La [fête], c'est [bizarre] (The [party] is [weird])

1 Starter activity:
C'est bon?

⏱ c. 5 mins 📖 AT1.2
AT2.2
O4.2 O4.4

Materials
Unit 6 Flashcards 1–6 (Food and drink), Unit 11 Flashcards
1–6 (More food and drink); other pictures of food, if possible

Description
Starter revision game, to give further practice in describing
food, using opinions covered so far.

Delivery
● Stick flashcards/pictures of food on the board.
● Point to one and ask *C'est bon?* to elicit and revise target
adjectives (*c'est bon, c'est délicieux, ce n'est pas bon, c'est
mauvais*). Give thumbs up/double thumbs up/thumbs
down/double thumbs down gestures to influence pupils'
answers accordingly.
● Continue until you have covered each target expression twice.

Support
Give pupils a choice of two phrases for each object rather than
leaving it open-ended, e.g. *C'est bon ou c'est mauvais?*

Extension
● Gently introduce the structure for this lesson by asking
pupils, e.g. *La pomme, c'est bon?* If pupils are feeling
confident, they can answer using this phrase as well.
● If you have time, briefly revise colour adjectives in the same
way as with the food flashcards, asking *C'est de quelle couleur?*
to elicit colours (*jaune, rouge, rose, marron, orange, bleu, vert*).
● Proceed as above until all cards or target adjectives have
been covered.

2 Presentation:
C'est comment?

⏱ c. 5–10 mins 📖 AT1.2
AT2.2 AT3.2
O4.2 O4.3
L4.1 L4.3

Materials
CD-ROM

Description
Click on the images to hear the different opinions about the
items on screen. Use the additional features to practise
sound/spelling links.

Delivery
● Invite pupils to click on one of the icons next to the screens,
which indicate *chouette* ('great'), *bizarre* ('weird') or *nul*
('rubbish').
● The scene will be animated, and pupils will hear the
corresponding audio description, e.g. *Le football, c'est chouette!*
('Football's great!').

● The scenes and icons can be selected in any order. Try to
direct the activity so that as many different options as possible
are presented, in order to reinforce the language.

Sounds
To further reinforce accurate pronunciation, and to introduce
some basic reading skills:
● Point to each word on the text bar and ask the class to say
the word.
● Focus on the text on screen, click on the *Sound* icon, and
click on the different highlighted sounds to hear the Virtual
Teacher saying them.
● Repeat all together.

3 Oracy activity:
C'est bizarre!

⏱ c. 5–10 mins 📖 AT1.2
AT2.2
O4.2 O4.4

Materials
CD-ROM

Description
Click on *Allez*. Watch the animation and listen to the audio
asking what something is like. Say what the correct answer
should be.

Delivery
● Click on *Allez* to start the activity. You will see and hear a
brief animation, and hear a question about it, e.g. *La musique,
c'est chouette ou c'est nul?* Click on *Encore* to hear the prompt
again, if needed.
● Pupils must give the correct answer (e.g. *La musique, c'est
chouette*).
● Click on the tick if their answer is correct, or the cross if not.
You can click on the audio check button in the speech bubble
to confirm the answer beforehand, if necessary.
● There is a reward animation for correct answers and the
Virtual Teacher will congratulate pupils. In the case of
incorrect answers, the Virtual Teacher will invite pupils to
have another try.
● Click on *Continuez* to go on to the next item.

Extension
Make two teams. Each team takes it in turn to answer a
question and scores a point for each correct answer.

4 Oracy activity: Les charades
⏱ 5 mins 📚 AT2.1 AT3.1 O4.2 L4.1

Materials
Optional: cards/strips of paper with the target adjectives (*bon, chouette, délicieux, bizarre, nul, mauvais*) written on.

Description
Charades game, in which pupils mime adjectives for the others to guess.

Delivery
● Model some standard mimes for the different types of opinions, e.g. holding tummy while doing thumbs up or down for food, or thumbs up or down without hand on tummy for general purposes.

● Invite pupils to the front and ask them to do a mime based on one of the adjectives covered so far (*délicieux, bon, pas bon, mauvais, chouette, bizarre, nul*). Either give them a strip of paper with the adjective written on, or whisper the adjective to them out of other pupils' earshot.

● The pupil who correctly guesses the adjective being mimed then comes out to the front to mime another one.

● Continue until all adjectives have been covered a couple of times.

Extension
● Write fuller phrases on the cards/paper, such as *La fête, c'est chouette* or *La pomme, c'est délicieux*. Then provide pupils with matching flashcards for each of the nouns used.

● When pupils read the phrases on the cards, they have to choose the correct flashcard and mime the opinion. The other pupils have to guess the whole phrase correctly.

5 Literacy activity: C'est délicieux!
⏱ c. 5–10 mins 📚 AT3.2 L4.1

Materials
CD-ROM

Description
Click on *Allez*, then click on the sentence which best describes each dish.

Delivery
● Click on *Allez* to see Madame Moulin present some food on a platter.

● In each case there are two sentences on screen; pupils click on the one which best describes the food presented. Click on *Encore* to hear her repeat the food item, if needed.

● If they are correct, there is an appropriate animation and the Virtual Teacher will congratulate pupils. If pupils click on the wrong panel, the Virtual Teacher invites them to try again.

● Click on *Allez* to proceed to the next item.

Extension
● Divide the class into two teams. Each team takes it in turn to select a sentence and scores a point for each correct answer.

6 Plenary activity: Qu'est-ce que c'est? C'est comment?
⏱ c. 10 mins 📚 AT1.2 AT2.2 AT4.2 O4.2 O4.4 L4.4

Materials
Small plastic plates; scarf or similar to use as blindfold; food samples – as many as possible of the following food and drink items introduced in this unit: *du pain* (bread), *du fromage* (cheese), *de la limonade* (lemonade), *de la crème* (cream), *des fraises* (strawberries), *des tomates* (tomatoes)

Description
Food tasting game to enable pupils to revise food vocabulary and to describe real food.

Delivery
NB. Ensure you follow relevant procedures to ensure that this activity is adapted for any pupils with food allergies or intolerances.

● Show the food and drink to the pupils and go through the words again if you feel this is required, otherwise start with the next step.

● Invite a pupil, or a couple of pupils, to come to the front. Blindfold them and offer them a food sample on a small plastic plate. The rest of the class ask: *Qu'est-ce que c'est?* and then *C'est comment?*

● The pupil at the front identifies the food item and says what they think of it (all in French, of course!): *C'est du pain. C'est mauvais!*

● Ask the rest of the class to say whether the food was identified correctly and take off the blindfold.

● Repeat with other pupils until all food items have been covered at least once.

Extension
● You may also wish to choose from food items covered in Unit 6: *un gâteau* (a cake), *une pizza* (a pizza), *une banane* (a banana), *un jus d'orange* (an orange juice), *un sandwich* (a sandwich), *une pomme* (an apple). You can extend this to other food types as required.

● Pupils could produce a chart listing the various food types against the number of different opinions, or with the food types listed against each pupil, who then writes in their own opinion.

Unit 11  Extra!

⏱ 10–15 mins 📖 AT3.1 AT4.1
L4.1 L4.4
Worksheet 1A

Description
Worksheet to give further practice in reading, writing, and talking about food and drink.

Notes
1 Give the class a couple of minutes to go through the words in pairs before having a whole-group discussion.
2 Give pupils a few minutes to do Activity 2 before going through the answers together.

Answers
2 a du fromage   e de la limonade
   b des gâteaux   f de la crème
   c des fraises   g des tomates
   d du pain   h des bananes

⏱ 10–15 mins 📖 AT2.2 AT3.1
AT4.1 O4.2
Worksheet 1B
L4.1 L4.3 L4.4

Description
Worksheet to give further practice in reading, writing, and talking about food.

Notes
1 Move around the class as pupils complete Activity 1 in pairs, to monitor progress and help with pronunciation as required.
2 Give pupils a few minutes to spot the differences between the baskets in Activity 2 before going through the answers together.

Answers
2 Je voudrais... des fraises, du pain, du fromage

⏱ 10–15 mins 📖 AT3.2
AT4.1
Worksheet 2A
L4.1 L4.4

Description
Worksheet to give further practice in reading and writing about food and prices.

Notes
1 Give pupils a few minutes to do Activity 1 before going through the answers together.
2 Move around the class as they complete Activity 2 to offer help as required.

Answers
1 a strawberries: 2€   c tomatoes: 4€
   b cakes: 2€   d cheese: 6€

⏱ 10–15 mins 📖 AT2.2 AT3.2
AT4.1 O4.4
Worksheet 2B
L4.1 L4.3 L4.4

Description
Worksheet to give further practice in reading, writing and speaking about food and prices.

Notes
1 Give pupils a few minutes to do Activity 1 before going through the answers together.

2 Give pupils another few minutes to do Activity 2 before going through the answers together.
3 Move around the class as pupils do Activity 3, to monitor the role-plays and offer help as required.

Answers
1

a	r	x	u	w	f	d	y	d	e	l	i
d	e	s	g	â	t	e	a	u	x	m	u
e	l	o	e	d	a	l	é	f	s	g	n
s	à	n	d	e	l	a	c	r	è	m	e
b	h	p	e	s	o	l	d	o	a	l	p
a	g	f	s	t	t	i	j	m	f	h	i
n	t	o	f	o	d	m	l	a	c	r	z
a	b	à	r	m	k	o	e	g	l	x	z
n	a	l	a	a	r	n	v	e	l	n	a
e	s	e	i	t	l	a	c	q	k	é	w
s	n	f	s	e	f	d	u	p	a	i	n
t	m	w	e	s	é	e	s	k	j	h	e
c	d	e	s	p	o	m	m	e	s	d	i

2 a – Je voudrais des **fraises**. C'est combien?
     – C'est **cinq** euros.
   b – Je voudrais du **fromage**. C'est combien?
     – C'est **six** euros.
   c – Je voudrais des **gâteaux**. C'est **combien**?
     – C'est deux euros.
   d – Je **voudrais** des tomates. C'est combien?
     – C'est quatre **euros**.

⏱ 10–15 mins 📖 AT3.1–2
AT4.1
Worksheet 3A
L4.1 L4.4

Description
Worksheet to give further practice in reading, writing, and speaking using *on* + verb.

Notes
1 Give the class a couple of minutes to go through Activity 1 in pairs before discussing the answers together. Then give pupils a few minutes to write in the answers.
2 Give pupils a few minutes to do Activity 2 before asking some of them to read out their 'plan'.

Answers
1 a On mange.   d On danse!
   b On boit!   e On chante!
   c On s'amuse.

⏱ 10–15 mins 📖 AT3.2
AT4.2 L4.1
Worksheet 3B
L4.4

Description
Worksheet to give further practice in reading, writing, and speaking using *on* + verb.

Notes
1 Give the class a few minutes to do Activity 1 before going through the answers together.
2 Give pupils a few minutes to do Activity 2 before asking some of them to read out their 'plan'.

Answers

1 a On danse à 4 heures.
   b On chante à 5 heures.
   c On mange et on boit à 6 heures.
   d On s'amuse beaucoup de 4 à 6 heures!

 Worksheet 4A   ⊘ 10–15 mins 📚 AT2.1 AT3.1
                                             AT4.1 O4.4
                                       L4.1 L4.3 L4.4

Description
Worksheet to give further practice in reading, writing, and speaking using *C'est* + adjective.

Notes
1 Give the class a few minutes to go through Activity 1 before discussing in pairs. Move around the class to monitor progress.
2 Give pupils a few minutes to prepare the questionnaire in Activity 2 and move around the class to help as required and monitor the pairwork.

 Worksheet 4B   ⊘ 10–15 mins 📚 AT2.2 AT3.1
                                             AT4.1 L4.1
                                       L4.3 L4.4

Description
Worksheet to give further practice in reading, writing, and speaking using *c'est* + adjective.

Notes
1 Give the class a few minutes to go through Activity 1 before discussing in pairs. Move around the class to monitor the activity.
2 Give pupils a few minutes to prepare the questionnaire in Activity 2, then move around the class to help as required and to monitor the pairwork.

 Project work: ⊘ c. 30–60 mins 📚 IU4.2
La nourriture en France

Description
Pupils prepare a poster or information sheet about a French dish or typical French produce.

Materials
Books and pictures about France, internet access, maps

Delivery
● Arrange the class in pairs or groups of three.
● Assign either a food/drink type (e.g. cheese, bread, seafood, meat) or a French region to each group.
● Ask pupils to find some pictures and information that they can make into a poster/leaflet for a wall display.
● Pupils could also be encouraged to compare these food types with what people eat in the UK.

Rigolo 1

Unit 12: Le cirque

National criteria

KS2 Framework objectives

O4.1   Memorise and present a short spoken text
O4.2   Listen for specific words and phrases
O4.3   Listen for sounds, rhyme and rhythm
O4.4   Ask and answer questions on several topics
L4.1   Read and understand a range of familiar written phrases
L4.2   Follow a short familiar text, listening and reading at the same time
L4.3   Read some familiar words and phrases aloud and pronounce them accurately
L4.4   Write simple words and phrases using a model and some words from memory
IU4.2   Know about some aspects of everyday life and compare them to their own
IU4.4   Learn about ways of travelling to the country/countries

QCA Scheme of Work

Unit 3   En famille
Unit 6   Le monde
Unit 10   Les vêtements

Language ladder levels

Listening:	Breakthrough, Grade 1–3
Speaking:	Breakthrough, Grade 1–2
Reading:	Breakthrough, Grade 1–3
Writing:	Breakthrough, Grade 1–3

5–14 guideline strands   Levels A–C

Listening
Listening for information and instructions	A, C
Listening and reacting to others	A–C

Speaking
Speaking to convey information	A, C
Speaking and interacting with others	B, C
Speaking about experiences, feelings and opinions	A, B

Reading
Reading for information and instructions	A, C
Reading aloud	A, C

Writing
Writing to exchange information and ideas	A, C
Writing to establish and maintain personal contact	A, C
Writing imaginatively/to entertain	n/a

Unit objectives

- identify various francophone countries
- talk about which languages you speak
- identify different items of clothing
- describe the colour of items of clothing

Key language

- Francophone countries: *la France* (France), *la Suisse* (Switzerland), *le Canada* (Canada), *la Martinique* (Martinique), *le Maroc* (Morocco), *le Sénégal* (Senegal)
- talking about languages: *Je parle anglais/français* (I speak English/French), *Je ne parle pas anglais/français* (I don't speak English/French)
- clothes: *un pantalon* (trousers), *une veste* (jacket), *une chemise* (shirt), *un t-shirt* (t-shirt), *un chapeau* (hat), *une jupe* (skirt)
- describing colour of clothes: colours met so far, plus *blanc(he)* (white) and *noir(e)* (black)

Grammar and skills

- give the names of various French-speaking countries
- use positive and negative phrases to talk about speaking languages
- describe various items of clothing, using colour adjectives

Unit outcomes

Most children will be able to:
- identify various French-speaking countries
- use single set phrases to say which languages they can speak
- describe colour of items of clothing, with some support

Some children will also be able to:
- use positive and negative phrases to talk about which languages they can speak
- apply the correct forms of colour adjectives to both masculine and feminine nouns

Unit 12  Lesson 1

Context
Talking about francophone countries

National criteria
KS2 Framework: **O4.2, O4.3, O4.4, L4.1, L4.2, L4.3, IU4.4**
Attainment levels: **AT1.1–3, AT2.1, AT3.1–3**
Language ladder levels:
 Listening: **Grade 1–3;** Speaking: **Grade 1;**
 Reading: **Grade 1–3**

Cross-curricular links
Geography, citizenship

Key vocabulary
Francophone countries: *la France* (France), *la Suisse* (Switzerland), *le Canada* (Canada), *la Martinique* (Martinique), *le Maroc* (Morocco), *le Sénégal* (Senegal)

Language structures and outcomes
C'est [le Maroc] (It's [Morocco])

 Starter activity: ⏱ 5–10 mins 📖 IU4.4
Le monde francophone

Materials
Unit 12 Flashcards 1–6 (Countries), large map of world

Description
Starter discussion about French-speaking countries.

Delivery
● Ask if anyone knows of any other countries where French is spoken, apart from France.

● Use the map and flashcards as visuals.

● You could ask pupils if they can suggest why people speak French in places as far away from France as Senegal and Canada (they were conquered by France and became French colonies in the 17th century).

● Explain that in some countries, French may be one of a number of languages spoken (e.g. the official languages of Switzerland are French, German, Italian and Romansch).

 **Animated story:** ⏱ 5–10 mins 📖 AT1.2–3
Le Grand Cirque AT3.2–3
International (1) 04.2 04.3
 L4.1 L4.2

Materials
CD-ROM, Unit 12 Flashcards 1–6 (countries)

Description
● Watch and listen to this interactive animated story presenting the language for Lessons 1 and 2 (introducing French-speaking countries).

● You can pause and rewind the story at any point.

Delivery
● This animated story can be used for both starter and plenary activities – the whole animation can be played at the end of the unit so that pupils can gauge their improved understanding.

● At this point pupils watch the first half of the story only; the second half is in Lesson 3.

Scene 1: Outside the Big Top
● Play the introductory scene through and ask pupils what sort of circus they think it will be, what sort of acts, etc.

Scene 2: Inside the Big Top
● Stick the country flashcards on the board and write the country names next to each one. Ask pupils to note in which order the countries appear in the animation.

● Play the scene through and check the answers: *le Sénégal, la Suisse, la Martinique, le Maroc, la France.*

Scene 3: The children and Bof in the circus audience

● Ask pupils to watch the scene and tell you what the characters are talking about.

● Play the scene and ask for a summary, to ensure they have understood the general gist.

● Play the scene again if required.

 Presentation: ⏱ c. 5 mins 📖 AT1.1
Les pays AT2.1 AT3.1
 04.2 04.3
 L4.1 L4.3

Materials
CD-ROM

Description
Click on the countries to hear a presentation of each one. Use the additional features to practise sound/spelling links, word classes and spelling.

Delivery
● Invite pupils to click on the countries, one by one. You will see a photo and the flag of the country, and the Virtual Teacher will say the country's name.

● Repeat each item a couple of times to reinforce learning. Click on *Encore* to hear each item again.

● Click on *Continuez*, and then select another country to see and hear it presented.

Spelling
● For groups who have already done the alphabet: Point to the word and ask the children to say/spell the word. Check answer by clicking on the word then on the *Spell* icon.

● To simply introduce the concept of spelling in French, click on an image, then on the *Spell* icon, and point to the letters as the Virtual Teacher says them. Repeat, this time asking the whole class to join in. Continue in the same way with all the words.

Word class
● Focus on a word and ask the group what type of word it is.

● Click on the *Word* icon to hear the Virtual Teacher say the word class.

● Repeat all together, copying the Virtual Teacher's gestures as you say the word class.

Sounds
To further reinforce accurate pronunciation, and to introduce some basic reading skills:

● Point to each word on the text bar and ask the class to say the word.

- Focus on the text on screen, click on the *Sound* icon, and click on the different highlighted sounds to hear the Virtual Teacher saying them.

- Repeat all together.

NB. If the *Sound* icon is not illuminated, that means it is not applicable for that particular word.

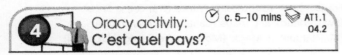

4 Oracy activity: C'est quel pays?   ⏲ c. 5–10 mins 📚 AT1.1 O4.2

Materials
CD-ROM

Description
Click on *Allez*. Listen to the audio prompt and click on the correct country from a choice of three illuminated on the map.

Delivery
- Click on *Allez* to start the activity. You will hear the name of a country, and see three of the six countries illuminated on the map.

- Pupils must click on the country they hear (you can replay the audio by clicking on *Encore* if required).

- If pupils' answer correctly, there is a reward animation, and the Virtual Teacher (if activated) will congratulate them. If their selection is wrong, the Virtual Teacher will invite pupils to have another try.

- Click on *Continuez* to go on to the next question.

Extension
- Make two teams. Each team takes it in turn to answer a question and scores a point for each correct answer.

5 Plenary activity: C'est le Sénégal ou c'est le Maroc?   ⏲ c. 10 mins 📚 AT1.2 AT2.1 O4.2 O4.4 IU4.4

Materials
Unit 12 Flashcards 1–6 (Countries)

Description
A guessing game using flashcards to give further practice in identifying francophone countries.

Delivery
- Hold up one flashcard at a time and ask, for example, *C'est le Sénégal ou c'est le Maroc?* to elicit *C'est [le Maroc]*.

- After going through all the cards in this way, progress to asking *C'est quel pays?* ('What country is it?') to elicit answers as above. After each question, stick the card face down on the board.

- When you have been through all the cards in this way, point to the cards (face down) on the board and ask the same question again – this time pupils' memory is tested as well!

Extension
- Divide the class into teams and play the above games, awarding points for each correct answer.

Lesson summary

Context
Talking about the languages we speak

National criteria
KS2 Framework: **O4.2, O4.3, O4.4; L4.1, L4.3, L4.4, IU4.2, IU4.4**

Attainment levels: **AT1.2, AT2.2, AT3.2, AT4.2**

Language ladder levels:
Listening: **Grade 2**; Speaking: **Grade 2**;
Reading: **Grade 2**; Writing: **Grade 2**

Cross-curricular links
Geography, citizenship, literacy, ICT

Key vocabulary
Talking about languages: *Je parle anglais/français* (I speak English/French), *Je ne parle pas anglais/français* (I don't speak English/French)

Language structures and outcomes
As above

1 Starter activity: ⏱ 5–10 mins 📖 IU4.4
Le monde francophone – revu!

Materials
Unit 12 Flashcards 1–6 (Countries), large map of world. For up-to date information on the countries covered you may wish to use the internet, e.g. the BBC website.

Description
Starter discussion about the languages spoken, other than French, in French-speaking countries.

Delivery
• Use the map and flashcards as visuals.

• Explain to pupils that in the countries they've met so far people speak French but sometimes other languages too.

• Of the countries featured, only France is more or less completely francophone, but Breton is spoken in Brittany and some other parts of France preserve their dialects alongside standard French.

• Senegal has its own language (*le wolof*) but uses French as an administrative language.

• The official language of Morocco is Arabic (*l'arabe*) but some French is spoken.

• Switzerland is essentially trilingual, depending on area, with most people speaking German (*l'allemand*), some French and a small percentage speaking Italian (*l'italien*) as well as a minority speaking Romansch.

• Canada is officially bilingual with French being the language of Quebec province.

• Martinique forms part of *la France d'Outremer*, that is, administratively it is considered part of France.

2 Presentation: ⏱ c. 5–10 mins 📖 AT1.2
Tu parles français? AT2.2 AT3.2
O4.2 O4.3
L4.1 L4.3

Materials
CD-ROM

Description
Click on the clowns to hear them say which language(s) they speak/don't speak. Use the additional features to practise sound/spelling links, word classes.

Delivery
• Invite pupils to click on the clowns, one by one.

• You will hear the clowns say which language(s) they speak/don't speak.

• Repeat each item a couple of times by clicking again on the clown, to reinforce the language.

• Click on another clown to continue.

Sounds
• This is a good opportunity to practise sound/spelling links. See the Introduction for notes on how to use this feature of the Language Presentation.

 Knowledge About Language

Negative forms
• Remind pupils that they have already met a negative phrase earlier in *Rigolo 1*, by writing *J'ai un animal* and *Je n'ai pas d'animal* on the board.

• Then write *Je parle français* and *Je ne parle pas français* on the board, asking pupils to tell you what they mean. Explain that we call a phrase like 'I speak English' a positive phrase, and one like 'I don't speak English' a negative one.

• Looking at the two pairs of phrases, can pupils work out how you take a positive phrase (like 'I speak English') and turn it into a negative one? If they are having trouble with this, underline the words *ne/n'* and *pas* in each phrase, and explain that you 'sandwich' the verb with these two words.

• If they have understood this, then you can follow this up by writing a few verb phrases they have met in *Rigolo* so far. Ask pupils to predict how you would say the opposite: *Je suis grand, Je regarde la télé, Je vais à Paris, Il fait beau.* The negative versions of these are *Je ne suis pas grand, Je ne regarde pas la télé, Je ne vais pas à Paris* and *Il ne fait pas beau.*

3 Oracy activity: ⏱ c. 5–10 mins 📖 AT2.2
Tu parles quelle langue? O4.2 O4.4

Materials
CD-ROM

Description
Click on *Allez*. Jake asks each clown what language they speak. Watch the clown who waves their flag(s), and say in French what their answer will be.

Delivery
• Click on *Allez* to start the activity. You will hear Jake ask each clown which language they speak. Click on *Encore* to hear him again, if necessary.

• Pupils must predict what the clown will say, using the visuals and audio as clues, saying *Je parle* + language or *Je ne parle pas* + language.

● Check their answers using the audio check button in the speech bubble, if required. Click on the tick if pupils' answer is correct, otherwise click on the cross.

● If their answer is correct, the clown becomes animated and the Virtual Teacher, if activated, will congratulate them. If their answer is wrong, the Virtual Teacher will invite pupils to have another try.

● Click on *Allez* to go on to the next question.

Extension
● Make two teams. Each team takes it in turn to answer a question and scores a point for each correct answer.

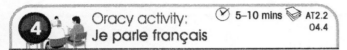

4 Oracy activity: Je parle français — ⏲ 5–10 mins 📖 AT2.2 O4.4

Materials
Puppets

Description
Speaking activity in which pupils ask and answer questions about the languages they speak.

Delivery
● Using the puppets, model a dialogue with the target expressions e.g. *Tu parles quelle langue?/Je parle anglais et français.*

● Ask a few pupils the same question, to reinforce the language.

● Divide the class into groups. Pupils must turn to the person to their left and ask them which language they speak. The second pupil answers the question before asking the pupil to his/her left the same question.

● If you know that some of your pupils speak other languages, give them the French for these before you start: e.g. *le gallois* (Welsh), *l'urdu* (Urdu), *le bengali* (Bengali), *l'hindi* (Hindi), *le polonais* (Polish).

5 Literacy activity: Je parle... — ⏲ c. 5–10 mins 📖 AT3.2 L4.1 L4.3

Materials
CD-ROM

Description
Drag the correct speech bubble to each character to describe what language(s) they speak.

Delivery
● The five characters are holding flags to denote the languages they speak, or flags crossed out to denote languages they don't speak.

● Pupils must select and drag the correct speech bubble to the corresponding character, to accurately describe what language(s) they speak or don't speak.

● If their sentence is grammatically correct and relevant to the character, the character will be animated. Otherwise the Virtual Teacher will invite pupils to try again.

● Click on *Allez* to proceed to the next question.

Extension
● Make two teams. Each team takes it in turn to compose a sentence and scores a point for each correct answer.

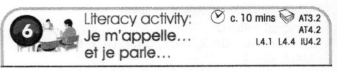

6 Literacy activity: Je m'appelle... et je parle... — ⏲ c. 10 mins 📖 AT3.2 AT4.2 L4.1 L4.4 IU4.2

Materials
Paper and pencils

Description
Literacy activity in which pupils write a brief profile of themselves, including which languages they speak.

Delivery
● Ask pupils to write two or three sentences about themselves, including saying what languages they speak.

● Write up target sentences on the board, e.g. *Je m'appelle.../J'ai [10] ans./Je suis [britannique]./Je parle...*

● Walk round the class to monitor pupils' writing.

● When pupils have finished, ask as many as time allows to read out what they have written to the rest of the class.

Extension
● This activity can be used in writing and sending emails to a partner school in a French-speaking country.

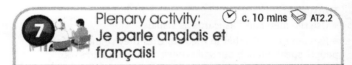

7 Plenary activity: Je parle anglais et français! — ⏲ c. 10 mins 📖 AT2.2

Materials
Union Jack and Tricolore flags (Unit 7 Flashcards 13–14, or bought/made in class)

Description
A team game to give further practice in saying which languages we speak/don't speak.

Delivery
● Demonstrate the target structures in the following way: Hold up one or both flags and say *Je parle [anglais/et français]*. Hold one flag down and say *Je ne parle pas [anglais/français]*.

● Divide the class into teams. One pupil from Team A comes to the front and holds either or both flags (in raised or lowered position). Their team must say the sentence that corresponds to the flag position and scores two points if they do so correctly. Offer a bonus point to the other team if their answer is incorrect.

● Repeat for Team B, and alternate between the teams as long as time allows.

Extension
● Encourage pupils to use *mais* ('but') if they are linking a negative phrase with a positive one, e.g. *Je parle anglais, mais je ne parle pas français.*

Unit 12  Lesson 3

Context
Identifying different items of clothing

National criteria
KS2 Framework: **O4.2, O4.3, O4.4, L4.1, L4.2, L4.3**
Attainment levels: **AT1.1–3, AT2.1, AT3.1–3**
Language ladder levels:
  Listening: **Grade 1–3;** Speaking: **Grade 1;**
  Reading: **Grade 1–3**

Cross-curricular links
n/a

Key vocabulary
Clothes: *un pantalon* (trousers), *une veste* (jacket), *une chemise* (shirt), *un t-shirt* (t-shirt), *un chapeau* (hat), *une jupe* (skirt)

Language structures and outcomes
As above

 Starter activity: Les couleurs — 5 mins — AT1.1 AT3.1 O4.4

Materials
Unit 2 Flashcards 1–14 (Classroom objects and Colours)

Description
Starter activity using flashcards to revise some colours.

Delivery
● Hold up the colour flashcards and ask pupils *C'est quelle couleur?*
● Encourage pupils to call out the colours. Keep the pace as brisk as possible.
● Continue until all of the colours have been covered: *marron, rose, rouge, jaune, orange, bleu.* You can also use 'green' (*vert*), which comes up in Unit 3.

Extension
● Move on to the classroom object flashcards; ask *Qu'est que c'est?* to elicit e.g. *C'est un sac.* If necessary, prompt pupils with *C'est de quelle couleur?* so that they say the colour and eventually *C'est un sac marron.*
● Continue until all the classroom object flashcards have been covered.

 Animated story: Le Grand Cirque International (2) — 5–10 mins — AT1.2–3 AT3.2–3 O4.2 O4.3 L4.1 L4.2

Materials
CD-ROM, Unit 12 Flashcards 1–6 (Countries)

Description
Watch and listen to this interactive animated story presenting the language for Lessons 3–4 (introducing clothes and some more colours). You can pause and rewind the story at any point.

Delivery
● This animated story can be used for both starter and plenary activities – the whole animation can be played at the end of the unit so that pupils can gauge their improved understanding.
● At this point pupils watch the second half of the story only; the first half is in Lesson 1.
Scene 4: Inside the Big Top
● Play the scene through as far as Madame Moulin's appearance.
● Summarise together the scene so far.
● Ask pupils what they think is going to happen next.
● Play the rest of the scene and summarise together, checking whose predictions were correct.
● Play the scene again if required.

 Presentation: Les vêtements — c. 5 mins — AT1.1 AT2.1 AT3.1 O4.2 O4.3 L4.1 L4.3

Materials
CD-ROM

Description
Click on the items of clothing to hear a presentation of each one. Use the additional features to practise sound/spelling links, word classes and spelling.

Delivery
● Invite pupils to click on the items of clothing on the washing line, one by one.
● You will hear the Virtual Teacher say the word and see the item of clothing become animated.
● Repeat each item a couple of times to reinforce learning.

Spelling
● For groups who have already done the alphabet: Point to the word and ask pupils to say/spell the word. Check answer by clicking on the word, and then on the *Spell* icon.
● To simply introduce the concept of spelling in French, click on an image, then on the *Spell* icon, and point to the letters as the Virtual Teacher says them. Repeat, this time asking the whole class to join in. Continue in the same way with all the words.

Word class
● Focus on a word and ask the group what type of word it is.
● Click on the *Word* icon to hear the Virtual Teacher say the word class.
● Repeat all together, copying the Virtual Teacher's gestures as you say the word class.

Sounds
To further reinforce accurate pronunciation, and to introduce some basic reading skills:
● Point to each word on the text bar and ask the class to say the word.
● Focus on the text on screen, click on the *Sound* icon, and click on the different highlighted sounds to hear the Virtual Teacher saying them.
● Repeat all together.
NB. If the *Sound* icon is not illuminated, that means it is not applicable for that particular word.

4 Oracy activity: Quel vêtement?

c. 5–10 mins AT2.1 04.4

Materials
CD-ROM

Description
Click on *Allez*. You will see an item of clothing highlighted; say what the item of clothing is.

Delivery
● Click on *Allez* to start the activity. An item of clothing will start to flash on one of the clowns. Pupils must say what it is using the structure *C'est [une veste]*. You can check their answers using the audio check button in the speech bubble, as required.

● If their answer is correct, click on the tick and the Virtual Teacher will congratulate them.

● If their selection is wrong, click on the cross. The Virtual Teacher will invite pupils to have another try.

● Click on *Allez* to go on to the next item.

Extension
● Make two teams. Each team takes it in turn to answer a question and scores a point for each correct answer.

5 Oracy activity: C'est une veste ou un pantalon?

c. 10 mins AT1.2 AT2.1 04.2 04.4

Materials
Unit 12 Flashcards 7–12 (Clothes)

Description
A guessing game using flashcards, to give further practice in saying items of clothing.

Delivery
● Hold up one flashcard at a time and ask, for example, *C'est une veste ou un pantalon?* to elicit *C'est [un pantalon]*.

● After going through all the cards in this way, progress to asking *Qu'est-ce que c'est?* ('What is it?') to elicit answers as above.

● After each question, stick the card face down on the board.

● When you have been through all the cards in this way, point to the cards (face down) on the board and ask the same question again. This time pupils' memory is tested as well!

Extension
● Divide the class into teams and play the above games, awarding points for each correct answer.

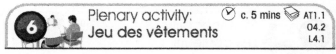

6 Plenary activity: Jeu des vêtements

c. 5 mins AT1.1 04.2 L4.1

Materials
Unit 12 Flashcards 7–12 (Clothes); box of dressing-up clothes: two pairs of trousers, two jackets, two shirts, two t-shirts, two hats, two skirts

Description
A dressing-up game, to give further practice in identifying items of clothing.

Delivery
● Ask a pupil to come to the front of the class.

● The other pupils call out items of clothing and the pupil at the front must select and wear the clothes as instructed. Write a list of the clothes on the board for the pupil at the front to use as reference.

● Repeat with other pupils.

● Alternatively, invite two pupils at a time to the front: they must try to be the first to find and put on the clothes. The winner is the one wearing the most items of clothing.

Extension
● Introduce some additional clothing items if you want to make the game more difficult, e.g. *des chaussettes* (socks), *des chaussures* (shoes), *un pull* (jumper).

Lesson summary

Context
Describing items of clothing

National criteria
KS2 Framework: O4.1, O4.2, O4.3, O4.4, L4.1, L4.2, L4.3, L4.4
Attainment levels: AT1.2, AT2.2, AT3.2, AT4.2
Language ladder levels:
  Listening: **Grade 2**; Speaking: **Grade 2**;
  Reading: **Grade 2**; Writing: **Grade 2**

Cross-curricular links
Music

Key vocabulary
Describing colour of clothes: colours met so far, plus *blanc(he)* (white) and *noir(e)* (black)

Language structures and outcomes
Noun + adjective: *une chemise blanche, un pantalon noir*, etc.

---

1 Starter activity: C'est quelle couleur?
⏱ 5 mins AT1.2 AT2.2 O4.4

Materials
Unit 2 Flashcards 9–14 (Colours)

Description
Team game using flashcards to revise colours previously learned.

Delivery
● Divide the class into teams.

● Hold up a flashcard to the first team and ask *C'est quelle couleur?* Award two points for a correct answer within 10 seconds, or a bonus point to the other team if the first team can't remember.

● Alternate questions between teams until all colours have been covered, adding *vert* (green) to the list as well.

2 Presentation: Les vêtements et les couleurs
⏱ c. 10 mins AT1.2 AT2.2 AT3.2 O4.2 O4.3 L4.1 L4.3

Materials
CD-ROM

Description
Click on the pots of paint to hear each colour presented, then on one of the items of clothing to hear it described using the relevant colour. Use the additional features to practise sound/spelling links, word classes and spelling.

Delivery
● Invite pupils to click on the pots of paint, one by one.

● You will hear the Virtual Teacher say the colour, and see an animation each time.

● Pupils repeat the word after the Virtual Teacher. Most of these words act as revision, as pupils should already be familiar with these colours. Focus longer on *blanc* and *noir*, which are newly introduced in this lesson.

● Repeat each item a couple of times to reinforce learning.

● Once you are confident that the class have remembered all the colours and learned the new ones, move on to clicking on the different clothes worn by the clowns. You will hear the clothing described using the appropriate colour here. Again, get pupils to repeat.

Spelling
● You can practise spelling using the language in this presentation. See the Introduction for notes on how to use this feature of the Language Presentation.

Sounds
● This is a good opportunity to practise sound/spelling links. See the Introduction for notes on how to use this feature of the Language Presentation.

Word class
● This is a good opportunity to practise word classes. See the Introduction for notes on how to use this feature of the Language Presentation.

Knowledge About Language

Adjective agreements
● Pupils last reviewed adjective agreements in Unit 7. You can remind them of this by writing up on the board: *un stylo bleu* and *une trousse bleue*.

● Ask pupils if they can remember why *bleu* is spelt differently with the two nouns. (There are two types of noun in French, those that take *un* – masculine – and those that take *une* – feminine. The adjectives describing the feminine nouns usually add an 'e' at the end.)

● Now follow this by writing *un chapeau* and *une chemise* underneath the other phrases on the board, checking with pupils what these words mean ('a hat' and 'a shirt'). Ask pupils how you would say and write 'a blue hat' and 'a blue shirt' (*un chapeau bleu* and *une chemise bleue*). You can continue this drill with various other clothes and regular adjectives, but avoid using *blanc, marron, rouge, jaune, rose* or *orange*.

● You may already have pointed out to pupils in Unit 7 that there are some adjectives that don't follow this usual pattern. There is another example of this here with *blanc* ('white'), which becomes *blanche* in the feminine form. This happens because adding an 'e' on its own is impossible to pronounce in French. In some other cases, like *rouge, jaune* and *rose*, as the masculine form already has an 'e' at the end, it is impossible to add another one so the feminine form remains the same.

3 Oracy activity: c. 5–10 mins AT1.2 04.2 04.3
Le bon vêtement

Materials
CD-ROM

Description
Click on *Allez*. Listen to the audio and click on the item of clothing described.

Delivery
● Click on *Allez* to start the activity.

● You will hear an item of clothing being described, e.g. *un chapeau noir*. Click on the *Encore* button to hear the audio repeated, if necessary.

● Pupils must click on the relevant item of clothing, in the correct colour.

● If their answer is correct the Virtual Teacher will congratulate them. Otherwise the Virtual Teacher will invite pupils to have another try.

● Click on *Allez* to go on to the next item.

Extension
● Make two teams. Each team takes it in turn to answer a question and scores a point for each correct answer.

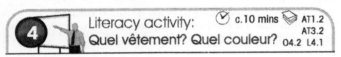

4 Literacy activity: c. 10 mins AT1.2 AT3.2 04.2 L4.1
Quel vêtement? Quel couleur?

Materials
CD-ROM

Description
Play bingo in teams, either using completed cards, or filling your own cards in on screen or using a printed grid. Then mark off the phrases on your card if you see them appear on-screen. The first player or team with all their phrases marked off wins.

Delivery
There are three ways of playing the bingo game:
● *Ready to go*: the computer automatically completes two grids for each team. Team members mark off phrases on their grid as pictures appear on-screen.

● *Make your own*: as above, but teams complete their grids with their choice of phrases on-screen.

● *Print your own*: as *Ready to go*, but print off blank lotto grids from the CD-ROM, which pupils fill with their choice of phrases from those listed on-screen.

● When you are ready to start the game, call up a member of each team to click on the card.

● Click on *Allez* to make each item appear. When pupils hear a phrase from their grid, they must either click on the relevant square or mark the square off on their printed grid.

● When the first on-screen grid is complete, there will be a celebratory animation.

● If playing with printed grids, then the first player to fill their grid calls out *Gagné!*

● Click on the *Jouez encore?* ✓ to play another game, if time allows.

Support
● You can play with or without sound. With sound on, pupils will hear each number spoken as it appears.

5 Song: 10–15 mins AT1.2 AT2.2 AT3.2 04.1 04.2 04.3 L4.1 L4.2 L4.3
Coco le clown

Materials
CD-ROM or Audio CD, track 18; Unit 12 Flashcards 7–12 (Clothes); Unit 2 Flashcards 9–14 (Colours); Bof puppet

Additional props if possible, e.g. picture of a custard pie (or simply a paper plate); water pistol

Description
Watch and listen to the interactive song practising colours and items of clothing. Choose either *Practice* or *Sing* mode: the former to go through the song line by line, the latter to sing it all the way through. Switch the music and words on or off as you prefer.

Delivery
● Stick all the flashcards on the board or wall.

● Play the first verse through and pause at the end. Invite pupils to come up and point to flashcards of items/colours that were featured in the verse. Chorally repeat the phrases.

● Do the same for the other verses.

● Divide the class into three groups. Each group will focus on one verse each.

● Divide the various props and flashcards between the groups according to their character.

● Play the song again. This time, each group must sing along to its designated verse, karaoke-style, and hold up the pictures and props as they are mentioned.

Extension
● Divide the class into groups of 6–8 pupils.

● Each group performs its own version of the song.

● The other groups can award points to see which version was the best.

See the Introduction for more notes on the Song features.

6 Plenary activity: c. 5–10 mins AT2.2 AT4.2 04.1 L4.4
Un défilé de mode!

Materials
Items of clothing (several sets if possible): trousers, jackets, shirts, T-shirts, hats, skirts

Description
A mini fashion parade in which pupils describe what another is wearing using colour and clothing vocabulary.

Delivery
● Divide the class into groups.

● Each group nominates a pupil to be the 'model'. The model puts on a few items of clothing (limit this to three items if time is short). The others note down what they are wearing e.g. *un chapeau bleu*.

● In turn, each group stands at the front and describes what their model is wearing.

Extension
● Ask pupils to describe each model using the phrases *il/elle porte* (he/she is wearing), e.g. *il porte un chapeau bleu*.

● Pupils can follow this up with their own written fashion parade, with drawings or magazine clippings of several models and a written description underneath.

Unit 12

Worksheet 1A

🕐 10–15 mins 📚 AT2.1 AT3.1
AT4.1
L4.1 L4.3 L4.4

Description
Worksheet to give further practice in reading, writing, and saying names of countries.

Notes
1 Give the class a few minutes to go through Activity 1 before going through the answers together

2 Do the same with Activity 2: when you go through the answers, ask pupils to spell out the complete words if possible.

3 Move around the class to monitor Activity 3.

Answers
1 a le Canada   d la Suisse
  b la Martinique   e le Maroc
  c la France   f le Sénégal

2 a MARTINIQUE   d MAROC
  b CANADA   e FRANCE
  c SÉNÉGAL   f SUISSE

Worksheet 1B

🕐 10–15 mins 📚 AT2.1 AT3.1
AT4.2 O4.4
L4.1 L4.3 L4.4

Description
Worksheet to give further practice in reading, writing, and saying names of countries.

Notes
1 Give the class a few minutes to go through Activity 1 before going through the answers together.

2 Give pupils a few minutes to do Activity 3 (this could be done in pairs) before checking through answers as a whole class.

Answers
1 a le Canada
  b la Martinique
  c la France
  d la Suisse
  e le Maroc
  f le Sénégal

2 a il pleut
  b il neige
  c il fait beau
  d il fait beau
  e il fait chaud
  f il fait froid

Worksheet 2A

🕐 10–15 mins 📚 AT2.2 AT3.2
AT4.2
L4.1 L4.3 L4.4

Description
Worksheet to give further practice in reading, writing, and saying *je parle* (I speak) + language.

Notes
1 Give the class a few minutes to go through Activity 1 before going through the answers together.

2 & 3 Move around the class to monitor these activities.

Answers
1 a Je parle français.
  b Je parle anglais et français.
  c Je ne parle pas anglais.
  d Je parle anglais et français.
  e Je parle français.
  f Je parle anglais et français.

Worksheet 2B

🕐 10–15 mins 📚 AT2.2 AT3.2
AT4.2
L4.1 L4.3 L4.4

Description
Worksheet to give further practice in reading, writing, and saying *je parle* ('I speak') + language.

Notes
1 Give the class a few minutes to go through Activity 1 before going through the answers together.

2–3 Move around the class to monitor these two activities.

Answers
1 a Je parle français.
  b Je parle anglais et français
  c Je ne parle pas anglais.
  d Je parle anglais et français.
  e Je parle français.
  f Je parle anglais et français.

Worksheets 3A & 3B

🕐 10–15 mins 📚 AT2.2 AT3.2
O4.4
L4.1 L4.3

Description
Worksheet to give further practice in reading and speaking about clothes and colours.

Notes
1 Quickly go through the words on the cards to ensure everyone remembers them.

2 Move around the class to monitor as pupils draw on the backs of the cards.

3 Hand out scissors and move around the class to monitor the games (e.g. pupils collect all cards of the same colour, or collect cards with the same name).

Worksheet 4A

🕐 10–15 mins 📚 AT2.2 AT3.2
AT4.2
L4.1 L4.3 L4.4

Description
Worksheet to give further practice in reading, writing and speaking about clothes and colours.

Notes
1 If necessary, go through the clothing of the first clown together, then give pupils a few minutes to colour in, before going on to do the next one. Otherwise, let the pupils get on with the activity, and move around the class to monitor progress and help as required for both sections.

2 Move around the class to monitor this activity.

Worksheet 4B

⏱ 10–15 mins 📖 AT2.2 AT3.2–3
AT4.2–3
L4.1 L4.3 L4.4

Description
Worksheet to give further practice in reading, writing and speaking about clothes and colours

Notes
1 If necessary, go through the clothing of the first clown together, then give pupils a few minutes to colour in, before going on to do the next one. Otherwise, let the pupils get on with the activity and move around the class to monitor progress and help as required for all sections.

2–3 Move around the class to monitor these two activities.

Mon projet:
Un pays francophone

⏱ c. 30–60 mins 📖 IU4.2
IU4.4

Description
Pupils prepare a poster or information sheet about a French-speaking country.

Materials
Books and pictures about French-speaking countries, internet access, maps, holiday brochures

Delivery
• Divide the class into pairs or groups of three.

• Assign a French-speaking country to each group (you may wish to use the countries that have been covered in this unit).

• Provide access to information via brochures or books and/or internet access, and ask each group to find some information on their assigned country.

• Pupils then do some research and turn their findings into a poster/leaflet for a wall display about French-speaking countries.

• Encourage them to add captions to any pictures in French where possible.

Extension
• Get pupils to present their project findings to the rest of the class. You can encourage them to use ICT, e.g. Microsoft PowerPoint, for this.

Support
• It may be a good idea to give some headings, e.g. population, location, countryside, food, etc. for pupils to work on. Pupils in each group could then focus on one aspect, and collate the information at the end.

Sound/spelling activity

⏱ 15–20 mins 📖 AT1.1
AT2.1 AT3.1
O4.2 O4.3 L4.3

Description
Practise listening out for and pronouncing the *an* and *eau* sounds. Then identify the sounds as you hear them in different words.

Delivery
• This sound/spelling activity focuses specifically on the *an* and *eau* sounds.

• There are two parts to the activity: the first (*Practice*) allows pupils to familiarise themselves with the two sounds and to compare their pronunciation with the Virtual Teacher model. The second part (*Activities*) contains two exercises: *Activity 1* is an exercise where pupils have to click on a button if they hear the *an* sound in a list of words; and *Activity 2*, where pupils do the same with the *eau* sound instead.

• Select *Practice* and click on *Next* to start this part. Then click on *Allez*. The Virtual Teacher will say the *an* sound first on its own, and then as part of three words that have already been

used in the units to date. For each of these, get the class to repeat the sound or word chorally several times, checking the model each time using the *Encore* button to see how close they are.

• Once you have finished this part, relaunch the activity and choose *Activities* from the selection menu to move on to test pupils' recognition of these sounds. Click on *Allez* to start *Activity 1*. Pupils will hear one of 20 words read out in random order, and must click on the *an* button before the timer runs out if they hear this sound in the word. If they do not hear the sound, they should click on the red cross. Pupils score a point when they correctly identify a word containing the *an* sound within the time allowed. You can click on *Encore* to hear the word again, and to restart the timer. Once they have completed each answer, you can use the *Encore* button to listen again, in order to review their understanding.

• Finally, in *Activity 2*, pupils must do the same as above, this time listening out for words using the *eau* sound.

• Repeat the activity again if you feel pupils need further practice.

Extension
• You can continue the practice activity using more words with these sounds if you feel that pupils have grasped this well, even words not yet covered in *Rigolo*. Pupils can then hold up cards marked with the sounds to show when they hear the appropriate one.

Assessment for Units 11–12

Écoutez!

Play the recording 2–3 times or more if necessary. Pause the recording during each activity as necessary.

Total marks for listening: 20. If pupils are getting 8–14/20, they are working at level 1. If they achieve 15–20/20, they are working towards level 2.

Activity 1   (AT1.1; O4.2)
Mark out of 5

Answers
(*example:* 1 € 5)
2 € 2
3 € 8
4 € 3
5 € 4
6 € 7

(*example:* 1 C'est combien? C'est cinq euros… cinq euros.)
2 C'est combien? C'est deux euros… deux euros.
3 C'est combien? C'est huit euros… huit euros.
4 C'est combien? C'est trois euros… trois euros.
5 C'est combien? C'est quatre euros… quatre euros.
6 C'est combien? C'est sept euros… sept euros.

Activity 2   (AT1.2; O4.2)
Mark out of 5

Answers
a4 b1 c2 d5 e3

1 Je parle français.
2 Je ne parle pas anglais.
3 Je parle français et anglais.
4 Je parle anglais.
5 Je ne parle pas français.

Activities 3a & 3b (AT1.2; O4.2)
Mark out of 10 (5 for 3a and 5 for 3b)

Answers
Ticked: (**1** *example:* smiley face + heart)
2 CD/music notes + heart crossed through
3 glass of water + heart
4 microphone/music notes + heart crossed through
5 knife/fork + heart
6 smiley face − heart

> *(example:* **1** On s'amuse. C'est chouette!)
> **2** On danse. C'est bizarre!
> **3** On boit. C'est bon!
> **4** On chante. C'est nul!
> **5** On mange. C'est délicieux.
> **6** On s'amuse. C'est super!

Parlez!

Pupils can work in pairs for the speaking tasks. If it is not possible to assess each pair, then assess a few pairs for each assessment block and mark the rest of the class based on the spoken work they do in class.

Total marks for speaking: 10. Pupils achieving 5/10 are working at level 1; Pupils achieving more than 5/ 0 are working towards level 2.

Activity 1 (AT2.1; O4.4)
5 marks

Answers
example: un pantalon, un chapeau, une veste, une chemise, un t-shirt, une jupe (*any 5*)

Activity 2 (AT2.2; O4.4)
5 marks. For more able pupils, encourage them also to ask about the price.

Answers
examples:
A Qu'est-ce que tu veux?   **B** Je voudrais du pain.
   extra!
B C'est combien?
A C'est 2 euros.
A Qu'est-ce que tu veux?   **B** Je voudrais des fraises.
   extra!
B C'est combien?
A C'est 4 euros. *etc.*

Lisez!

Total marks for reading 20: Pupils achieving 8–14 are working at level 1. Pupils achieving 15 or more are working towards 2.

Activity 1 (AT3.1; L4.1)
Mark out of 10

Answers
(example: ✗) a ✓ b ✗ c ✓ d ✓ e ✗ f ✗ g ✓ h ✓ i ✗ j ✗

Activity 2 (AT3.2; L4.1, *extra!* L4.3)
Mark out of 10 (5 for each picture)

Answers
A *Pupils to colour clown as follows:* yellow trousers, green hat, red jacket, blue t-shirt and orange shirt
B *Pupils to colour Nathalie as follows:* blue skirt, black hat, blue t-shirt, white shirt and pink jacket

Écrivez!

For the writing tasks, the copying of words can be approximate.

Total marks for writing: 20. Pupils achieving 8–14/20 are working at level 1. Pupils achieving 15 or more out of 20 are working towards level 2.

Activity 1 (AT4.1; L4.4)
Mark out of 10

Answers
a Canada	**f** chapeau
b France	**g** chemise
c Suisse	**h** jupe
d Maroc	**i** pantalon
e Sénégal	**j** veste

Activity 2 (AT4.2; L4.4)
Mark out of 10 (any opinion is acceptable); 2 for each correct sentence and 2 for general accuracy.

Answers
(example: **a** On boit. C'est bon)
        b On danse. C'est…
        c On chante. C'est…
        d On mange. C'est…
        e On s'amuse. C'est…

Unit 1: Bonjour

Lesson	Objective	Context/language	Grammar/skills	National criteria
1	Greet and say goodbye to someone	Greetings: *bonjour* (hello), *salut* (hi), *au revoir* (goodbye)	• Social conventions	Framework: O3.1, O3.2, O3.3, O3.4, L3.1, L3.2, L3.3, IU3.1, IU3.2, IU3.3 Attainment levels: AT1.1, AT2.1, AT3.1 Language ladder: Listening: Grade 1; Reading: Grade 1; Speaking: Grade 1
2	Ask someone's name and say your own	Greetings: *Comment t'appelles-tu?* (What's your name?), *Je m'appelle...* (My name is...)	• Ask and answer questions	Framework: O3.2, O3.3, O3.4, L3.1, L3.2, L3.3 Attainment levels: AT1.1, AT2.1, AT3.1, AT4.1 Language ladder: Listening: Grade 1; Reading: Grade 1; Speaking: Grade 1; Writing: Grade 1
3	Ask how someone is and respond to same question	Asking and saying how you are: *Ça va?* (How are you?), *Oui, ça va bien* (Yes, I'm well), *Comme ci comme ça* (I'm so-so), *Non, ça ne va pas* (No, I'm not doing well)	• Ask and answer questions	Framework: O3.1, O3.2, O3.3, O3.4, L3.1, L3.2, L3.3, IU3.3 Attainment levels: AT1.1–2, AT2.1–2, AT3.1–2, AT4.1 Language ladder: Listening: Grade 1–2; Reading: Grade 1–2; Speaking: Grade 1–2; Writing: Grade 1–2
4	Learn some basic nouns	Instruments: *un tambour* (drum), *une guitare* (guitar), *un piano* (piano), *une trompette* (trumpet), *une flûte à bec* (recorder) Miscellaneous: *une fille* (girl), *un garçon* (boy), *un dragon* (dragon)	• First notions of gender • Cognates	Framework: O3.1, O3.2, O3.3, O3.4, L3.1, L3.2, L3.3 Attainment levels: AT1.1, AT2.1, AT3.1, AT4.1 Language ladder: Listening: Grade 1; Reading: Grade 1; Speaking: Grade 1; Writing: Grade 1
5	Count numbers 1–10	Numbers 1–10: *un, deux, trois, quatre, cinq, six, sept, huit, neuf, dix*		Framework: O3.1, O3.2, O3.3, O3.4, L3.1, L3.2 Attainment levels: AT1.1, AT2.1, AT3.1 Language ladder: Listening: Grade 1; Reading: Grade 1; Speaking: Grade 1
Extra	• Further practice for Unit 1 • Project work: French châteaux	Summary of above language		Framework: O3.3, L3.1, L3.3, IU 3.3 Attainment levels: AT2.1, AT3.1, AT4.1 Language ladder: Speaking: Grade 1; Reading: Grade 1; Writing: Grade 1

Unit 2: En classe

Lesson	Objective	Context/language	Grammar/skills	National criteria
1	Identify classroom objects	Classroom objects: *une trousse* (pencil case), *un stylo* (pen), *une règle* (ruler), *un crayon* (pencil), *un cahier* (exercise book), *un livre* (text book), *un sac* (bag), *une gomme* (rubber)	• Gender • Ask and answer questions	Framework: O3.1, O3.2, O3.3, O3.4, L3.1, L3.2, L3.3 Attainment levels: AT1.1, AT2.1, AT3.1, AT4.1 Language ladder: Listening: Grade 1; Reading: Grade 1; Speaking: Grade 1; Writing: Grade 1
2	Identify colours, and describe an object's colour	Colours: *rouge* (red), *rose* (pink), *bleu* (blue), *jaune* (yellow), *marron* (brown), *orange* (orange). Revision of classroom objects from Lesson 1.	• Basic word order	Framework: O3.2, O3.3, O3.4, L3.1, L3.2 Attainment levels: AT1.1, AT2.1, AT3.1–2, AT4.1–2 Language ladder: Listening: Grade 1; Reading: Grade 1–2; Speaking: Grade 1; Writing: Grade 1–2
3	Say your age	Giving your age: *J'ai ... ans*	• Using context to determine meaning • Comparing languages	Framework: O3.1, O3.2, O3.3, O3.4, L3.1, L3.2, L3.3 Attainment levels: AT1.1–2, AT2.1–2, AT3.1–2, AT4.1–2 Language ladder: Listening: Grade 1–2; Reading: Grade 1–2; Speaking: Grade 1–2; Writing: Grade 1–2
4	Recognise and repeat classroom instructions	Classroom instructions: *écoutez, regardez, lisez, asseyez-vous, levez-vous, écrivez, chantez*		Framework: O3.1, O3.2, O3.3, O3.4, L3.1, L3.2 Attainment levels: AT1.1, AT2.1, AT3.1 Language ladder: Listening: Grade 1; Reading: Grade 1; Speaking: Grade 1
Extra	• Further practice for Unit 2 • Project work: Contact with a French school • Sound/spelling activity for Units 1–2 • Assessment for Units 1–2	Summary of above language, and Unit 1	• Recognise how sounds are represented in written form • Practise pronunciation	Framework: O3.2, O3.3, O3.4, L3.1, L3.2, L3.3, IU3.4 Attainment levels: AT1.1–2, AT2.1–2, AT3.1–2, AT4.1–2 Language ladder: Listening: Grade 1–2; Speaking: Grade 1–2; Reading: Grade 1–2; Writing: Grade 1–2

Unit 3: Mon Corps

Lesson	Objective	Context/language	Grammar/skills	National criteria
1	Identify parts of the body	Parts of the body: *les yeux* (eyes), *le nez* (nose), *la bouche* (mouth), *les oreilles* (ears), *les cheveux* (hair), *la jambe* (leg), *le bras* (arm), *la tête* (head)	• Gender • The definite article	Framework: O3.1, O3.2, O3.3, O3.4, L3.1, L3.2 Attainment levels: AT1.1, AT2.1, AT2.2, AT3.1 Language ladder: Listening: Grade 1; Reading: Grade 1; Speaking: Grade 1
2	Describe eyes and hair appearance	*J'ai les cheveux/les yeux* + [adjective] Parts of the body: *les yeux* (eyes), *les cheveux* (hair) Colours: *vert* (green), *rouge* (red), *marron* (brown), *jaune* (yellow), *bleu* (blue) Adjectives: *long* (long), *court* (short)	• Simple word order • Simple descriptions • Comparing languages	Framework: O3.2, O3.3, O3.4, L3.1, L3.2, L3.3 Attainment levels: AT1.2, AT2.1–2, AT3.2, AT4.2 Language ladder: Listening: Grade 1–2; Reading: Grade 1–2; Speaking: Grade 1–2; Writing: Grade 1–2
3	Recognise days of the week	Days of the week: *lundi, mardi, mercredi, jeudi, vendredi, samedi, dimanche*		Framework: O3.1, O3.2, O3.3, O3.4, L3.1, L3.2 Attainment levels: AT1.1, AT2.1, AT3.1–2 Language ladder: Listening: Grade 1–2; Reading: Grade 1–2; Speaking: Grade 1
4	Give basic character descriptions	Adjectives describing character: *Je suis… grand(e), petit(e), timide, bavard(e), drôle, sympa* Summary of above language	• Basic notion of adjectival agreements (for brighter pupils)	Framework: O3.2, O3.3, O3.4, L3.1, L3.2, L3.3 Attainment levels: AT1.1–2, AT2.1–2, AT3.2, AT4.2 Language ladder: Listening: Grade 2; Speaking: Grade 1–2; Reading: Grade 2; Writing: Grade 2
Extra	• Further practice for Unit 3 • Project work: Famous French people			Framework: O3.3, L3.1, L3.2, L3.3, IU3.3 Attainment levels: AT2.1–2, AT3.1–2, AT4.1–2 Language ladder: Speaking: Grade 1–2; Reading: Grade 1–2; Writing: Grade 1–2

Unit 4: Les Animaux

Lesson	Objective	Context/language	Grammar/skills	National criteria
1	Identify animals and pets	*J'ai* + [animal] *je n'ai pas d'animal* Animals: *un chien* (dog), *un chat* (cat), *une tortue* (tortoise), *un lapin* (rabbit), *un oiseau* (bird), *une souris* (mouse), *un dragon* (dragon)	• Genders • Recognise negative form	Framework: O3.1, O3.2, O3.3, O3.4, L3.1, L3.2 Attainment levels: AT1.1–2, AT2.1–2, AT3.1–2 Language ladder: Listening: Grade 1–2; Speaking: Grade 1–2; Reading: Grade 1–2
2	Recognise and use numbers 11–20	Numbers 11–20: *onze, douze, treize, quatorze, quinze, seize, dix-sept, dix-huit, dix-neuf, vingt*	• Counting numbers up to 20	Framework: O3.1, O3.2, O3.3, O3.4, L3.1, L3.2, L3.3 Attainment levels: AT1.1–2, AT2.1–2, AT3.1–2. AT4.1–2 Language ladder: Listening: Grade 1–2; Speaking: Grade 1–2; Reading: Grade 1–2; Writing: Grade 1–2
3	Give someone's name	*Il/Elle s'appelle...* (S/he's called...)	• Giving names in the third person (he/she)	Framework: O3.1, O3.2, O3.3, O3.4, L3.1, L3.2 Attainment levels: AT1.1–2, AT2.1–2, AT3.2 Language ladder: Listening: Grade 1–2; Speaking: Grade 1–2; Reading: Grade 1–2
4	Describe someone	*Il/Elle est...* (S/he's ...) Adjectives describing character: *grand(e)* (tall), *petit(e)* (small), *drôle* (funny), *sévère* (strict), *timide* (shy)	• Basic notion of adjectival agreements • Giving descriptions in the third person (he/she)	Framework: O3.2, O3.3, O3.4, L3.1, L3.2, L3.3 Attainment levels: AT1.2, AT2.1–2, AT3.2, AT4.2 Language ladder: Listening: Grade 2; Speaking: Grade 1–2; Reading: Grade 2; Writing: Grade 2
Extra	• Further practice for Unit 4 • Project work: Pets • Sound/spelling activity for Units 3–4 • Assessment for Units 3–4	Summary of above language, and Unit 3	• Recognise how sounds are represented in written form. • Practise pronunciation.	Framework: O3.2, O3.3, O3.4, L3.1, L3.2, L3.3 Attainment levels: AT1.1–2, AT2.1–2, AT3.1–2, AT4.1–2 Language ladder: Listening: Grade 1–2; Speaking: Grade 1–2; Reading: Grade 1–2; Writing: Grade 1–2

Unit 5: Ma famille

Lesson	Objective	Context/language	Grammar/skills	National criteria
1	Identify family members	Family members: *ma mère* (mother), *mon père* (father), *mon frère* (brother), *ma sœur* (sister), *mes parents* (my parents)	• Genders	Framework: O3.1, O3.2, O3.3, O3.4, L3.1, L3.2 Attainment levels: AT1.1–2, AT2.1, AT3.1–2 Language ladder: Listening: Grade 1–2; Speaking: Grade 1; Reading: Grade 1–2
2	Recognise and spell with letters of the alphabet	Letters of the alphabet a–z, plus some accented letters	• Spell words using the French alphabet	KS2 Framework: O3.1, O3.2, O3.3, O3.4, L3.1, L3.2 Attainment levels: AT1.1, AT2.1, AT3.1 Language ladder: Listening: Grade 1; Speaking: Grade 1; Reading: Grade 1
3	List household items	Household objects: *le CD* (CD), *le lecteur CD* (CD player), *l'ordinateur* (computer), *le jeu vidéo* (video game), *le DVD* (DVD), *la machine* (machine), *la table* (table), *la chaise* (chair)		KS2 Framework: O3.1, O3.2, O3.3, O3.4, L3.1, L3.2, L3.3 Attainment levels: AT1.1–2, AT2.1, AT3.1–2, AT4.1 Language ladder: Listening: Grade 1–2; Speaking: Grade 1; Reading: Grade 1–2; Writing: Grade 1
4	Use basic prepositions *sur* and *dans* to describe position	*Le CD est dans le lecteur de CD* *Le jeu vidéo est sur la table* Prepositions: *dans* (in), *sur* (on)	• Classifying words into different types • Describe position using basic prepositions *sur* and *dans* and familiar language	KS2 Framework: O3.2, O3.3, O3.4, L3.1, L3.2, L3.3 Attainment levels: AT1.2, AT2.1–2, AT3.1–2, AT4.1–2 Language ladder: Listening: Grade 2; Speaking: Grade 1–2; Reading: Grade 1–2; Writing: Grade 1–2
Extra!	• Further practice for Unit 5 • Project work: Alphabet chart	Summary of above language		KS2 Framework: O3.3, L3.1, L3.2, L3.3 Attainment levels: AT2.1–2, AT3.1–2, AT4.1–2 Language ladder: Speaking: Grade 1–2; Reading: Grade 1–2; Writing: Grade 1–2

Unit 6: Bon anniversaire!

Lesson	Objective	Context/language	Grammar/skills	National criteria
1	Recognise and ask for snacks	*Qu'est–ce que tu veux?* *Je voudrais…* Snacks: *une pomme* (an apple), *une banane* (a banana), *un jus d'orange* (an orange juice), *un sandwich* (a sandwich), *une pizza* (a pizza), *un gâteau* (a cake)	• Genders	KS2 Framework: O3.1, O3.2, O3.4, L3.1, L3.2, L3.3 Attainment levels: AT1.1–2, AT2.1, AT3.1–2, AT4.1 Language ladder: Listening: Grade 1–2; Speaking: Grade 1; Reading: Grade 1–2; Writing: Grade 1
2	Give basic opinions about food	Simple opinions (about food): *C'est délicieux* (it's delicious), *C'est bon* (it tastes nice), *Ce n'est pas bon* (it doesn't taste nice), *C'est mauvais* (it tastes bad)	• Understand and reply to question on food wanted	KS2 Framework: O3.2, O3.3, O3.4, L3.1, L3.2, L3.3 Attainment levels: AT1.1, AT2.1–2, AT3.1–2, AT4.1–2 Language ladder: Listening: Grade 1; Speaking: Grade 1–2; Reading: Grade 1–2; Writing: Grade 1–2
3	Use numbers 21–31	Numbers 21–31	• Count numbers up to 31	KS2 Framework: O3.1, O3.2, O3.3, O3.4, L3.1, L3.2, L3.3 Attainment levels: AT1.1–2, AT2.1, AT3.1–2, AT4.1 Language ladder: Listening: Grade 1–2; Speaking: Grade 1–2; Reading: Grade 1–2; Writing: Grade 1
4	Recognise and use the months	Months: *janvier* (January), *février* (February), *mars* (March), *avril* (April), *mai* (May), *juin* (June), *juillet* (July), *août* (August), *septembre* (September), *octobre* (October), *novembre* (November), *décembre* (December)	• Use numbers up to 31 together with months to form dates	KS2 Framework: O3.1, O3.2, O3.3, O3.4, L3.1, L3.2 Attainment levels: AT1.1–2, AT2.1–2, AT3.1–2 Language ladder: Listening: Grade 1–2; Speaking: Grade 1–2; Reading: Grade 1–2
5	Form dates	*C'est quand, ton anniversaire?* (When is your birthday?) Dates: [C'est] le…[mars, etc.] [It's the… [March, etc.])	• Question forms	KS2 Framework: O3.1, O3.2, O3.3, O3.4, L3.1, L3.2, L3.3 Attainment levels: AT1.2, AT2.1–2, AT3.1–2, AT4.1 Language ladder: Listening: Grade 2; Speaking: Grade 2; Reading: Grade 1–2; Writing: Grade 1
Extra	• Further practice for Unit 6 • Project work: French name days • Sound/spelling activity for Units 5–6 • Assessment for Units 5–6	Summary of above language, and Unit 5	• Recognise how sounds are represented in written form • Practise pronunciation	Framework: O3.2, O3.3, O3.4, L3.1, L3.2, L3.3 Attainment levels: AT1.1–2, AT2.1–2, AT3.1–2, AT4.1–2 Language ladder: Listening: Grade 1–2; Speaking: Grade 1–2; Reading: Grade 1–2; Writing: Grade 1–2

Unit 7: Encore!

Lesson	Objective	Context/language	Grammar/skills	National criteria
1	Revise ways of describing people	Descriptive vocabulary: *Il/Elle a (He/She's got)… les cheveux courts/longs (short/long hair), les yeux bleus (etc.) (blue eyes, etc.), un chien (a dog), sept ans (is seven), un frère/une sœur (brother/sister)*	• Revision of variety of *avoir* phrases • Recognise and use third person singular (*il/elle*) with *avoir*	Framework: O4.1, O4.2, O4.3, O4.4, L4.1, L4.2, L4.3 Attainment levels: AT1.2–3, AT2.2, AT3.2–3 Language ladder levels: Listening: Grade 2–3; Speaking: Grade 2; Reading: Grade 2–3
2	Revise ways of describing people	Descriptive vocabulary: *Il/Elle a (He/She's got)… les cheveux courts/longs (short/long hair), les yeux bleus (etc.) (blue eyes, etc.), un chien (a dog), sept ans (is seven), un frère/une sœur (brother/sister)*	• Revision of variety of *avoir* phrases • Recognise and use third person singular (*il/elle*) with *avoir*	Framework: O4.1, O4.2, O4.3, O4.4, L4.1, L4.2, L4.3 Attainment levels: AT1.2–3, AT2.2, AT3.2–3 Language ladder levels: Listening: Grade 2–3; Speaking: Grade 2; Reading: Grade 2–3
3	Describe someone's nationality	Nationalities: *français(e) (French), canadien(ne) (Canadian), britannique (British)* *Il/Elle est (He/She is)… + nationality*	• Use *être* phrases with adjectives • Recognise and use third person singular (*il/elle*) with *être* • Recognise different adjective endings	Framework: O4.2, O4.3, O4.4, L4.1, L4.2, L4.3, L4.4, IU4.4 Attainment levels: AT1.1–3, AT2.2, AT3.1–3, AT4.1–2 Language ladder levels: Listening: Grade 1–3; Speaking: Grade 2; Reading: Grade 1–3; Writing: Grade 1–2
4	Describe people using various adjectives	Adjectives: *intelligent(e) (clever), sportif (sporty), sévère (strict), français(e) (French), canadien(ne) (Canadian), britannique (British)* *Il/Elle est (He/She is)…*	• Use *être* phrases with adjectives • Recognise and use third person singular (*il/elle*) with *être* • Recognise different adjective endings	Framework: O4.1, O4.2, O4.3, O4.4, L4.1, L4.2, L4.3, L4.4 Attainment levels: AT1.2, AT2.1–2, AT3.1–2, AT4.2 Language ladder levels: Listening: Grade 2; Speaking: Grade 1–2; Reading: Grade 1–2; Writing: Grade 2
Extra!	• Further practice for Unit 7 • Project work: Describing someone	Summary of above language		Framework: O4.1, O4.2, O4.3, O4.4, L4.1, L4.3, L4.4 Attainment levels: AT2.1–2, AT3.1–3, AT4.1–2 Language ladder: Speaking: Grade 1–2; Reading: Grade 1–2; Writing: Grade 1–2

Unit 8: Quelle heure est-il?

Lesson	Objective	Context/language	Grammar/skills	National criteria
1	Talk about activities	*Je regarde* (I am watching)... *la télé* (TV), *un DVD* (a DVD) *J'écoute* (I am listening to)... *mes CD* (my CDs), *la radio* (the radio) *Je joue* (I'm playing)... *au football* (football), *au tennis* (tennis)	• Use several present tense verbs to describe activities • Produce short phrases orally	Framework: O4.2, O4.3, L4.1, L4.2, L4.3 Attainment levels: AT1.2–3, AT2.2, AT3.1–3 Language ladder levels: Listening: Grade 2–3; Speaking: Grade 1–2; Reading: Grade 1–3
2	Talk about activities	*Je regarde* (I am watching)... *la télé* (TV), *un DVD* (a DVD) *J'écoute* (I am listening to)... *mes CD* (my CDs), *la radio* (the radio) *Je joue* (I'm playing)... *au football* (football), *au tennis* (tennis)	• Use several present tense verbs to describe activities • Produce short phrases orally and in writing	Framework: O4.1, O4.2, O4.4, L4.1, L4.2, L4.3, L4.4 Attainment levels: AT1.2–3, AT2.2, AT3.2–3, AT4.2 Language ladder levels: Listening: Grade 2–3; Speaking: Grade 2; Reading: Grade 2–3; Writing: Grade 2
3	Tell the time	Numbers 1–12 Telling time *Quelle heure est-il?* (What time is it?) *Il est... [cinq] heures* (It's...[five] o'clock)	• Express the time	Framework: O4.1, O4.2, O4.3, O4.4, L4.1, L4.2, L4.3, L4.4 Attainment levels: AT1.2–3, AT2.1–2, AT3.2–3, AT4.2 Language ladder levels: Listening: Grade 1–3; Speaking: Grade 2; Reading: Grade 1–3; Writing: Grade 2
4	Talk about what time you do activities	Activities: *Je regarde* (I'm watching)... *la télé* (TV), *un DVD* (a DVD) *J'écoute* (I am listening to)... *mes CD* (my CDs), *la radio* (the radio) *Je joue* (I'm playing)... *au football* (football), *au tennis* (tennis) Times: *...à [trois] heures*	• Use several present tense verbs to describe activities • Produce short phrases orally and in writing • Express the time separately and in phrases with other verbs	Framework: O4.2, O4.3, O4.4, L4.1, L4.3, L4.4 Attainment levels: AT1.2, AT2.2, AT3.2, AT4.2 Language ladder levels: Listening: Grade 2; Speaking: Grade 2; Reading: Grade 2; Writing: Grade 2
Extra!	• Further practice for Unit 8 • Project work: Finding out about famous French people • Sound/spelling activity for Units 7–8 • Assessment for Units 7–8	Summary of above language, and Unit 7		Framework: O4.2, O4.3, O4.4, L4.1, L4.3, L4.4, IU4.2 Attainment levels: AT1.1–2, AT2.1–2, AT3.1–2, AT4.1–2 Language ladder: Speaking: Grade 2; Reading: Grade 1–2; Writing: Grade 1–2

Unit 9: Les fêtes

Lesson	Objective	Context/language	Grammar/skills	National criteria
1	Talk about festivals and dates	Festivals: *le Nouvel An* (New Year), *la Fête des Rois* (The Feast of Kings/Epiphany), *la Saint-Valentin* (St Valentine's day), *Pâques* (Easter), *la Fête Nationale* (Bastille Day), *Noël* (Christmas) *Le [nouvel an], c'est le [premier janvier]* ([New Year] is on the [1st January])	• Give dates for festivals through the year	Framework: O4.2, O4.3, O4.4, L4.1, L4.2, L4.3, IU4.1 Attainment levels: AT1.1–3, AT2.1–2, AT3.1–3 Language ladder levels: Listening: Grade 1–3; Speaking: Grade 1–2; Reading: Grade 1–3
2	Talk about presents at festivals	Presents: *un vélo* (bike), *un jeu* (a game), *un livre* (a book), *un ballon* (a ball), *un Père Noël en chocolat* (chocolate Father Christmas), *un œuf de Pâques* (Easter egg) *Qu'est-ce que tu veux [comme cadeau]?* (What [present] would you like?) *Je voudrais [+ nom]* (I'd like [+ noun])	• Give more dates for festivals through the year • Ask for various presents	Framework: O4.2, O4.3, O4.4, L4.1, L4.3, L4.4 Attainment levels: AT1.1–2, AT2.1–2, AT3.1–2 Language ladder levels: Listening: Grade 1–2; Speaking: Grade 1–2; Reading: Grade 1–2; Writing: Grade 2
3	Count from 31–60	Numbers 31–60	• Count up to 60	Framework: O4.2, O4.3, O4.4, L4.1, L4.2, L4.3 Attainment levels: AT1.1–3, AT2.1, AT3.1–3 Language ladder levels: Listening: Grade 1–3; Speaking: Grade 1; Reading: Grade 1–3
4	Give and understand instructions	Instructions: *touchez le nez/les pieds!* (touch your nose/feet!), *comptez!* (count!), *sautez!* (jump!), *levez les bras!* (raise your arms!), *tournez!* (turn around!)	• Understand and give imperative instructions • Recognise plural forms	Framework: O4.1, O4.2, O4.3, O4.4, L4.1, L4.2, L4.3, L4.4 Attainment levels: AT1.1–2, AT2.1–2, AT3.1–2, AT4.1 Language ladder levels: Listening: Grade 1–2; Speaking: Grade 1–2; Reading: Grade 1–2; Writing: Grade 1
Extra!	• Further practice for Unit 9 • Project work: Festivals	Summary of above language		Framework: O4.2, O4.4, L4.1, L4.3, L4.4, IU4.1 Attainment levels: AT1.2, AT2.1–2, AT3.1–2, AT4.1–2 Language ladder: Listening: Grade 2, Speaking: Grade 1–2; Reading: Grade 1–2; Writing: Grade 1–2

Unit 10: Où vas-tu?

Lesson	Objective	Context/language	Grammar/skills	National criteria
1	Talk about going to French cities	Où vas-tu? (Where are you going?) Je vais à (I'm going to)… Paris/Bordeaux/Strasbourg/Nice/Grenoble	• Recognise various French cities • Ask and answer where you are going, using je vais à…	Framework: O4.2, O4.3, O4.4, L4.1, L4.2, L4.3, IU4.4 Attainment levels: AT1.1–3, AT2.2, AT3.1–3 Language ladder levels: Listening: Grade 1–3; Speaking: Grade 2; Reading: Grade 1–3
2	Give and understand basic directions	Directions: tournez à droite (right), tournez à gauche (left), allez tout droit (straight on), arrêtez (stop)	• Understand and give imperative instructions for directions	Framework: O4.2, O4.3, L4.1, L4.3, IU4.4 Attainment levels: AT1.1–2, AT2.2, AT3.2 Language ladder levels: Listening: Grade 1–2; Speaking: Grade 2; Reading: Grade 2
3	Talk about the weather	Weather: Quel temps fait-il? (What's the weather like?) il fait beau (it's sunny), il fait froid (it's cold), il fait chaud (it's hot), il pleut (it's raining), il neige (it's snowing)	• Form weather expressions using impersonal il… expressions	Framework: O4.2, O4.3, O4.4, L4.1, L4.2, L4.3, IU4.4 Attainment levels: AT1.2–3, AT2.2, AT3.1–3 Language ladder levels: Listening: Grade 2–3; Speaking: Grade 2; Reading: Grade 1–3
4	Talk about the weather and places in France	Weather: Quel temps fait-il? (What's the weather like?) À Paris/Bordeaux/Strasbourg/Nice/Grenoble, il fait beau/il fait froid/il fait chaud/il pleut/il neige (In Paris [etc.], it's sunny/cold/hot/raining/snowing) À [Paris] [il pleut] (It's [raining] in [Paris])	• Recognise various French cities • Form weather expressions using impersonal il… expressions • Describe the weather in a certain location in a short sentence	Framework: O4.1, O4.2, O4.3, O4.4, L4.1, L4.2, L4.3, IU4.4 Attainment levels: AT1.2, AT2.2, AT3.2, AT4.2 Language ladder levels: Listening: Grade 2; Speaking: Grade 2; Reading: Grade 2; Writing: Grade 2
Extra!	• Further practice for Unit 10 • Project work: Une ville française • Sound/spelling activity for Units 9–10 • Assessment for Units 9–10	Summary of above language, and Unit 9		Framework: O4.2, O4.3, O4.4, L4.1, L4.2, L4.3, L4.4, IU4.2, IU4.4 Attainment levels: AT1.1–2, AT2.1–2, AT3.1–2, AT4.1–2 Language ladder: Listening: Grade 1–2; Speaking: Grade 1–2; Reading: Grade 1–2; Writing: Grade 1–2

Unit 11: On mange!

Lesson	Objective	Context/language	Grammar/skills	National criteria
1	Go shopping for food	Food items: *du pain* (bread), *du fromage* (cheese), *de la limonade* (lemonade), *de la crème* (cream), *des fraises* (strawberries), *des tomates* (tomatoes) *Qu'est-ce que tu veux?* (What do you want?) *Je voudrais [du pain]* (I'd like [some bread])	• Ask what someone wants • Say what you want • Talk about food using partitive article	Framework: O4.2, O4.3, O4.4, L4.1, L4.2, L4.3, IU4.2 Attainment levels: AT1.2–3, AT2.1–2, AT3.2–3 Language ladder levels: Listening: Grade 2–3; Speaking: Grade 1–2; Reading: Grade 2–3
2	Ask how much something costs	Using money: *C'est combien?* (How much is it?) *C'est [cinq] euros* (It's [five] euros)	• Ask how much something costs • Ask what someone wants • Say what you want • Talk about food using partitive article	Framework: O4.1, O4.2, O4.3, O4.4, L4.1, L4.3, L4.4, IU4.2 Attainment levels: AT1.1–2, AT2.1–3, AT3.2, AT4.2 Language ladder levels: Listening: Grade 1–2; Speaking: Grade 1–2; Reading: Grade 2; Writing: Grade 2
3	Talk about activities at a party	Party activities: *on boit* (we are drinking), *on mange* (we are eating), *on danse* (we are dancing), *on chante* (we are singing), *on s'amuse* (we are having fun) *Qu'est-ce qu'on fait pour la fête?* (What are we doing for the party?) *On [danse]* (We are [dancing])	• Use *on* to talk about first-person plural activities	Framework: O4.1, O4.2, O4.3, O4.4, L4.1, L4.2, L4.3, L4.4 Attainment levels: AT1.1–3, AT2.1–2, AT3.1–3, AT4.1 Language ladder levels: Listening: Grade 1–3; Speaking: Grade 1–2; Reading: Grade 1–3; Writing: Grade 1
4	Give opinions about food and various activities	Opinions: *c'est chouette* (it's great), *c'est nul* (it's rubbish), *c'est bizarre* (it's weird) *La [fête], c'est [bizarre]* (The [party] is [weird])	• Give basic opinions about activities and food	Framework: O4.2, O4.3, O4.4; L4.1, L4.3, L4.4 Attainment levels: AT1.2, AT2.1–2, AT3.1–2, AT4.2 Language ladder levels: Listening: Grade 2; Speaking: Grade 1–2; Reading: Grade 1–2; Writing: Grade 2
Extra!	• Further practice for Unit 11 • Project work: *La nourriture en France*	Summary of above language		Framework: O4.2, O4.4, L4.1, L4.3, L4.4, IU4.2 Attainment levels: AT2.1–2, AT3.1–2, AT4.1–2 Language ladder: Speaking: Grade 1–2; Reading: Grade 1–2; Writing: Grade 1–2

Unit 12: Le cirque

Lesson	Objective	Context/language	Grammar/skills	National criteria
1	Discuss francophone countries	Francophone countries: *la France* (France), *la Suisse* (Switzerland), *le Canada* (Canada), *la Martinique* (Martinique), *le Maroc* (Morocco), *le Sénégal* (Senegal) *C'est [le Maroc]* (It's [Morocco])	• Give the names of various French-speaking countries	Framework: O4.2, O4.3, O4.4, L4.1, L4.2, L4.3, IU4.4 Attainment levels: AT1.1–3, AT2.1, AT3.1–3 Language ladder levels: Listening: Grade 1–3; Speaking: Grade 1; Reading: Grade 1–3
2	Discuss the languages we speak	Talking about languages: *Je parle anglais/français* (I speak English/French), *Je ne parle pas anglais/français* (I don't speak English/French)	• Use positive and negative phrases to talk about speaking languages	Framework: O4.2, O4.3, O4.4; L4.1, L4.3, L4.4, IU4.2, IU4.4 Attainment levels: AT1.2, AT2.2, AT3.2, AT4.2 Language ladder levels: Listening: Grade 2; Speaking: Grade 2; Reading: Grade 2; Writing: Grade 2
3	Identify different items of clothing	Clothes: *un pantalon* (trousers), *une veste* (jacket), *une chemise* (shirt), *un t-shirt* (t-shirt), *un chapeau* (hat), *une jupe* (skirt)	• Describe various items of clothing	Framework: O4.2, O4.3, O4.4, L4.1, L4.2, L4.3 Attainment levels: AT1.1–3, AT2.1, AT3.1–3 Language ladder levels: Listening: Grade 1–3; Speaking: Grade 1; Reading: Grade 1–3
4	Describe items of clothing	Describing colour of clothes: colours met so far, plus *blanc(he)* (white) and *noir(e)* (black) Noun + adjective: *une chemise blanche, un pantalon noir,* etc.	• Describe various items of clothing, using colour adjectives	Framework: O4.1, O4.2, O4.3, O4.4, L4.1, L4.2, L4.3, L4.4 Attainment levels: AT1.2, AT2.2, AT3.2, AT4.2 Language ladder levels: Listening: Grade 2; Speaking: Grade 2; Reading: Grade 2; Writing: Grade 2
Extra!	• Further practice for Unit 12 • Project work: *Un pays francophone* • Sound/spelling activity for Units 11–12 • Assessment for Units 11–12	Summary of above language, and Unit 11		Framework: O4.2, O4.3, O4.4, L4.1, L4.3, L4.4, IU4.2, IU4.4 Attainment levels: AT1.1, AT2.1–2, AT3.1–3, AT4.1–3 Language ladder: Speaking: Grade 1–2; Reading: Grade 1–3; Writing: Grade 1–3

KS2 Framework mapping grid

Rigolo 1 units

Year 3 objectives

	1	2	3	4	5	6	7	8	9	10	11	12
O3.1: Listen and respond to simple rhymes, stories and songs	✓	✓	✓	✓	✓	✓						
O3.2: Recognise and respond to sound patterns and words	✓	✓	✓	✓	✓	✓						
O3.3: Perform simple communicative tasks	✓	✓	✓	✓	✓	✓						
O3.4: Listen attentively and understand instructions, etc.	✓	✓	✓	✓	✓	✓						
L3.1: Recognise some familiar words in written form	✓	✓	✓	✓	✓	✓						
L3.2: Make links between some phonemes, rhymes, spellings	✓	✓	✓	✓	✓	✓						
L3.3: Experiment with the writing of simple words	✓					✓						
IU3.1: Learn about different languages spoken in the school	✓											
IU3.2: Locate country/countries where language is spoken		B										
IU3.3: Identify social conventions at home and in other cultures	✓	B		B		B						
IU3.4: Make contact with countries where language spoken	✓					✓						

Year 4 objectives

	1	2	3	4	5	6	7	8	9	10	11	12
O4.1: Memorise and present a short spoken text							✓	✓	✓	✓	✓	✓
O4.2: Listen for specific words and phrases							✓	✓	✓	✓	✓	✓
O4.3: Listen for sounds, rhyme and rhythm							✓	✓	✓	✓	✓	✓
O4.4: Ask and answer questions on several topics							✓	✓	✓	✓	✓	✓
L4.1: Read and understand a range of familiar written phrases							✓	✓	✓	✓	✓	✓
L4.2: Follow a short familiar text, listening and reading at the same time							✓	✓	✓	✓	✓	✓
L4.3: Read some familiar words/phrases aloud and pronounce accurately							✓	✓	✓	✓	✓	✓
L4.4: Write simple words/phrases using model and words from memory							✓	✓	✓	✓	✓	✓
IU4.1: Learn about festivals and celebrations in different cultures								B	✓	✓	✓	B
IU4.2: Know about aspects of everyday life and compare to their own										B	✓	✓
IU4.3: Compare traditional stories												
IU4.4: Learn about ways of travelling to the country/countries							✓					✓

✓ Objective is covered in this unit on the CD-ROM and/or in the corresponding Big Books

B Objective is covered for this unit in the corresponding Big Books

5–14 guidelines mapping grid

Strands and attainment targets		Rigolo 1 units					
		1	2	3	4	5	6
Listening:	Listening for information and instructions	A, C	A, C	A, C	A, C	A, C	A, C
	Listening and reacting to others	A, B, C	A, B, C	A, B, C	A, B, C	A, B, C	A, B, C
Speaking:	Speaking to convey information	A, C	A, C	A, C	A, C	A, C	A, C
	Speaking and interacting with others	B, C	B, C	B, C	B, C	B, C	B, C
	Speaking about experiences, feelings and opinions	A, B	A, B	A, B	A, B	A, B	A, B, C
Reading:	Reading for information and instructions	A, C	A, C	A, C	A, C	A, C	A, C
	Reading aloud	A, C	A, C	A, C	A, C	A, C	A, C
Writing:	Writing to exchange information and ideas	A, C	A, C	A, C	A, C	A, C	A, C
	Writing to establish and maintain personal contact	A, C	A, C	A, C	A, C	A, C	A, C
	Writing imaginatively/to entertain	n/a	n/a	n/a	n/a	n/a	n/a